As technologies and globalization reduce the need for labour in the advanced economies, we find a higher portion of the nation's wealth is passed to the owners of capital at the expense of the rest of the population. This inevitably leads to greater income differential and ultimately to creating a class of the few, who have, and the rest, who have not.

Author, businessman, and intellectual adventurer Mahmoud Nafousi was born in Nineveh in the '40s.

He grew up in a conservative culture and in 1963, at the age of seventeen, moved to the UK to complete a degree in Economics and Accounting at Bristol University. He then qualified as a Chartered Accountant with KPMG and returned to Iraq in 1972. At the age of twenty-nine, he became the youngest Controller General in charge of auditing all the publicly owned companies including all the banks and the oil companies. He then left Iraq in 1979 with his wife Kathy who started her Ph.D. in Histopathology at Oxford University.

He occupied major positions in Saudi Arabia, the UK, and the UAE as a senior executive of international companies. He has travelled widely and has deep interest in cultural, religious, and scientific issues of the day.

Encounter in Nineveh

MAHMOUD NAFOUSI

Encounter in Nineveh

A Route to Personal Enlightenment

Vanguard Press

VANGUARD PAPERBACK

© Copyright 2014
Mahmoud Nafousi

The right of Mahmoud Nafousi to be identified as author of
this work has been asserted by him in accordance with the
Copyright, Designs and Patents Act 1988.

A CIP catalogue record for this title is
available from the British Library.

ISBN: 978-1-84386-991-7

*Vanguard Press is an imprint of
Pegasus Elliot Mackenzie Publishers Ltd.*
www.pegasuspublishers.com

First Published in 2014

**Vanguard Press
Sheraton House Castle Park
Cambridge England**

Printed and bound in Great Britain

This book is dedicated to my loved ones who stood by me during my frequent moves between the many countries my destiny drove me to since I left Iraq in the early part of 1980.

A special place in my heart is to my father, the widower, who brought up eight children on his own.

Acknowledgements

This book is dedicated to all political activists who seek the truth behind deceptive appearances in public life, who tirelessly campaign to ensure that world leaders remain true servants of justice, world peace and prosperity for the many.

The book is also dedicated to all those who volunteer their time and money to see those who are less fortunate on this planet are pulled out of poverty and ignorance.

Above all, this book is dedicated to my wonderful family who have put up with my isolation for many months while I wrote this book.

Last but not the least: this book is also dedicated to all those who believed in me and encouraged me to commit my deepest thoughts into writing.

Contents

Foreword

This is one book that will set your pulse racing as the author Mahmoud Nafousi weaves a tale of the utmost significance to modern man. It is a tale that will awaken your soul and you will feel the dawn of a "new enlightenment" as you continue reading the book.

The book is not just for people who have a religious bent of mind. In fact, it has universal appeal. The book takes the form of a great dialogue that discuses many problems that afflict modern societies. The author Mahmoud Nafousi also offers plausible solutions to some of the burning issues of today. Great minds from the past are brought together in one single "Encounter" with the author to send a message that will alter the way we think about our faiths and the way we look at life.

This book is not meant to replace any holy book. It is not the intention of the author to offend any faith but to offer a better way of life through the adherence to various faiths. The author offers a new way of looking at and interpreting the various faiths, keeping in mind the changing world order and the emergence of a materialistic society.

This is truly a classic and it is a book that should adorn your bookshelf for generations to come. This book is highly recommended for anyone who wants to re-examine his or her life and how they should go about their lives.

Jitendra K Bharai
[Editor]

Preface

Ever since I was ten years old, I have loved to reflect on everything I observe. I have had great fascination for how major civilizations rise and then fall almost with certainty. Growing up in a conservative society of Mosul in Iraq, religion should always have played a major role in my life. It did for a while without stopping me in my search for the truth. Applying rational thinking and absorbing what Darwin's theory of evolution was all about, I refused to be buried in rigid customs and orthodox behavior. At the age of seventeen, I moved to the UK in the sixties with its completely different culture. This is when I realized that what matters most in this world is for one to be open-minded. One must look beyond appearances to discover the true, underlying forces shaping events.

My desire was to bring science and religion together and this desire guided me to search for a common ground to discover the truth. I developed a great love of investigating new ideas on the most challenging subjects. I refused to accept that contradictions couldn't be resolved. I refused to accept that everything came out of nothing because we cannot explain it rationally. This search for a simple and rational explanation took a giant leap forward in 1984. This is when I was able, according to my personal understanding at least, to simplify all existing theories in physics by the unique idea that photons can be bent into two tiny radii to form protons and electrons.

Being deeply interested in the subject of genetics and with the help of many medical doctors in the family, I started to question the accepted theory that evolution is a matter of random mutation. I started to ask how humans could sustain life on other planets. The only practical way I could think of is by creating seeds of life and then to get them delivered to new planets in the universe via some comet. If human ingenuity can achieve that, then why should we deny this capability to the Great Designer of the Universe? For a seed to turn into talent, it must have a built-in program to guide its evolution. This is where the idea of the existence of a monitoring gene came from.

This search to find rational answers then extended to questions such as; why has God bothered to create intelligence? How does God manage everything in the universe? If the universe is run by strict laws, does that make God's powers limited? How could a photon vibrate in empty space? What is gravity? What is time? Why is there no general theory of physics to explain everything in a simple manner? Is the universe eternal? Is the universe expanding, contracting, or both? What is a black hole? Are black holes necessary for a stable universe? Are black holes continuously created and then destroyed through big bangs to recreate new galaxies? Can man neutralize the effects of gravity? Can man bend a photon to create something out of energy?

The questions became endless once I moved to questions the rationale behind various faiths. They all claim to have a monopoly to the absolute truth. Does God really exist? What is the Holy Spirit? Is Jesus truly the son of God? Are we to believe in everything we are told in all the holy books? How could we then reconcile the contradictions? What is faith? Why does it create rigidities in the mind? How can we change our beliefs? What does it take to be one of "God's Chosen People"? Do angels exist and who are they? Is there eternal life? What is the concept of Heaven and Hell? Why do religions need this concept? What is Soul? Why do we need to pray? What are the fundamentals used to establish and sustain a new religion? Can dreams tell the future? What is the Kingdom of Heaven? Can the mysterious sayings of Jesus in the Gospel of Thomas be explained with the new understanding of how the universe works? What is the basis of Hindu religion? How does it differ from Buddhism? Is there something that we can learn from prophets and religions to create world class socio-economic institution.

Then, I turned to practical questions affecting human beings in their everyday life. Why are there so many wars and conflicts? Why has man not rid himself of the evils of greed and the craving for power? Why is democracy not working as it used to or as it should? Does a shadow government exist? Who are the masters of the universe? Is money corrupting politics? Is the media dominated by the few? Are the majority of people destined to live in bondage of extreme poverty? How do we deal with failing states? How do we deal with a 'nanny state' mentality? What are the roles of charities and retirees in the building of states? What are the evils of casino banking and speculation? Can we create truly independent international bodies with their own tax system? Can economic cycles be eliminated by understanding the changes in human psychology and the associated fear and greed? Can we find a solution to the Middle East problem? Can human beings truly create a 'Just World Order'?

The questions are endless. The need to find a theory that can explain all these questions, through the application of the art of questioning and deductions from first principles, is great and urgent. Human beings have been trying to do so over thousands of years without addressing the serious deficiencies in human virtues and lack of rational thinking. A new deep and philosophical approach is needed to commit thoughts to paper as a trigger for wider debates to address these and many more urgent issues afflicting man.

The answer to all these questions and more were offered during an encounter in Nineveh, while I was apparently in a state of a coma and was approached by what appeared to me five wise holograms. These shadows were given the task of providing humanity with rational explanations for all his natural and supernatural observations. They appeared in the names of Newton, Abraham, Darwin, Plato and Adam Smith. Each will devote one day to pass knowledge to humanity. Any gap in knowledge that cannot be provided by them was left to the last day of the encounter. This would be given through a conference call with Moses, Jesus and Mohammed. Their answers are meant to provide the foundation for religious dialogue and to explain that not all of what one reads in holy books should be taken literally. They call for the application of a rationality test. If what is written is not rational and does not serve the well-being of humanity as a whole, then the interpretation of the message must evolve to meet current human intellects and needs. One should consider that those messages could have been distorted, reported out of context or they were mere statements of traditions instead of being divine instructions. Many quotes from the holy books have been used to support the new rational approach expressed in this work.

The book is full of inspirational quotes and calls for a mass movement to bring the huge change required to create a democracy that will serve the many. Global action is required to bring about lasting peace on earth. Only then, human beings will have the chance to fulfil their divine role in completing their evolution and thus rid themselves of their negative emotions. This will allow humans to be trusted with more divine knowledge and to recreate the seeds of life for the rebirth of talents on new planets.

Mahmoud Nafousi

Chapter 1

A Trip to Iraq

September 11th, 2001 was a turning point in recent human history. The senseless act and savagery committed against innocent civilians in the most powerful country in the world was not to pass without a great response. There was unanimous worldwide approval for President Bush to commit forces against the perpetrators who were holed up in Afghanistan. Unfortunately, the dominant pressure groups behind the scenes in the US started to set in motion wider war objectives to include other countries.

To my surprise, Iraq, after years of the most severe international boycotts in human history, was included as a prime target of the American "War on Terror". The UK, under Tony Blair's premiership was ready to support whatever George W. Bush and his nondescript vice president Dick Cheney would order in this respect. "Old Europe", as Donald Rumsfeld, (the defense secretary and the chief warmonger) called France and Germany, stood against extending the war to include Iraq, without any clear evidence of the existence of WMD (Weapons of Mass Destructions) and without a UN mandate.

In the early part of 2003, my wife Kathy and I left our home in Oxford to join one of the largest demonstrations ever to take place in London against the intended war in Iraq. It was clear that George W. Bush and Tony Blair were planning for the war at any cost and in a clear violation of international law. That was the first demonstration we ever attended. We thought it was time to stand up for what we believed in. We hoped that making the effort to express our opinion with millions of Brits would make the misguided and deluded Tony Blair sit up and listen to the voices of wisdom.

It was one of the most emotional days of our lives. We saw millions of people, young, old, males, females who came from all walks of life, caring so much about the fate of my country of birth, Iraq. They were clearly aware of what the war would unleash in terms of destruction and personal tragedies. The demonstrators' collective good judgments must have been correct compared to the small foreign policy study groups in the US, who were scheming and spreading misinformation to subvert public opinion for widening the war. My wife and I wondered how a small unelected group could hijack democracy and the will of the people with impunity. Many politicians, once in office, start to tow the lines dictated to them by shadowy elites who do most of their work behind closed doors and away from public scrutiny. The primary aim of these politicians was to ensure that money and media support continued for their egotistical hunger for power.

I asked a friend of mine if he knew what happened to the Labour Party's ethical foreign policy that was in their manifesto before they came to power. It's no surprise that almost 50% of the UK and USA electorate have lost faith in politics in general and the election process in particular. The elected governments don't seem to be accountable to the people except in appearance. In reality, they are at the mercy and guidance of those who fund them.

I seriously thought that in a democratic country and without a mandate from the UN, Tony Blair wouldn't dare commit UK troops and billions of pounds to an illegal and unpopular war just to please George W. Bush and the neo-conservative party in the US. I also believe that Tony Blair was naïve to think that by invading Iraq he could get democracy to flourish in a region of the world where the necessary foundations for democracy are very weak. Those who have no desire to see democracy flourish in the Middle East are the same people who pushed for the invasion of Iraq. The heart of their agenda was to dismantle the country and create chaos for many years to come.

After the demonstration, it was clear that the drums of war were getting louder. It was quickly becoming apparent that the war was inevitable once the war machines had finished their preparations. We had to make the agonizing decision of whether to send our youngest daughter Roxie, who was only sixteen years old, to see my sick elder sister in Iraq. We felt that she may never have the chance to see her if she did not make this trip. I put my hesitation behind me, as I remembered the words of a great philosopher who once said, "There is nothing worse than fear itself". I finally managed to persuade my wife to allow Roxie to make her first trip to our country, although there was no direct flight to Iraq. I seriously thought that the war would not start until mid-April. Planning Roxie's trip was a major task. She flew to Istanbul, and then from there she had to travel by car to Kurdistan in northern Iraq. Getting to Mosul (where my sister lived) from Erbil (the capital of Kurdistan) was the most difficult part of the journey. Iraq was practically a divided country. The north had been under a "no fly zone" for many years and autonomous from the rest of Iraq. Finally, she got to Mosul. It was practically a war zone with Sadam's army completely demoralized and with no one knowing what would happen next. I was pleased that she had made it in one piece. Regardless of what might happen after that, Roxie received a great reception from my sister and our extended family. She was meeting everyone for the first time and they were very excited to see her. A few days after Roxie arrived in Mosul, the war broke out. We became extremely concerned about her safety. I decided that I had no choice but to make the trip myself to bring her back. Everyone thought that I was crazy to have let her go in the first place. I was blamed harshly for the stupid decision I had made. I must admit the whole plan was unforgiveable. I have no idea what made me make such a decision. It was completely out of character.

I waved my wife and three older children, who were full of tears, goodbye at Heathrow Airport. It was a very sad and emotional send-off. In Turkey, I had to pay many people to organize my getting smuggled into Iraq. The borders were closed and we had to follow the smugglers' routes. During this trip, I was accompanied by a young Iraqi man called Sami. He had just graduated from Harvard and was about to return to his home with the excitement of starting a new life. I learned that all of his family in Baghdad had been torn to pieces by the heavy bombardment of the capital before the ground troops moved in. My difficulties seemed rather minor relative to his tragedy.

Once I was in Iraq, I quickly realized that nothing was normal. The whole country appeared to have been dismantled over the last twenty years due to wars and harsh economic boycotts. I felt I was lucky to have arrived in Mosul (Nineveh Province) in one piece, while heavy bombardment and horrendous destruction was taking place in the south of Iraq and Baghdad.

I spent most of the time in my sister's garden trying to avoid thinking about the disastrous scenarios that could play out next. I started to recall my previous visits to the ruins of Nineveh and my tour of the British Museum that houses a big collection of artifacts from that period of ancient history. My tour of the museum confirmed that Nineveh was one of the oldest and greatest cities in antiquity. The area was settled as early as 6000 BC. By 3000 BC, it had become an important religious centre for the worship of the goddess Ishtar. The city grew dramatically in size, grandeur and fame under the reign of King Sennacherib (704–681 BC) who made Nineveh the capital of his Assyrian Empire. He built great walls around the city with fifteen gates. He created public parks, gardens, aqueducts, irrigation ditches, canals and greatly expanded upon and improved the structure of the city. His palace was the most magnificent building known in ancient times. It had eighty rooms and he proclaimed it to be "The palace without rival".

In 612 BC the city of Nineveh was ransacked and burnt down by the allied forces of the Medes and Babylonians who then proceeded to divide the region between them. The area was sparsely populated thereafter and, slowly, the ancient ruins became buried in the earth. I was wondering if history was about to repeat itself and whether the town would meet the same fate by the modern allied forces led by George W. Bush and Tony Blair. It was clear that this war had a religious dimension to it and this made it a very sad story in human history.

Nineveh was best known through the Christian era by the central role it played in the Hebrew composition known in the Bible as "The Book of Jonah".

The ruins lay buried until they were uncovered and excavated to reveal the magnificent scope of this once great city. The Royal Library of Ashurbanipal (the last great king of the Neo-Assyrian Empire), had a collection of thousands of clay tablets and fragments containing texts of all kinds from the 7th century BC. Among them was the famous epic of Gilgamesh. These materials were found in the archaeological site known as "Kouyunjik".

Today, Nineveh's location is marked by excavations of five gates, part of the walls on four sides, and two large mounds known as the hill of Kouyunjik and hill of Nabi Yunus. On the hill of Nabi Yunus, there is a Muslim shrine dedicated to Prophet Jonah. Mosul is well known for its heritage of receiving Divine visitors. Locally, it is known to house the tombs of almost forty prophets.

This fascination for Nineveh and its genealogy was probably passed to me from my grandmother. She outlived my mother who died when I was six years old. My grandmother (who was in her eighties) looked after my seven siblings and me for a while. I was the youngest boy in the family. I remember her as a mystical old woman. She used to have vivid dreams that truly foretold the future. I recall her wise smile and the excitement in her voice as she told me that we were the direct descendants of Younis. The descendants of Younis belong to a group of ancient mystic people blessed to receive divine wisdom. Of course, I did not understand what that meant nor did I take it seriously at the time. I wondered if this gift of having vivid dreams had been passed on to my generation. I remembered my youngest sister asking me not to travel to Iraq as she saw our dead father visiting her in a very disturbing dream. He told her in a very sad voice that there would be widespread destruction in Iraq that would last for more than twenty years.

The many stories and interpretations of dreams I heard from my grandmother, planted in me the love to be receptive to the concept of supernatural happenings all around us. Such events could manifest themselves in the multiple prophets who had appeared in this area in particular. These stories helped me to be open-minded and reflective. I sounded older than my age at the time. As far as I can remember, I always tried to ignore appearances and searched behind what looked obvious, to find the true explanations. At school, I was fascinated by Darwin's theory of evolution and this influenced my thinking for the rest of my life. I always did well in my studies and I ended up graduating from Bristol University in the 60s and later qualified as a chartered accountant from KPMG, one of the big four international firms of auditors.

I quickly became bored, as there was very little to do in Mosul. I left my sister's house, where my daughter and I were staying and decided to visit my favorite childhood historical site of the ruins of Nineveh. I used to spend many hours there, between the ages of nine and fifteen. I used to climb Mound Kouyunjik. It was made up from the ruins of this once greatest city on Earth. Deep inside me, I was trying to be a young archaeologist searching the caves with the hope of finding some ancient artifacts of historical significance.

It was a cloudy cold Saturday and it was still early in the morning when I reached the ruins of Nineveh. A prolonged shiver passed through my spine as I realized it had been almost forty years since my last visit. As I sat under the shadow of a tree, I remembered the story of Jonah (Younis) in the Bible: Then the word of the Lord came to Jonah: "Go to the great city of Nineveh and proclaim to it the message I give you". After some hesitation, Jonah obeyed the word of the Lord and went to Nineveh. Jonah began by going on a day's journey into the city, proclaiming, "Forty more days, and Nineveh will be overthrown". As a result, the Ninevites repented and started to believe in God. A fast was proclaimed, and all citizens, from the greatest to the humblest, put on sackcloth. When Jonah's warning reached the King of Nineveh, he rose from his throne, took off his royal robes, covered himself with the sackcloth, and sat down in the dust. The King and his people obeyed God's command. He decreed that everyone should call urgently on God. The King ordered them to give up their evil ways and their violence so that God may yet relent. God would, with compassion, turn from His fierce anger so that they will not perish. When God realized what they did and how they had turned from their evil ways, he relented and did not bring on them the destruction he had threatened. This act of compassion upset Jonah as he was expecting that God would ultimately relent, and renders his trip to warn them futile.

I was rather scared of the thought that God was subjecting the Iraqis to the same test. Are the Iraqis being punished for their wicked ways for the last twenty-four years as they are ruled by a brutal dictator? Are they going to be subjected to even greater destructions by the incredible might of the invaders who are regard themselves as God on Earth? Are the invaders going to be merciful and compassionate as "God, the Almighty" or will those who called for the extension of the war on terror to include Iraq be like Jonah has no interest in mercy?

I felt rather sad and very gloomy as to what was going on. I started to recall all about the various caves I used to explore long ago. As I was walking, I heard American bombers flying very low. I was terrified as I could be easily spotted on the mound since no one else was there. I ran for cover towards the nearest cave as the bombs started to drop nearby. The ground shook below my feet and then I believe I lost consciousness.

The next thing I remember was seeing a string of flashing lights at the dark end of the cave. First, I took no notice thinking that it was the result of the heavy bombing outside. However, as the blinding bright light continued to flash without any sound of the bombs, I decided to investigate as to what the hell was going on. After some twenty minutes of paralyzing fear, I continued to see more of the same. I quickly realized that what I was seeing could not be explained by lightning or exploding bombs. There must be another reason behind this mystery. I thought that it might be some military underground operation manned by Saddam Hussein's forces to defend the city from the invading armies. It was a tormenting few moments that seemed like hours at the time. I had to decide my next move quickly. I thought of three choices: to run out of the cave as fast as I could and shout for help, to stay and hide wherever I could and watch the unfolding drama, or to move nearer to the source of the light and investigate. At that moment, I remembered the wise words of a great poet: "Those who fear climbing mountains will live forever in ditches".

Remembering all the stories about the past mysteries of this ancient and mysterious place, I decided to do the bold thing and investigate. At this moment I recalled my grandmother's prediction that I was blessed and protected from all evils and that I should always follow my heart. She also told me once that only with courage I would live my life to the full. As the light became permanent with differing dazzling colours, I started to realize that whatever lay behind this mystery must be part of some advanced technologies. I started to think that it could be an American team conducting some secret surveillance before the army arrived. This thought was less scary than the other alternatives I was imagining. I could easily communicate with the Americans and ask them to help me leave the country with my daughter back to the UK. Hope started to replace fear. I told myself, I must build hope in this scary situation by focusing on the lovely bright colours and not focus on the unknown. As they say *Whatever will be, will be!*

My heartbeat returned to normal and I was no longer very scared. I started to walk very slowly towards the source of the light. At the same time, I continued to look back to see if there was any sign of movement outside the cave. I wondered whether this could be a trap and if the small exit could be blocked by someone or something. I could end up dying here without anyone being able to find me. In those days, no mobile phones where allowed in Iraq by Saddam Hussein's regime. The only mobile phone that worked was through a satellite connection called Thuraya. This was a very expensive device and anyone found with such a phone would be accused of espionage and could be imprisoned or, worse, paraded on TV as a spy and then shot.

I managed to silence the doubts within me as I kept moving deeper into the cave. From my recollection of what happened, I must have fallen into a well-lit space. I hit the ground with a painful bang and must have lost consciousness again. I had no idea how long I was in that state. Due to the searing back pain, I couldn't move at all once I did regain consciousness. I had the strangest feeling that I was in the presence of some extraordinary company. I was too scared to open my eyes, hoping that I may hear some reassuring voices first. I felt for sure that this was the end of my time, as everything happening seemed very surreal. Only a few days ago I was in Oxford, discussing with my wife the need to get our daughter back before the war starts. Now here I was in a very strange situation and too scared to open my eyes, in the ruins of Nineveh.

I waited for a few minutes but it seemed forever. I could no longer ignore the situation, as the irresistible urge to investigate was overwhelming. I tried to gather strength and pluck the courage to examine my situation. I remembered that one's greatest strength is to overcome hesitations.

Chapter 2
Alien Holograms

The light was unusually bright and I still could not work out its source. I truly thought that I might have been buried alive with an unknown energy that seemed brighter than the sun. I tried to stand up but my head ached so severely that I immediately knew that I must have been badly shaken up from the incident.

With my eyes half closed to reduce the damage to my sight, I wondered if I could work out where the brightness was coming from. Then I could try to plan my exit. This situation lasted for what seemed to me almost an hour. I was still hopeful of hearing some reassuring voices as the silence was killing me, or even better to wake up from a dream and find myself in bed. However, I was to have no such luck. I tried to move again and this time I realized the pain had subsided. I was able to sit upright and I tried to grasp onto something in my surroundings. I accepted the conclusion that, whatever was happening to me was not normal by any standard. Many things were very mysterious and beyond any rational explanation. It was not normal to see such a strong light in what appeared to be an empty cave with no exit. I looked up to determine how I could've fallen but there seemed to be no hole to indicate how it had happened. I thought that this was all very strange and it defied all possible explanations. My mind started to go blank. I did not know what to think or what to make of the situation I found myself in. I must have fainted again as this is usually part of the body's defensive mechanism to preserve sanity.

I don't remember for how long I was unconscious. To my shock, I was awakened by strange voices. I could not understand the language being spoken, but the very possibility that I was hearing human voices seemed the best gift I could've hoped for in this situation. Suddenly, I was stunned to see five respectable, unusually dressed men staring back at me. Even though they looked very reassuring, I was still uncomfortable with the whole situation. I was deeply puzzled by the manner in which they were dressed. I extended my arm hoping that I would get help from one of them to stand up. As I tried to hold onto the hand that extended towards me, I realized that there was nothing to actually grab hold of. I felt very confused and scared. This sort of thing only happens in dreams, but I knew I was not dreaming. I pulled my hand back quickly trying to see the reaction on their faces, as they were scrutinizing me in great detail.

After a few minutes of silence, I plucked the courage to say, 'Please explain where I am, and who you are?'

I was not expecting an answer, as they seemed to have no physical form or hand to hold onto. They mumbled to each other as if they were debating how to address me and who would be selected as their spokesman. As I spoke to them in English, they realized that this was my preferred language for communicating with them.

Then, to my surprise one of them said in a soft voice and in perfect English, 'Don't fear us, don't fear us Mahmoud. We are here with a message of peace and goodwill for the human race. You will be called Mac for short.'

I stayed silent and took a very deep breath to absorb what I had just heard. They knew my name and they had come with a message of peace and goodwill, not for me, not for Iraq, but to the entire human race. They appeared to be like human holograms and yet they possessed technology to create floodlights all over the cave without any obvious type of power generator.

Seeing the surprise and confusion on my face, they tried to put me out of my misery.

'Mac,' one of them said, 'Please relax and let us explain by introducing ourselves first. I am Plato, as you can probably see from my ancient Greek outfit. The one on my right is Darwin with his nineteenth-century English clothes.'

Then Plato introduced Abraham who was dressed in a very ancient tribal dress that resembled the current Bedouin dressing more than any other earlier period.

'Newton and Adam Smith are the ones standing just behind me,' said Plato as he pointed to them. They all appeared to be very friendly and courteous.

Plato smiled and continued, 'I think you are familiar with our names. To help you recognise us we have dressed in accordance to the era we lived in.'

After some hesitation I said, 'I do not understand. How could I be familiar with your names unless you mean you are whom I think you are supposed to be? But this cannot be happening as you are all dead and belong to different eras.'

'That is right,' answered Plato. 'We have borrowed these names to bring home the message of goodwill we are trying to pass onto humanity.'

'Since you are not human beings, please tell me first if you are angels or some sort of aliens?' I asked.

'You could say so,' Plato replied. 'We are not humans nor are we in a physical form. This is why you could not hold our hands or touch us physically. We are, as you may have guessed,

33

holograms. We wanted to enable you to recognise us and feel at home as we spend the next few days together.'

'What?' I screamed, 'Few days? You cannot be serious! My daughter and sister's family will be worried to death wondering if something serious had happened to me.'

'Relax Mac; you should feel very privileged to be selected for this assignment. The quicker you accept it and focus on our teachings the deeper your understanding and enlightenment will be after this encounter,' Plato said reassuringly.

'OK,' I responded half-heartedly. 'First I'd like to know if I am here by accident or if all this had been planned? I would also like to know what you hope to achieve from this encounter.'

Abraham came and sat next to me and said, 'We don't leave things to chance. Everything had been planned, including Roxie's visit to Mosul. I am sure you know that it was out of character for you to send your daughter to Iraq. After all, you are an accountant who has an aversion to risks and you coldly calculate everything before implementing. You must have known that the war was about to start at any moment. Yet you did. We planted the idea in your subconscious and then engineered for you to follow her.'

'I suppose you also refreshed my memory to visit the Ruins and be in this cave!' I said, trying not to sound sarcastic.

Plato laughed and said, 'Now you are beginning to get it. You are bright after all. This encounter has been planned for a long time. Would you like to know why you have been chosen? I am sure you remember your grandmother's supernatural stories.

'You have come from a family that is tuned to receive divine messages. Initially, we were not sure of your capabilities to tune in until we tested you in 1984 when you were in Jeddah. We established that you not only got our messages loud and clear but also acted on them. I am sure you remember the general theory of physics that we passed on to you. We recall when you named that moment as "The Eureka Moment". Actually, you didn't only receive our message with great passion, but also you did something about it. You extensively researched the subject and wrote a paper on the topic.'

I put my hand on my head, and said in shock, 'Please don't play with my mind. Although what you are saying is absolutely true, I cannot believe that I had been put under your observation for over such a long period of time. It has been almost twenty years. I still have the paper I wrote. I sent it to many potential publishers at the time and I have the response from some of them. I am very proud of it, as it was my first attempt to commit abstract ideas to writing. I actually made many cosmic predictions that later came true. I remember the great efforts I put in writing that paper to see if what I formulated amounted to a general theory of physics. I tried to find out if other scientists had felt similarly. It was great fun trying to find a public library in Jeddah. I ended up in the University of King Abdulazziz's library for my research. To my pleasant surprise, everything I read appeared to be separate models to explain the observed universe and supported the general theory I had just worked out. I thought it was so simple, yet no one had put it that way. Therefore, Abraham, you are telling me that you have been observing me and that you were aware of my love for science and religious harmony all along? Please tell me that you have not been planting all those ideas in my head.'

Abraham laughed and said, 'While some people come up with original ideas and are considered very creative, others may get help from divine messengers.

'Before I opened my mouth to interrupt," he continued, 'I suppose that we have to provide you with reasonable explanations of how such divine messages are transmitted to reach certain individuals, otherwise you will be too embarrassed to even mention it.'

I realized that these shadows could read the millions of neurons that were firing in my brain before I even knew myself.

Newton, looking serious, said to his colleagues, 'Let us put Mac out of his misery and explain how he will survive with us during the coming few days. Let us also entertain Mac by showing him a thirty-minute film about his life from birth to date.'

They all looked at me for a reaction as if they knew they had thrown a bombshell.

'How are you going to look after me when you know very well that we are stuck in this deep hole with no food or water? Do you have some logistic support on the outside to ensure that we are adequately supplied? How you are going to show me a tape about my life since birth?'

Darwin looked rather serious and said, 'We do not need anything to survive as we are not in a physical form as you must have guessed by now. As to how we can supply you with anything that comes to your mind, you leave that to us.'

'So you do mean what you have just said? But surely only God and his agents have such powers,' I said.

'Let us call it a miracle for the time being. You humans insist on finding an answer for everything. With your limited knowledge, if you cannot explain what is being observed, you will say, "This is an act of God". Only then you can put your mind at ease,' Darwin continued, 'This is why once the human mind was redesigned to have the frontal lobe, it started to simulate concepts and ask "What if" questions, i.e. man became inquisitive. If the brain is subjected to some contradictory observations or messages, it will not rest and inner harmony will not get re-established until an answer is found to resolve the contradictions.'

I responded, 'I think I understand. This is why most human beings find faith and the existence of God in their lives very comforting. God is the answer to all our known unknowns.'

Abraham added, 'The real risk of all religions is to stop the inquisitive minds from questioning the unknowns. This is probably why some societies throughout history have experienced a lengthy period of darkness. Believing in God is very comforting and necessary for human survival and their social development. That does not mean that one has to be rigid in his thinking. There are some believers who get brainwashed. They accuse anyone who challenges them with blasphemy.'

I could see Plato was getting concerned with Abraham's comment. He said, 'We are moving away from a structured approach to the various subjects planned for the days that lie ahead. Let us leave these details to appropriate lectures in order to enable us to stick to our program.'

I interrupted Plato, 'I have been promised to be shown a video of my life from birth to the present day. Is this true or is it a joke?'

Before I finished the sentence, Newton stared at me and responded, 'We don't joke during such serious encounters.'

'Humans believe in life after death and also believe that God knows every move we make and every thought we have. So is this a confirmation that you had some godly assistance in making this tape? How come it is only thirty minutes then?' I enquired.

In a rather relaxed voice Plato said, 'I am sure you wouldn't want to see the long version of your life. With the passing of time, most of the minor events and even some of the major ones would have been forgotten by you. We are only going to play some of the memorable situations in your life. We hope to refresh some memories which relate to why you have been selected for this task.'

I was full of excitement and disbelief. I felt incredulous that I was about to see a replay of the main events of my life, going back to a period when just taking a black and white picture would have been a major technological marvel. They all sat down as if they were in a movie theatre. There it was, our old house. I recognized my grandmother standing up in the top room. She looked very happy, as my mother had just delivered a healthy baby boy. Many children were playing in the background. The year was 1947 and it was a cold wintery day. There were few scenes showing how I grew up with my siblings. Next, I was six years old walking from school to the house where there were many women crying and wearing black clothes. My father was telling me that my mother had just died and that he now had to take care of his eight children on his own. I started to accompany my father to his shop after school. We had an education system similar to that in Britain and we were continuously tested before we moved to the next level. They showed the time I used to spend hours on my own in the ruins of Nineveh. My grandmother used to tell me stories about her special mystical powers.

Then the movie showed my first trip out of Mosul to travel to England for my studies. I was happy to see my life during the swinging sixties in the UK, mostly in Bristol. The tape reminded me of my Danish wife whom I met in Bristol and my daughter Anna who was born in Denmark in 1972 while I was in Iraq. They came to Iraq briefly but I then lost contact with Anna and her mother after they returned to Denmark in 1973. After twenty-five years, in 1997 Anna found me via an Internet chat room. It was a tearful reunion at Heathrow Airport. The tape also refreshed my memory of my life in Saudi Arabia as a senior executive in the eighties. It also showed how I worked on my general theory of physics. The First Gulf War started and I had to leave Saudi Arabia and move to the UK, as I was a holder of an Iraqi passport. The tape continued onto September 11, 2001 and then to the present day. I was dying to know how they could make such a tape as they claimed that this was only an extract from a much more detailed one.

Newton looked at me and said, 'We promise, you will know how such tapes are made and you will be shocked when you realize how easy it is to make them. I also make a personal promise that if you do not work out the answer for yourself after the first two sessions, I will spend extra time with you to explain it.'

Although I was reassured, I was rather surprised at the level of promises they were making. Even if they did tell me, how am I going to recall all of it, keeping in mind my poor memory? Then we spent a very relaxing time discussing some heavenly powers and revelations.

All of a sudden, I had the urge to ask a rather serious question. 'Are you about to re-confirm Genesis as it was told in the Old Testament?'

They whispered to each other and then Abraham responded by saying, 'You may call it "Genesis Revisited". Please try and keep your questions to a minimum for today.'

Then Abraham continued to recite Genesis revisited:

'Genesis 1) God said, "Let creation commence" and there were two completely dark bundles of solid photons (singularities or black holes) rotating at the speed of light in opposite directions.

Genesis 2) God said, "Let there be light and let time and space commence" and the two black holes collided creating the expanding universe.

Genesis 3) God said, "Let there be atoms" and some of the photons started to bend and rotate around themselves in very small and stable radii and in doing so created the physical universe.

Genesis 4) God said "Let there be gravity" and all the physical universe (atoms and black holes) started to interact with the Divine Dimension.

Genesis 5) God said, "Let there be seeds of life" and the seeds were created and spread around the universe.

Genesis 6) God said, "Let the seeds evolve to create intelligent beings in my image as the Creator" and the genes' instructions started to evolve to create intelligent beings.

Genesis 7) God said, "Let the living organisms have Soul" and the Divine Dimension started to interact with the vibrating genes.'

Hoping to inject some humor after such big revelations, I said, 'I know I am not supposed to ask questions but did God design these tasks over seven days? Did God forget his day of rest?'

They all laughed and Abraham continued, 'You humans take what you read in your holy books very literally. This is the real failing of the human mind. It is the main reason why many people prefer to be atheists rather than be hardwired to such rigidities. There is a third way to bring science and religions together and we hope to guide you to it.'

Thinking about what I had just heard, I could not stop wondering if they are going to answer humanity's dream by disclosing hidden knowledge. What would it mean if they revealed the "Ultimate Theory of Everything"? Would it bring to an end the long human struggle to understand the universe? Would it simplify understanding of the laws that govern the universe? Would science be simplified so that ordinary people could understand it? At present, few people can keep up with the rapidly advancing knowledge, while the rest of us are mere spectators.

Would the new knowledge change our understanding of the unlimited power of God even if there were a unified theory that is just a set of rules and equations? Why did God bother to create the universe and all living things? Does the unified theory need a Creator; as spelled by Genesis above and if so, does He have any control on the universe other than being responsible for its creation? The philosophers have not been asking these questions, as they are unable to keep up with the advancement of scientific theories. However, in the nineteenth and twentieth centuries, science became too technical and mathematical for the philosophers or anyone else, except for a few specialists. Is it time for the philosophers to make a comeback to awaken humanity from their complacency?

I lifted my head to look at my guests. I realized that they were all watching me with deep interest as they were fully absorbing my line of thinking.

Plato laughed loudly, looked at Newton, and then said to me, 'You are really making Newton nervous as you seem to have identified many areas you'd like him to cover tomorrow. You are also touching on religion and philosophy and we realize now how ambitious you are in your expectations of this encounter. We hope to provide humanity with an almost complete theory. We expect that it will be widely debated, challenged and, in time, understood broadly by the many and not just by the few who specialize in physics. This will lead to the triumph of both rationalism and religion. God will make a great comeback in the minds and the hearts of people.'

It was getting late on Saturday and I was very hungry. I was guided to another part of the cave where all the different foods that I normally enjoy had been prepared. I had a wonderful dinner while they joined me pretending that they were dining with me. At the dinner, they did not want to waste any time and started to explain how they will handle the next five days of training and the final, concluding day.

Plato eyed me carefully for the slightest reaction and then said, 'I suppose you would now like to know why we have selected the names and appearances of well-known people from history? Let me explain what will happen over the next few days.

'Tomorrow, Newton will start with the amplification of the physical dimension and the unifying theory of physics. We will all be present and you will be able to request any clarification you like. We will respond according to our disciplines. If there is anything you do not absorb, then please interrupt and ask for an explanation so that we can expand on the issues concerning you.

'Abraham will be devoting Monday to the explanation of the Divine Dimension and the role religions play in human life. As you know, Abraham is the father of all three monolithic

42

faiths. Effectively, Abraham will remind us that this Encounter is to comply with the first *surah* handed to Mohammed in the Quran.

'Darwin will start on Tuesday. He'll enlighten you with his revised theory of evolution. The real Darwin would love to come back to modern times and rewrite his book. He will devote a great deal to the role of genes in his theory of evolution. During the encounter, you will be reminded that the concept of the seeds of life is not new but is mentioned in the Bible and other holy books.

'Wednesday will be devoted to me, Plato. I will explain the various political systems and also why all of them have their shortcomings. I will discuss how democracy has been hijacked by the few. I will then tell you about the plan being drawn for Jerusalem in the Kingdom of Heaven.'

'Thursday will be allocated to Adam Smith. He will explain the problems with the current economic practices and casino banking. He will also explain why they are failing humanity. He will disclose the solution of how to fund the new "Just World Order" and at the same time he will deal with the issues of major economic imbalances.'

'Finally, on Friday we will have a general question and answer session with important guests that would include Moses, Jesus and Mohammed via a conference call. They will clarify how to deal with issues of blind faith. They will call for multi-faith dialogue. This will be followed by a farewell handshake. Each of the guests will make a few revelations as to what will happen to humanity in the centuries to follow.'

I looked at Plato with overwhelming emotions as he mentioned the names of the greatest men that have ever walked on this planet.

'Your promises are getting wilder by the second. Even if they are going to happen as you say, how are you expecting me to absorb all this high-level stuff in five days plus one? I recall that Plato used to keep his students in the academy for more than twenty years just to absorb the little knowledge which existed at that time.'

They all laughed and Plato quickly responded, 'We are not expecting you to become a physicist, a priest, a biologist, a philosopher or an economist. Our objective is to lay the foundations for a philosophical debate that may awaken human minds to be more creative, just, tolerant and compassionate way of thinking. We trust that this will also create better understanding of science and the acceptance of God's existence. We hope to show the importance of religious tolerance and the need for peace on Earth for the Great Designer's plan to be fulfilled.'

Abraham added, 'Mac, we promise that anyone who will read in full with open mind and reflect on our teaching during this Encounter will be a different person by the end of it. If you know what is ahead of you, then what is hidden from you will be revealed. For there is nothing hidden that won't be revealed.'

I took a deep breath and said, 'Oh yes that sounds very biblical in scale. I wish I hadn't asked the question. You want me to have some deep understanding of all that is hidden?'

Plato looked rather serious and said, 'Not all that is hidden but most. The rest will come when man can be trusted to handle the hidden knowledge. Mac, remember that the biggest enemy to success is inner doubt. It is not enough just to have a dream or a vision. You must also have the inner strength and discipline to convert the knowing into doing. You must kill the whispering doubt and replace it with an "I can" attitude. With a will of steel, you can move mountains. Hesitation is the enemy of success.'

I looked at the rest to help me stop Plato, as he seemed to love preaching in any area of human frailty. Surely, he must have detected my self-doubt?

Looking at me Abraham said, 'Let me remind you of a verse from Surah Bee 2, in the Quran: The Lord sent Angels (in the spirit) by his command, to any human as he pleases, to warn that, "there is no God but I, so listen to my teaching".'

I noticed that Abraham was trying to imply that while I may think that they are angels, in fact they are Senior Souls (from the Spirit) acting as agents of the Lord to elaborate on some of existing teachings in all the holy books. In the Kingdom of Heaven (the Divine Dimension) Angels and Souls dwell as already revealed in many holy books.

Newton, looking rather serious, winked at me and said, 'Mac, I don't want you to be too tired for tomorrow, as there will be a lot to absorb. What I have to say will be the foundation for the rest of the Encounter.'

Then he stood up and recited:

O man! Wake up and see.
How much works lie ahead for you to be.
Put Courage and Wisdom in your heart.
The long march for salvation must start.

The light dimmed slowly and all of us went to sleep. I say all went to sleep or appeared to do so, for this was as far as my consciousness could make of this strange situation.

Chapter 3

Newton's Day
The Working of the Universe

It was Sunday morning and we were ready for breakfast. I was taken aback by the layout of the surroundings. It was more beautiful than anything ever created by man and truly out of this world. Plato noticed the big shock on my face.

'I know you have a lot of questions as we noticed yesterday. Please leave them for later as Newton is getting anxious to start. He is apprehensive of the big task ahead. It is not easy to pass so much knowledge in one day and make it comprehensible.'

Newton stood up and said rather impatiently, 'Let us start?'

It being the first day in the process of illumination, I was not sure what to expect. I didn't know how serious they were in keeping all the promises they had made the previous day regarding the knowledge and wisdom they were going to impart to me.

Before Newton could open his mouth, Plato said, 'I have always found it useful in such situations to put an individual in the correct picture.'

From my body language it must have been clear to Plato that I did not understand what was going on.

'To absorb knowledge,' Plato continued, 'you need to be open-minded and reflective. Only then, what you hear and see will be understood and absorbed into your permanent memory.

Human history is full of stories where someone has seen a Divine Revelation. Then that becomes hardwired in the brain and changes their personality forever.'

I interrupted, 'What are you saying? Do you expect me to accept everything you are going to tell me as gospel and not to challenge it just because I am having an unusual experience?'

Abraham realized the harshness in my tone and stood up to calm me down. 'On the contrary, we want you to be very inquisitive. Please challenge everything we say. Most of Mankind's evils are the result of rigidities and dogmas when it comes to the subject of faith and divine experiences. All that Plato has requested is for you to be open-minded and reflective.'

I was regretful of my outburst and said, 'Apologies if I misunderstood Plato. There are so many idiots on our planet who are trying to impose their beliefs on others.' I turned to Newton and said, 'Please start as you are very keen that we don't waste any more time.'

Newton responded, 'Thanks Mac. Let me summarize the current human knowledge regarding the working of the universe. I must say it is an immense topic and therefore I will be very brief. I will start with Aristotle who was born in the year 384 BC.'

Plato could not help saying, 'He was my best student at that time. Aristotle was the first philosopher and scientist to introduce a rational and systematic process for investigating all aspects of life. He dismissed the reliance on beliefs that the universe was created by some magic. He applied rational thinking to explain the natural world. He opened the doors for humanity to challenge the status quo. He applied logic and research to explain all that was needed to be explained. His work constituted the encyclopaedia of scientific knowledge for many centuries after his death. The move to the age of

47

enlightenment started when some open-minded thinkers liberated themselves from the dogma of religions. They started to apply Aristotle's rational thinking to all issues under investigation. The real breakthrough came with the theoretical work of Newton who was born in 1642 in England. Newton's most prominent achievements were in the field of mathematics and the laws of motion that have many practical and universal applications in the real world. He then presented his law of Gravity that predicted the motion of the planets precisely. This was followed by his great achievement in the study of heat and acoustics.'

Newton keen to regain control of his lecture said, 'According to present human knowledge there are a number of partial theories explaining how the universe works. These include the general theory of relativity, the partial theory of gravity, and the partial theories that govern the weak forces, the strong forces, and the electromagnetic forces. All current attempts to have a unified general theory of physics are not very satisfactory because they do not include gravity. Let me now briefly mention the scientific contributions of the greatest mind ever, and that is Albert Einstein. He propounded the theory of relativity, the general theory of relativity and the law E (energy) = M (mass) times C^2 (where 'C' is the Speed of Light). He was the first to postulate the existence of photons, or particles of light to explain the observed electromagnetic waves of light. This opened the door to quantum theory.'

I could see the excitement on the faces of all my respectable teachers as we were approaching a crucial point on the foundation of the general theory of physics.

Newton continued, 'It is important that I explain what is already known about the photon as you will hear this word several times today and during the rest of this Encounter. The photon (or more commonly known as light) is the most basic elementary particle. The quantum of light, electromagnetic forces and all other forms of electromagnetic radiation are subjects covered under this heading. It is also known that the photon has zero mass. According to the quantum theory, the photon exhibits wave-particle duality.'

I was restless and raised my voice saying, 'This is getting too technical for me. It's starting to sound like a normal physics lecture and not a simplification by some mysterious shadows as promised.'

Newton responded, 'You are right. I will keep it simple. Imagine the photon as a dot (.) without mass and moving at the constant speed of light. As the dot moves, it vibrates. This vibration creates a wavelength and frequency. Photons have zero mass and usually move in a straight line. If a photon is bent and locked into a very tiny stable radius in circular motion, then and only then does it start to have an observable mass. Therefore, this is how energy can change to mass and mass to energy. This is how to explain the law $E=MC^2$ as I will expand on this principle in more detail later. There are only two radii at which the rotating photons would be stable. The very small radius generates the proton and therefore the greater mass relative to the electron. On the other hand, the electron is bigger in size and has a smaller mass relative to the proton. This means that the mass detected depends on how many times the photon rotates around itself per millisecond. Researchers have noticed that in some experiments the photons may have a different radius from the two stable ones. In this case, a different mass is detected for a very short time and then it disappears as the rotating photon converts back to its straight line motion and becomes massless.'

Everyone was shocked to see me jump from my chair and shout, 'You cannot be serious. Are you telling me that the entire universe with all of it wonders, colours, heat and variations are nothing but massless dots moving constantly at the speed of light? Since we are made of the same substance, then life including human beings is nothing but rotating photons. I am sure you have more to say.'

Newton looked at me, 'I expected this to be difficult to accept. Why don't we take a break? This will allow you to reflect on what I have just revealed so far. We can then continue after you have had something to drink and eat.'

During the break, hundreds of questions started to hit me. If the physical universe is nothing but rotating photons then all that appears to be solid is not in reality so at all. This must explain how we receive mobile and other signals that pass through walls and through objects that appear to be solid. To human eyes, many things appear to be solid but in reality are transparent, as far as the photons are concerned and they can pass through them. I wanted to know more about the photon. If the dot is in continuous motion in empty space, then how does it vibrate? What force locks the photon into such a small radius? Why do we say that the electron has a different charge from the proton?

As I was deep in thought, Abraham put his hand on my shoulder, 'Relax Mac, we will answer all these questions.'

'Excellent,' I replied as I was very keen to get the lecture restarted.

Newton stood up and said, 'Let me expand on the properties of the photon. The photon, which vibrates as it moves, creates an infinite number of wavelengths. Each wavelength creates different frequencies and different photon energies. The shorter the wavelength the greater is the frequency and therefore the higher is the energy. You can see how the Creator of the photon established the foundation for the most observable wonders in the universe by giving it the flexibility to have different frequencies. All experiences such as light, colours, radiation, heat, etc are the result of the vibrating photons. However, if these were all the properties of the photons then the physical universe would not have existed in its current form and no life would have been created. Another incredible characteristic of the photon is the way it gets to bend into two stable circular radii. This means that the photon does not stay moving in a straight line but it can also be forced into a curvilinear motion and be locked into a stable radius. Current human knowledge expresses photon energy mathematically and it almost a negligible value. I am not here to teach you physics or to explain the various useful properties of photons. All electromagnetic radiation, as in the case of medical imaging, lasers, light, photography and many other applications are all examples of photon application.

'Let us now move to the core of our teaching for today. All observable mass is made from a combination of:

'(1) Photons rotating in a very small and stable radius to form the proton with its positive charge

'(2) An electron that is bigger in size and has a negative charge

'The mass of the proton is 1838 times that of the electron and it is all due to the difference in the relative size of their radii. With this knowledge, scientists can measure the relative length of the electron's radius to that of the proton.

'(3) A neutron is the interlocking of the proton with another particle. It is also made of a rotating photon, but with an opposite charge to that of the proton. This other particle could be seen as an electron with a much smaller radius. The combination of these two particles makes the neutron slightly heavier than the proton and it has no charge. The proton and the neutron form the nucleus of the atom with electrons rotating around it. The number of the rotating electrons will depend on the number of the protons in the nucleus. You cannot have a stable nucleus without a neutron, as the gravity it generates is necessary to bind the protons together inside the nucleus. Now you can see how the vibrating dots, as they are forced into a stable circular motion, become a mass, and thus we have the observed physical universe. Different numbers of neutrons and protons are combined together to form stable nuclei of the various atoms.

'From the various atoms all the known substances in the universe are made. Symmetry and binding force are necessary for all stable nuclei. When a nucleus has too many protons and neutrons or lacks symmetry it becomes unstable and easily breaks up into smaller nuclei and radiates energy in the process. This is why Uranium, the heavy atom was used to create the nuclear bomb. This is known as atomic fission or the breaking up of the nucleus. In the process of splitting the heavy Uranium atom, some photons lose their stable radii. In so doing, they are thus converted into energy. While we are at it, you must also know that one could force two light atoms to be combined together to create a heavier nucleus and in the process release many photons. This process is known as atomic fusion. This is the concept behind the hydrogen bomb. In this way, greater energy is generated. Fusion is the main nuclear reaction that takes place in the core of stars including our sun. The atoms get highly excited and start to wobble violently. As the lighter atoms collide strongly, they fuse together to form heavier atoms. For example every four hydrogen nuclei join together to form a very stable helium nucleus. Helium is known as the building block for other heavier atoms. As the process of fusion continues within the stars, other atoms are created until the energy of the star dissipates and some stars will eventually turn into planets.'

I stood up half dazed with all this information. 'Please have mercy on my Soul and let me absorb what you are telling me. I am not sure if I want to laugh or cry.'

They all looked at me not knowing why I had said that.

I continued, 'It seems that we as human beings are nothing more than a cluster of photons (energy) locked in a given space. If some force is applied on our bodies we could evaporate into thin air.'

Plato stared at me, 'This is surely not new to you. You have always known that if a nuclear bomb is thrown on any city, as the US bomb was thrown on Hiroshima, thousands of people and objects would convert back to energy.'

Abraham understood the difficulty I was facing in adjusting to this new paradigm and said, 'Now you see why the Architect of the Universe has blessed humans with an eternal Soul. You have to be patient and wait for the rest of our teaching.'

It was really comforting to hear that the journey of our life will not end up as nothing due to the nature of the photon.

Abraham continued, 'Blessed are those who see the light within; blessed are those who are creative and virtuous to become eternal.'

After a prolonged silence that allowed me to reflect on what sounded akin to a verse from a Holy Book, I commented, 'I am sure you will explain at some stage the meaning of this quote. For now you are telling me that all matters are nothing but rotating photons and if someone can find a way to force the photons into a stable radii in a pre-known combination, then one can generate anything from thin air.'

Plato replied with a confident smile, 'Not from thin air, but from random radiations (photons floating continuously in space).'

I saw them laughing and then Adam Smith added, 'Now do you realize how you are getting your food in this cave?'

I was so puzzled and said, 'But you don't have any machines or other equipment to force photons to bend into a circular radius and generate food.'

'Let us not digress as the time has not come to explain how you are getting your food. At the right moment this will be made clear to you and it will appear to be very easy and logical,' said Plato.

I looked at Plato and said with some sarcasm in my voice, 'I can't wait. Can we return to the lecture and get Newton to explain the charge of the proton and electron? You have said the proton has a positive charge and the electron a negative charge.

So, much is determined by the charge of these particles. Can you explain what that means?'

Newton replied, 'To explain that, I will need to make another major revelation. I will explain how the photons and electrons are created in the first place and how the living universe works.'

They looked at each other and Plato added, 'We will be brief on this matter today as more will be explained tomorrow by Abraham.'

Newton continued, 'The entire observable universe by Mankind can be called the photon or physical universe as explained earlier. The photons did not appear by accident as atheists like you to believe. This type of thinking is the result of the inability of some scientists to accept the existence of a Great Designer as they struggle rationalise the concept of His existence. This sounds illogical to us. We are not going to tell you who created God as this will lead us to a never-ending debate. You are always going to end up asking who created the first Creator. At this stage, I only want to give an explanation of the working of the universe based on the existence of the Great Designer and His role in the process of creation. We are confident that what you will hear from us during this encounter will logically explain all the observations made by Mankind, both natural and supernatural.'

I looked at Newton with consternation and said, 'You are making a huge claim. Did God have a choice in creating the universe? Does the universe have a boundary? Did He have the freedom to choose the laws that the universe is obeying?'

Newton responded, 'There is only one complete unified field theory that explains the physical universe and allows the existence of intelligent beings in perpetuity. Let me spell it out for you, Mac. God has full knowledge of the properties of the substance from which the photons were released. God determined the constant speed at which the photons move (the speed of light) in order to have values which support the formation of a stable universe. Once He completed his creation, He no longer remained involved in the details of his creation. He creates processes that are strictly governed by predetermined laws. He then sits back and observes the wonders of His creation unfold. Some would argue that this infringes on God's freedom to change His mind and to intervene in the world. It will become clear during the encounter how God is not bothered by how the physical universe works. He is more interested in the wonderful things intelligent beings are capable of doing. More on that will come later.'

Newton continued, 'For our purpose at this stage, we know that the photon is made up of a dot or, as scientists call it, a singularity, and this photon is governed by strict laws as it vibrates. For an object to vibrate there must be some substance to make the vibration possible. Sound does not exist in vacuum because it needs molecules to create the vibration. The existence of a universal substance in space was the original thinking of the scientists until it was dismissed for not being able to prove its existence. To solve the problem of how the photon vibrates in emptiness, scientists assumed that the photon is a "string"-like and not a "dot"-like particle. This was a convenient way to explain the wave characteristic of the photon without the need to explain the existence of an undetectable dimension.

'Well, that undetectable dimension does exist. We call it the Divine Dimension (DD). The vast emptiness of the universe is made of the Divine substance. This cannot be detected by any instrument made by humans as all such instruments are made of photons. Mankind's current difficulties in arriving at a theory of everything are due to rejecting this fact. The existence of the DD is essential to explain many other observations regarded as supernatural by rationalists.'

I stood up and spoke with some hesitation, 'If I report these claims to scientists who have dismissed the existence of God and the existence of an undetectable universal substance, they will say this is a cheap attempt to acknowledge the presence of God through the back door.'

Newton replied without any reluctance, 'It seems that scientists are buried in their rationalism and thereby ignoring their mental limitations. They know that string theories require space-time to have ten or twenty-six dimensions, instead of the usual four. We are proposing only one additional dimention to explain most of the universe mysteries. Scientist also don't yet know whether all the infinities generated by the string theories' formulations cancel each other out. In fact, they also don't know how exactly to relate the waves on the string to the particular types of particle that they observe.'

Newton continued, 'You see Mac, the current skepticism of scientists is mainly due to the wild claims made by various religions. These religions try to instil blind faith through miracles and irrational explanations. Religions have exaggerated supernatural observations to such a degree so as to make any fair-minded person very doubtful. The God of the gaps principle, i.e. explaining every unknown as being created by God, is the most commonly used evidence by atheists for doubting the existence of a Creator. Many things that were claimed to be the work of God can now be given a simple and rational explanation.'

With some unwillingness on my part I asked, 'Are you telling me that some religions make wild claims regarding miracles? If you are not a figment of my imagination, isn't your presence with me a big miracle? Does it not defy any rational explanation?'

Newton replied, 'I suggest that you make up your own mind at the end of this encounter. Don't question our teachings and your observations without hearing us conclude our enlightenment. We assure you that you will become an advocate of the rational and of what is today regarded as irrational. You will call on scientists to recognise their limitations. You will show them that for the total understanding of how the cosmos works, they need to accept the existence of the DD.'

I kept silent, waiting for the explanation of the charge of particles and of how the photon was created in the first place.

Newton went on, 'The photons were created from splitting of a substance in the DD to create two very dense singularities. Each singularity is made up of dense photons or dots rotating at the speed of light. Some photons rotate clockwise while an equal number of photons rotate anticlockwise. It is the direction of these rotations that will give the particles their charge. Therefore, when we say the proton has a positive charge, it means that it is rotating, say, clockwise. Therefore by definition, the electron would rotate in the opposite direction, or anti-clockwise.'

I interrupted, 'If this is the case then there must be equal number of particle and anti-particles in the universe.'

'Well observed Mac,' Plato said. 'This is the case if we consider the whole universe. When the designer of the universe created the two singularities rotating at the speed of light, he actually created the first two black holes.

'Remember in Genesis God said, "Let creation commence" and there were two completely dark bundles of photons, singularities or black holes, rotating at the speed of light in opposite directions.'

Plato continued, 'As these two singularities with unimaginable masses and gravity, rotated at the speed of light in opposite directions, they gravitated towards each other. This was the first Big Bang that created a large number of galaxies speeding away from the point of the original impact. This is how the expanding universe started and at the same moment, time and space began. I can talk for days about black holes, as they have been the biggest mystery to scientists. They cannot be observed but their existence is known and required to give a rational explanation of the working of the universe. We could explain that the existence of a Great Designer and a DD is also necessary to give a rational explanation to everything being observed at the natural and supernatural levels.'

Newton resumed his lecture, 'We are not advocating that Mankind stop searching for the truth. On the contrary, we are providing a "Theory of Everything" and we ask humans to apply all their mental capacity to prove or disprove these claims. We hope that the debate that should follow, will lead to a new age of awakening, especially among orthodox and conservative cultures. You see, what I have just said also explains: Genesis 2) God said, "Let there be light and let time and space commence", and the two black holes collided and created the expanding universe.'

I could see that they were waiting to see how far I needed Newton to continue on this subject. I confirmed that I was overwhelmed and added with a smile, 'You are opening the unknown "unknown" box in my mind.'

They all laughed at my comment.

'Go ahead. Let us know which unknown of your mind you want it to be known?' Plato said.

I added, 'I will raise few questions but not in any structure as I am thinking aloud. I think I understand now how the universe started, and what it is made up of. Firstly, could you tell me why at the black hole level, the laws of Quantum Physics do not apply?

'Secondly, do black holes have any useful role in the universe beyond the original creation? Why are they called black holes and can we measure their mass? Can a black hole get created without the intervention of the Creator?'

Newton looked very sombre as he said, 'I am not sure how I am going to fit all the explanations in one day. We have not yet spoken about gravity and other aspects of the workings of the universe.'

'No problem, we can borrow some time from the other lectures,' I replied innocently.

All the other four holograms jumped in objection and shouted passionately and in one voice, 'No way! We hardly have enough time for our own lectures as it is.'

I realized that we would be wasting valuable time discussing the timetable and therefore asked Newton to carry on as he saw fit and proper.

Newton continued, 'You are right to ask these questions. The laws of quantum mechanics do not apply at the black hole level. The photons do not vibrate until they are released from the black hole in the Divine Dimension and therefore they have zero radii. You see, the observed universe relies on a few properties of the photons: vibrations, radii when they are locked in circular motion and their directions. At the black hole level, there is neither photon vibration nor a circular radius. This is why applying quantum physics at the black hole level would lead to zero or infinite values. Scientists need to develop different laws at the black hole level taking into account the explained characteristics of these bundles of photons.'

Abraham referred to Genesis 3 as explained above by Newton. God said "Let there be atoms", he reminded me, and how some of the photons started to bend and rotate around themselves in very small and stable radii and in so doing created the physical universe.

Newton then continued to answer my questions, 'For your information Mac, black hole or dark matter in the universe is a name given by scientists to this object, as nothing, not even light, can escape its tremendous gravity. Without the black holes, the universe cannot maintain its existence. Let me explain further. A black hole is found at the centre of each galaxy. Its gravitational force stops the constituents of a galaxy from breaking up and drifting away. In the long run, a proportional relationship exists between the mass of the black hole and the total mass of the galaxy. As a black hole is continuously growing in mass by absorbing all the objects that are trapped within its gravitational field, the galaxy must also grow in time. It does this by attracting other celestial bodies that approach its growing field of gravity. If a black hole has a relatively low mass to the size of the galaxy then the distant bodies, the planets and stars, will lose their orbit around that black hole due to any passing celestial object. You see, black holes keep the universe in stable clusters of stars and planets to stop them from drifting away and getting lost in space. Another important role for the black hole is to collect the photons and the out-of-orbit celestial objects. In doing so, a black hole acts as a cosmic vacuum cleaner and stabilizer. The growth of some black holes and their gravitational fields accompanied by the paths they follow in space, would ultimately lead to a new big bang and therefore new galaxies will be created.

'Let me now explain how a new black hole could come into existence. As a star of great energy is burned out, its core becomes very dense. The pressure at its core leads to the break-up of the photons' stable radii. As the photons cannot escape the dense core of the star, they convert back to their singularities. The resulting increased gravity at the core causes the adjacent photons to follow through by breaking out of their stable radii and joining the black hole fetus. This is the moment when the growing gravity of the infant black hole accelerates the break-up of other photons out of their stable radii and joins the core. In the process, many photons manage to escape creating a sudden burst of great energy. This will lead to the observation of the sudden burst of energy followed by complete darkness over a relatively short period of time in cosmic measurements.'

I looked at Newton with deep interest and asked, 'Why did you say only a star of a large size could turn into a new black hole?'

'This is a good question.' Newton responded. 'Only if the size of the star has such a huge pressure at its core can the photon be forced back into its singularity. If this is not the case then some of the stars would end up becoming planets.'

Plato was getting uncomfortable as he could observe the volume of information being thrown at me as if I were an experienced astronomer. He wanted to give me the chance to absorb what is being explained so far and requested a rest. I really needed the break and thanked him for his suggestion. During the break, I could not stop thinking about the huge amount of knowledge and power these visitors have. I wondered if they could show me some drawings or videos as teaching aids.

Newton obliged, 'This is a convenient time to move onto the important area of explaining the working of the universe and the resulting gravity. Without incorporating gravity into our teaching, you will not have a unified field theory of physics. Let me show you an example of what the DD may look like and how curvatures are shown as expression of gravity.'

A picture of infinite space with a transparent jelly-like substance was shown to me. This transparent jelly-type structure changed shape by shrinking and twisting as photons and black holes rotate. This shrinking and twisting of the substance of the DD is how individuals' experiences measures gravity. What I saw was unexpected. In some areas of this structure there were deep cone-like holes. At the bottom of the cones were the black holes. Everything, including light was being sucked down as they reached the edge of the curvature. This is similar to the folding of space as Einstein correctly postulated. For an object to escape gravity must moves at a speed faster than the shrinkage in the DD (space). Therefore, the force needed to escape gravity depends on the curvature created in the DD and the direction and speed of the object trying to escape such shrinkage (gravity). Einstein expressed this as the general theory of relativity.

'Therefore, if space is made up of emptiness, you will not have curvature related to gravity nor vibration of photons. This is important evidence that space is made of a substance we are calling it the Divine Dimension. This substance is necessary for a rational explanation of the working of the observable universe. As we proceed additional comments will be made in this regard.'

Abraham could not help reminding me of Genesis 4) God said "Let there be gravity" and the entire physical universe, with its atoms and black holes, started to interact with the Divine Dimension.

I couldn't keep quiet any longer. 'I understand now. You are here to use science as a means of contradicting atheists in their denial of the existence of God.'

They were all pleased with this observation and Abraham wanted me to expand on my comment and wondered if I had any problem with that?

After a period of silence and a great deal of hesitation on my part, I said, 'Why don't you follow the well tested methods used with all the previous prophets or messengers of the Lord? Give me the power to perform some miracles and all the people will experience a paradigm shift and will convert to the new message with ease. This is the time when the news of such miracles will be transmitted around the world in seconds to billions of people.'

Detecting a sarcastic note in my tone, Newton said, 'You are absolutely right. If we were here to propose a new faith, we would have done just that. The time of delivering new faiths based on miracles is no longer appropriate in the age of reason. You see, every era of human civilization requires a different approach. We are here to assist in Mankind's awakening based on rational thinking. Without this new knowledge man will not be on track to fulfil his Divine mission as will be made clear later.'

Abraham interrupted and said, 'We are running out of time so let us discuss these matters tomorrow. I am sure Mac has many more questions regarding science.'

I took a deep breath as I looked at Newton and said, 'Let me see. Firstly, could you explain what space and time are? Then I would appreciate a summary of how this information will improve my understanding of how the world around me works?'

'You are right,' Newton responded. 'Space and time are a very complex concept to explain and I will try to keep it simple.

'Space is understood by humans to be the distance between observed objects. When they say the universe is very vast, it means the distance between observed celestial objects is enormous. When the universe expands it means those objects in space are getting further away from each other. So space or the DD has no boundaries and at the same that time has no defined limits.'

Then Newton moved on to the difficult concept of time. He explained, 'Time only exists if you have motion or if objects are moving. This is why we said that time started at the point the black holes were created. Time is the property of the universe that God has created. Therefore, you can say that time is the by-product of motion. Time can be seen as a mean of measuring the change due to motion in any observed space. To measure time, you need to agree on the unit of measurement first. That unit must have a fixed value and easy to be comprehended by those conducting the measurements. On Earth, the most common unit of measuring time is one rotation of Earth around itself. Once this is agreed, it is broken down into hours and seconds. Another unit is selected for a longer period and that is the time needed for the Earth to revolve around the sun. In many cultures, the lunar rotation around the Earth is used as it was easier to observe the lunar months.'

Abraham interjected, 'Where there is no space and time, you want to be. Where there is space and time, you are on a journey. Use the "Here and Now" wisely and you will be rewarded amply.'

I looked around to see if he was talking to someone else.

Plato with a wide smile on his face said, 'Keep this saying in mind. All will be revealed before the end of this encounter.'

Newton continued, 'Now let me try and expand on what has been said so far regarding the working of the universe. I will try to clarify how this could help you understand the world around you. As the photons hit the atoms making up the substance, they get excited. In effect, short wave photons excite molecules greater than long waves as the former stay relatively longer within the atoms, including human tissues. This can also explain why long exposure to the sun can cause skin cancer, if humans do not filter out certain short wave photons that exist within sunlight. This filtration could be achieved through the colour of the skin or the use of appropriate sun cream. Heat is nothing but photons exciting the atoms within any substance. The amount of heat will depend on the number of photons bombarding the substance and the wavelength of those photons.'

I interrupted to ask about what is meant by the excitement of the atoms.

Newton clarified, 'You are right to ask this question. Let me explain. As light or energy bombards the atoms, the rotating photons making up the atom start to wobble. This wobbling at the core of the atoms leads to expansion of the substance and weakening of the binding force joining the molecules. As a result of this expansion, the binding force weakens and the substance turns into liquid and then into vapour. If you apply plenty of heat, by photon bombardments, on the lighter atoms, then their increased wobbling and colliding would lead to the formation of heavier molecules and the conversion of some rotating photons back to energy as it is continuously happening in the sun under a process called fusion, as I have explained earlier.'

I noticed Plato whispering to his colleagues. 'Mac, are you sure you are absorbing all the clarifications made by Newton?' he asked.

After some hesitation I responded, 'Why didn't you choose someone who is an expert in physics instead of picking an accountant for this assignment?'

The reply came quickly, although I don't recall who made it. 'The key is not what you know, but how open-minded and reflective you are to absorb the new concepts. The worst students for new ideas are those who are pre-loaded with preconceived beliefs. The ideal way to learn is to focus on the concepts and principles and not on what is said. Mac, as a final step in finishing the lecture, would you mind if we were to ask you a few practical questions? We hope that you will apply deductive reasoning and apply the information we have just given you, in arriving at the answers.'

With a great deal of indecision I replied, 'Please go ahead.'

'How do you explain various substances having different colours? Why do some substances change their colours when they are heated?' Plato asked.

I stared at Plato, 'Let me try. Visible light is nothing but a spectrum of photons. The wave's length or frequency determines the visible colour in our brain. So as the light falls on objects with different levels of atom excitement, the frequencies of the reflected photons may differ.'

I continued, 'I have heard that different colours may affect human thoughts and moods. This must also be due to the fact that the brain is made of atoms and different vibrations must affect the brain atoms differently.'

Then they asked me to define absolute zero i.e. when the substance is at a temperature of -273 centigrade.

I ventured the following answer, 'If heat is generated due to the photons exciting the substance, then absolute zero must be achieved by the complete absence of photons within that substance. This is usually difficult to obtain as photons are everywhere in the form of background radiation.'

Newton was happy with the progress made so far. He was obviously delighted that I was able to make these responses based on the simple explanation given today.

He continued, 'We have definitely made the right choice in selecting you Mac. We trust that the approach you have just used will assist you and others to be interested in science for its simplicity. It will also put scientists in the right direction to combine quantum mechanics and the theory of gravity to create a general theory of physics. After all, behind the entire observed complexity of the universe, is a very simple explanation. It is the vibrating photons moving at the constant speed of light in straight lines or in two stable radii that makes up the entire observable universe. The movement of the photons interacts with the DD. The photons move either clockwise or anti-clockwise. Symmetry in the way atoms are structured is part of that simplicity.

'All the planets and stars rotate in clockwise or anti-clockwise motion depending on the direction of the photons making up the protons. In other words, the direction of the planets' and stars' rotation around itself is determined by the direction of the smaller radius making up the proton in those celestial bodies. The number of photons rotating clockwise is the same as the number of the electrons rotating anticlockwise as each atom has a similar number of electrons and protons in total. It is worth noting that all celestial bodies in any galaxy are rotating around themselves in the same direction including the black hole at the centre of the galaxy. If this is not the case then those with differing directions will crash once they come within one another's gravitational fields.'

I looked at Newton trying to understand how the new knowledge can explain the tremendous heat at the core of the Earth and why the Earth rotates around itself.

Newton discussed the matter with his colleagues to ensure that it was not part of the forbidden knowledge and said, 'Current human explanations for the heat deep in the core of the earth are: (1) heat from when the planet formed and accreted, which has not yet been lost; (2) frictional heating, caused by denser core material sinking to the centre of the planet; and (3) heat from the decay of radioactive elements. This explanation does not provide the full answer. At the core of the planet, with its huge pressure, the electrons (being less stable than the proton) start to lose their stable radii and turn into energy. This energy leads to initial heating of the core. With the atoms losing their electrons, they become positively charged and act like magnets and attract the iron to the core. As more iron accumulates and lose their electrons, they become huge magnets rotating in the direction of the spinning photon within the protons. The heat generated is due the continuous repulsive force trying to push the proton away from each other as they are all positively charged. The tremendous pressure pushes them back and stops them from converting into liquid or escaping from the core. You see Mac, if humans can replicate these conditions on the surface of the planet, they will have a continuous supply of energy from the repulsive force of the positively charged atoms and the great pressure pushing them back, provided that some force is applied to stop a state of equilibrium being established.'

They all looked at me to see if I would buy this explanation. Everyone knows that energy cannot be generated from nothing. There must be more to it than that. Being able to read my mind Newton smiled and said, 'You are right. You need us to expand on this to make this explanation more rational. I am sure that you have seen a wristwatch which works on the motion of the hand when it is worn. The source of energy at the core works on the same principle. You see, as long as the sun is heating the planet, there are changes on the surface of the Earth in terms of water distribution, earth movements, wind and so on. These changes lead to the slight movements at the core of the planet to stop the pushing and pressing forces from getting into a state of equilibrium. This is how this kinetic energy at the core keeps the atoms wobbling and hence generating the heat.

I wasn't sure what to make of this explanation, although it appeared more rational than the current human explanation. To change the subject I asked, 'Is there only one black hole in each galaxy?'

The answer was quick, 'No. Some small black holes may have their own planetary system and at the same time, they are part of a big galaxy. The living universe is continuously giving birth, followed by maturity and death of galaxies. Newer and smaller-sized galaxies are created in the expanding universe. This expansion continues until a time comes when some of these galaxies, due to the path they follow, start to have a contracting space between them. This contraction will ultimately lead to these galaxies joining together leading to a complete upheaval until a new order is re-established with bigger galaxies being the result.'

In conclusion, Newton said, 'The Great Designer has bar coded each photon in order to track and keep a record of all the activities of the physical universe.'

'Wow!' I exclaimed. 'As everything is made of photons including our thoughts and every photon is bar-coded then this makes God an all-knowing Creator. I suppose this is how you were able to play a record of my life history?'

They all looked at me and Plato said, 'We told you that you would work it out for yourself due to its simplicity.'

'Now I see how Genesis revisited is a summary of the Creator's will. I suppose more will be revealed in the coming days,' I replied.

Abraham looked at his colleagues and said, 'Before Mac goes to bed let us have dinner.'

As we stood up, the scenery changed completely to a big white palace overlooking a lake. I was shocked at the beauty and greatness of what I was observing. I rubbed my eyes to reassure myself that I was not dreaming.

Darwin came close and whispered, 'You are not dreaming. This is not a physical reality. It is all in the mind.'

I responded, 'You know, all of this is not good for my mental health. I'm starting to lose track of what is real and what is not. If it wasn't for the existence of gravity everything, including life, would be nothing but a hologram.'

Darwin replied, 'Don't worry; insanity is experienced when the human mind fails to find explanations to sudden changes to his reality.'

'Exactly and this is precisely what I feel happening to me right now,' I quickly observed

All of them overheard what I had just said and joined the conversation. They were very patient in reassuring me that what I was experiencing was all in the mind.

'It makes no difference as perception is reality as far as I am concerned.'

I looked at Newton and continued, 'If you have lectured me to explain about every observation in the universe, please explain the science behind what I am experiencing.'

Newton spoke with some firmness in his voice to re-assure me, 'There is no gap in the information passed on to you. Mac, what I explained earlier was in respect of the observable physical universe. What you are experiencing here is of a different dimension and therefore not subject to the normal laws of physics. Therefore, this is not covered by our teaching. Humans have to accept the limitation of the dimension they are living in and stop trying to make sense of something which does not belong to their dimension.'

With some hesitation, I accepted that answer. In my heart, however, I was sure that this would be seen as a cheap way of avoiding the question.

Newton continued, 'Believe me, if we debate this subject, the Known "Unknown" will multiply millions of times. Then humanity will not tolerate their increased ignorance. Knowledge evolves and humans must be ready to receive what is revealed to them in stages. Do you think, if the revised Genesis we revealed to you, were revealed earlier to Mankind, it would have been understood?'

I was quick to respond, 'Are you telling me that what I am observing are acts of God or miracles? If you are, then you are no different from all those who claim to be angels arriving with miracles.'

They could all sense the dilemma I was in. I needed worldly explanations and not a divine one.

Abraham came to my rescue and said, 'We can see your dilemma. You are living in the age of rational thinking. There is no room for fairy tales.'

'Exactly, thank you for your understanding,' I replied

To prevent this subject from taking too much time, as it was getting late, Plato said, 'Can we park this subject till tomorrow? I trust that you will have a better understanding of what is bothering you then. Let us enjoy the panoramic views as you finish your meal. By the way, you will notice one of the supporting proofs of the existence of the Great Designer, is the beauty and simplicity that underlie all the observed complexities including intelligence. Everything in the universe is in continuous motion and evolving. These continuous processes start with birth, maturity and death followed by rebirth. They apply to everything to guarantee the eternity of the universe and life in the universe, as Darwin will explain.'

As we were approaching the end of our dinner, I looked at Adam Smith and said jokingly, 'You will be out of business soon.'

They all looked very surprised and waited for me to expand.

I continued, 'If humans find a way to bend photons into atoms, then we can say to anything "let it be", and "it will be". So why do we need to study economics and work?'

They all laughed and said, 'It will be a long time before humans can develop such technologies.'

I was rather surprised by their answer as it implied that it is possible to do so.

They continued, 'A few years ago humans got excited in thinking that they can create energy through cold nuclear reaction, or cold fusion. This was not to be. You humans are always in a hurry to get results without following the correct path. After many visits like these, humans may get such advanced technology.'

I ignored the comment as it meant that humans needed to be continuously visited in order to advance their knowledge. I also did not understand what they meant by not following the correct path.

Adam stared at me and said, 'How come you did not also ask about how to create anti-gravity and in so doing would be able to float in the universe?'

They were all stunned by this comment as they were trying to avoid such difficult questions. I detected for the first time their difficulties in trying to answer all my questions without Adam adding another one.

Plato tried to save the situation by saying, 'This may require a philosophical response. Mac, you know humans started on the road to enlightenment only during the last 12,000 years. This is why there is no record of human civilization before that period. Humans have been assisted with similar visitations every now and then to direct them to the correct moral codes. One of the key conditions for passing on advanced knowledge is that humanity should be able to prove to the Lord that they have become trustworthy. To reach that state, they must demonstrate that they are adhering to the Lord's moral code. To prove that, human beings must inhabit this planet without wars or conflicts for at least several generations. Darwin will clarify this the day after tomorrow. This was the purpose of all the previous visitations by angels to numerous prophets. The objectives of all religions have been to guide humanity to live in harmony with one another. This has proved rather difficult to date. Unfortunately, there is a fundamental fault in the mental evolution of human beings. It seems that it will take much longer than expected to enable humans to control the evils within. The pursuit of money and power keeps creeping up at the expense of full compliance with Universal Virtues.'

I asked, 'Is this why you came in full force? Is it to enlighten humanity in various disciplines? I assume that you will not pass the technology necessary to possess real powers until humans are trusted as team players at the galactic level.'

Plato smiled, 'So now you can see Mac, why all the lectures have their importance as the tasks ahead are rather onerous and very long.'

With some sadness in his eyes Abraham said, 'Humans do not have a long time left to acquire the level of knowledge which will allow them to escape from Earth's gravity. The past 12,000 years have been very disappointing, taking into account the level of wars and destructions from Sumerian, Babylonian and Ancient Egyptian times to the present day. The sciences were very advanced during those civilizations too. This was followed by a period of ancient knowledge getting lost and a deep freeze in scientific progress.'

Abraham continued with this thought to put me on notice as to what I would expect tomorrow. He said, 'When you are two you will become one. When you are one what will you do?'

74

All of them smiled realizing that I did not understand its meaning and that it might keep me awake.

Darwin injected some hope into the conversation, 'Let us not be very gloomy, as the door for human evolution has not yet closed provided that man follows the correct path. I am sure that what Abraham will say tomorrow will be very important in this respect.'

Abraham then stood up and recited:

O Man! Wake up and shout.
What are we doing? Are we Mad!
The war and destruction will spill out.
Find me the activists with Mandela and Gandhi's vision.
Who will work tirelessly to stop the wicked with mission?

All of us then went out for a walk and continued to discuss some of the concerns I had regarding this encounter before going to bed.

Chapter 4

Abraham's Day
The Divine Dimension (DD)

The morning of Monday appeared fine and serene. Scenes of tranquility were filled with special feelings of true love. This was what Abraham had organized for his teachings on God, the DD and religion. I could see how everyone was very excited. They all expected the subject to be lively. They expected that it would get me engaged.

Abraham with his colorful robe, white hair, beard and a glowing face looked like a true angel.

After a quick breakfast, everyone was in place to hear what Abraham had in store for us. They were looking at me to see if I wanted to start with any comments to help Abraham structure his lecture. As I was very disillusioned with some aspects of religion due to their rigidities and the deadly behaviors of some extremists, I decided to make no comment.

Adam broke the silence with a passion that I had not noticed during the previous days. 'You will see the extent of religious influence on many aspects of human life, including the economy and politics in most societies.'

Abraham was very excited and stood up to start the day and said, 'This is going to be an interesting and long day. I will challenge many of the existing religious rigidities that are not serving the image of God well. I will start by making a short introduction to Middle Eastern politics and show the role of religions in the current conflict in Iraq. I will explain the reasons for religious revivals and why this has become the reason for wars instead of being a driving force for peace. I would like you, Mac, to actively participate and ask questions. As you know, humanity is living in difficult times due to bigotries and extremism from all sides. I will also touch upon what God expects of humans and how this can be achieved.'

I could not hold myself from saying again, 'I hope that you are not coming up with a new religion. We have enough religions in the world and there is no room for another one.'

They all nodded their approval.

Abraham replied, 'Don't worry; there will be no new religion. To create a new religion we have to stay on Earth as in the case of Jesus, or make repeated visits as in the case of the other prophets and we have to come up with some miracles. As you probably know, towards the end of nineteenth century the Islamic world was ruled by the Turks under the Ottoman Empire. During the First World War the Arabs sided with the Christians from Western Europe against the Muslim Khalifa. It was clear that they put freedom and justice ahead of religion. These values continued to be the motivating forces until 1967. During this period many secular values were introduced and accepted in this region including Nationalism and Socialism.

'While the Arabs were aspiring to build their nations on a non-religious basis, the secular Jews in Europe and around the world were using religion as a basis for building their Jewish state in Palestine. The Arabs were defeated in 1948 and the state of Israel was created. To defend themselves, the Arabs galvanized themselves under the banner of Arab Nationalism. This led to their disastrous defeat during the Six Day War in June 1967. The speed with which victory was gained led to a dramatic increase in Jewish fundamentalism all around the world as it renewed the belief that the Jews are still in favour with God and that they were truly God's Chosen People. Some newborn Christians started to spread the message that the Messiah's return was near. The building of the Temple of Solomon, which was predicted in their teachings, has become a matter of time only. The Muslims reacted to their defeat by re-examining their secular values. They realized that one can only challenge aggression based on religious prophesies with adherence to their faith.'

Plato interrupted, 'How very true this is. Man's core values are derived from faith and traditions. To know people well, one must get to know their core beliefs. When people are desperate, they seek any common ground to unite. There are many historical examples of the power of religion and its institutions in galvanizing the masses and acting as a unifying force.'

Abraham continued, 'The process of Islamic revival was encouraged by the West, as Islam was seen as a strong barrier against the expansion of Socialism and Communism which were spreading very fast at that time. In the 1980s, Islamic jihadists were encouraged with arms and money to fight the USSR in Afghanistan. In Iran, the creation of the Islamic state was also assisted by some Western powers enabling those acting behind the scenes to plant the seeds of the division between the two main branches of Islam: Sunni Islam and Shiite Islam. This was the result of the Arab world's biggest political mistake by using oil as an economic weapon during the 1973 war with Israel. Destabilizing these countries for the next fifty years or so was seen as an effective way to recycle the huge wealth derived from oil. This was also seen as a tool to allow Israel to march relentlessly and annex most of the territories won in the Six Day

War. The rebuilding of the Temple of Solomon was almost a reality.'

I was rather impressed by this socio-political introduction. To those unfamiliar with the politics of the region, this introduction will sound more like a conspiracy theory than a true analysis of what has really happened in recent history.

I looked at Abraham and said, 'Are you also going to tell me that the 9/11 attack was assisted by some shadowy groups in America? We all know that to create the correct paradigm shift at worldwide level, some major incident must be the trigger.

'You cannot ask the rest of the world that you are either "with us" or "against us" unless you have been invaded by aliens. This is exactly what George W. Bush said when he addressed the world to join him with the new war on terror.'

Abraham responded to my comment in a matter of fact way, 'No, 9/11 was definitely not a conspiracy. However, the CIA and other intelligence agencies within the US administration could have stopped it. They had enough information to conclude that something big and involving airplane hijacking was being planned. They thought this would be the usual airplane hijacking, which would be enough to give the neoconservatives headed by VP Dick Cheney and Ronald Rumsfeld the pretext to start the war on terror. Some pressure groups in the US advocated the deepening of the sectarian war between the two branches of Islam by extending the war on terror to include Iraq and handing this country to their apparent enemy, Iran.'

Abraham continued, 'The wars and destruction in the region started with the creation of the Islamic Republic of Iran. It was very quickly followed by some Western Powers, acting through the Gulf countries, encouraging the dictator of Iraq, Saddam Hussein to attack Iran in August 1980. That war lasted eight years as the West ensured a balanced power of incompetence to achieve the maximum destruction on both sides and to sell weapons using Gulf money. The whole world knows the Iran-Contra affairs, the scandal that came to light during November 1986 where the US secretly sold arms to Iran to ensure the continuation of the bloodshed. The plan was and still is for the sectarian war to last for fifty years from the date the new regime in Iran came to power. This involves the whole region including all the Gulf countries and Turkey. By 2020, it is hoped that most of the religious fundamentalists including Al Qaida and their affiliates, Iran's Revolutionary Guards and Hezbollah will be sucked into this civil war until they are destroyed from within. This is similar to the way the USSR was dismantled. The plan is for the Gulf countries to fund this war in the same way they funded the First Gulf War and the Mujahedeen fighting the Soviet Union in Afghanistan during the eighties.'

I reflected deeply on what I had just heard and thought that this was very depressing. Those who understand human nature deeply and the cultural differences of these countries are not ashamed to use any means to achieve their objectives.

After some silence, I looked at Abraham and said, 'I hope that this long introduction will lead to something new, as what you have just told me so far could be deduced by any fair minded observer.'

Plato asked me to be patient and said, 'Mac, Abraham is trying to inform you that religion can be manipulated for political reasons. As you will see, religions are greatly abused by those who seek to retain power for their selfish reasons. People with strong religious beliefs become like robots and are manipulated by those with evil agendas. Faith demands few questions to be asked and encourages blind obedience. You should not be surprised to hear that the most fundamental Islamic teachings are being encouraged by the enemies of Islam. Some of the extremist opinion formers have been deliberately planted and those who hear them think they are following their saviors.'

I looked at Abraham, 'You speak like an atheist with your attack on religions. I wouldn't be surprised if you have changed your name to Abram, your original name before God spoke to you.'

They all looked very surprised at my outburst.

Plato mumbled, 'This is why the Quran has asked the faithful to be patient more than forty times. Mac, please remember that those who are slow to anger will ultimately prevail.'

Abraham stood next to me and put his hand on my shoulder. 'Please relax, all will be revealed in good time. If you live in haste you will live in poverty, but if you are wise, you will excel and you will test eternity.'

I looked at him wondering what the last quote was about, and offered him my sincere apologies and requested him to continue.

Abraham obliged, 'I am sorry that this introduction has taken so long. I want to you to be in the correct frame of mind before I get to the heart of today's teachings. I quoted something about the virtue of patience and eternal life. I hope you will be able to absorb its meaning.'

Abraham continued, 'When some people believe that they have a monopoly to the absolute truth, in reality it is mostly blind faith. Let me start correcting the myth that Adam was created from clay and Eve from his rib. God created the living organism process in the form of seeds, as Darwin will explain tomorrow. Humanity must continue to seek knowledge until he is able to recreate the seeds of life and pass them on to new planets in the universe. Jesus has told his disciples the "Parable of Talent" which says in clear language what we are trying to clarify. This parable supports the view that God has tasked human beings to do something with their talent during their life on Earth. Matthew 25:13-30, "For it is like a man going on a journey, who summoned his slaves and entrusted his property to them. To one he gave five talents, to another two, and to another one, each according to his ability. Then he went on his journey". The talent is the intelligence God has trusted with humans at different degrees. The two who used their talents and expanded their knowledge were rewarded. The one who did not use his talent was condemned.'

I was very excited to see that most of the teachings from my visitors were not new at all. They were only clarifying what had already been revealed in various holy books. They only needed to give the correct interpretations. Therefore, God's objective is for humans to be creative. This can only be achieved in the spirit of cooperation and peaceful co-existence. I also remembered that it couldn't be a coincidence that the first words of the angel to the Prophet Mohammed were "Read in the name of your Lord the Creator".

Abraham continued with a quote to call all the faithful of various religions to return to their religion in moderation and with their eyes fully open. He said, 'This is the Lord your God calling upon you to return to the Shepherd of Moderation. Those who are talented will not test death. Those who are blind by their faith will not live."

82

Abraham then continued, 'There is a built-in mechanism in all humans to seek God and ultimately acknowledge His existence. This mechanism is simply the result of human desire to find explanations to all observations. The neurons will not stop searching for the truth until all the questions are answered. This search for answers to all the known 'unknowns' has led to the reliance on God's unlimited powers as the explanation. It is assumed that God gets involved in all the details of the running of the universe including the evolution of life with all its diversity and wonders. According to some faiths, nothing is done by the individual or done to him, without God's direct order. They deny that man's destiny is determined by his genes, by his environment or by what has been stored in his brain from the contacts, experiences, and reflections he makes during his life span. The problem with many people is that when it comes to issues of faith, they create a fortress culture wherein only news supporting their beliefs is communicated. They wear very dark glasses to deny the existence of light outside their faiths.'

I interrupted Abraham, 'Are you telling me that God does not influence our life? Then why do we pray to Him and ask for His favors? What would be left in any religion if God is not at hand to assist those who deserve His assistance?'

Abraham looked at me with concern as he realized that his teachings completely contradicted some of my established beliefs. He tried to tread very gently as he introduced his clarifications, 'God creates processes and leaves his creations to unfold as per his original master plan. The Ultimate Creator has left any assistance that the mortals may need, to come from Souls and Angels in the DD. You see, this is the beauty of the total automation of the processes. Those Souls that pass the test of ethical conduct (in current terminology they go to Heaven) are given the power to assist their loved ones. Some exceptional

Souls are selected to become God's Agents (in current terminology, Angels).'

I looked at all the shadows as if I had been given the impossible task of re-arranging my belief system over a few days. I said, 'Abraham, I don't really get it yet. However, I promise you that I will listen reflectively and with an open mind. If I see your clarifications present a more rational alternative than my current understandings, then I will gladly re-consider. This is especially so if it provides a rational explanation to counter the atheist's attacks on religions.'

They were all very satisfied with this promise. Plato confirmed that if everyone listened with openness to discuss his or her beliefs, the world would be a much better place.

He added, 'The surest way to brainwash the youth is to instil the virtues of blind obedience and to appreciate those who think alike more than those who may differ.'

Abraham looked at me and said, 'I may be digressing a bit, but I think it will ultimately become clear to you. An architect may design the most wonderful building but the end result will depend on the workmanship of those implementing the plan. Compliance with universal virtues is akin to workmanship when it comes to perfection in utilizing the talent humans are entrusted with. Pursuit of happiness in any society requires a true adherence to the correct upbringing of all individuals. The greatest gift parents can give to their children is to awaken their hidden talents. It is this gift which will turn them into useful adults.'

Plato interjected again to assure me that Abraham would ultimately get to the point. 'Mac, you know that so much has been spoken and written about religions. Please be patient while

Abraham refers to the fundamental building blocks of his clarifications. He will explain his concern with the current religious beliefs. He will show you how the "Straight and Narrow" paths of various religions need to evolve to comply with current human needs and developments.'

Plato smiled and continued, 'By the way, do you know that Abraham is one of your compatriots from the City of Ur in Iraq? He was the first prophet to advocate the complete oneness of God. Followers of the three main religions Judaism, Christianity and Islam regard him with reverence. So try not to be too hard on him.'

Abraham thanked Plato and continued. 'The second observation I need to make is that faiths are processed differently from science or other areas of knowledge in the human brain. The way faith is stored in the human mind gets hardwired and stronger filters are created to prevent its change. This is the case due to the perceived reward and punishment associated with most religious teaching. For this reason it is very difficult to change religious beliefs once firmly wired, while a scientist could accept a new explanation to any theory with minimal hesitation.'

I asked Abraham to elaborate as to why this is the case. I understand how difficult it is for one to change his religious beliefs.

Abraham replied, 'Faith is the compass guiding every individual in almost all walks of daily life. Faith is the sum and substance of things hoped for. It is all about believing in things you have not yet seen. It is important that the faith of any individual be stable and not change frequently, yet ready to assess new knowledge. For faith to be absorbed or changed, the mental filter must be opened. This is not easily done unless the person, who is making the approach, is accepted by the recipient as a man of authority in that religious orientation. For example, it is often difficult for parents or friends outside a given cult to stop an individual from becoming susceptible to the destructive forces of the cult in which they are. On the other hand, the cult leader can command the individual to commit suicide and he gets complete obedience.'

Plato looked at Abraham, 'Let me point out the key reason why faith gets hardwired. Every instruction or teaching if linked to reward and punishment becomes part of one's belief system. Once that perception is created, then real joy or fear is associated with compliance or non-compliance as the case may be. This is why every religion needs the concept of Heaven and Hell to provide the basis for hard wiring the brain. Without Heaven and Hell there would be no hard wiring of the brain, no faith and no religion.'

Plato continued, 'I am sure Darwin will say more on that tomorrow. I think it is the time to expand on Genesis revisited and what has been said in the last two days. We have shown the role of the Divine Dimension in the creation of the universe. I am sure that Abraham will expand soon on our explanation on the existence of God and on the Divine Dimension. I strongly insist all those who believe that their holy books contain some hidden knowledge, to examine the relevant texts taking into account our new approaches of looking at the universe, life and the DD. I promise you they will be pleased and surprised at how much more sense those verses will make.'

He then looked at Abraham and apologized for the interruption.

Abraham looked back at Plato and said, 'I will continue with Genesis Revisited focusing this time on the Great Designer and the Divine Dimension. You may think that we are making statements or claims to fit the observed facts in the universe. Please be patient until we finish and consider our explanation in totality. You may find our teachings based on assumptions that cannot be substantiated. This may be the case. However, it should be more appealing to the human mind in comparison to the claim that everything ultimately came out of nothing or out of pure random actions. Knowledge progresses by postulating a theory around the observed or perceived evidence and then continues with further tests to see if it fits all the facts.

'In Genesis 1) God said, "Let creation commence" and there were two completely dark bundles of solid photons (singularities or black holes) rotating at the speed of light in opposite directions.

'Newton has explained how the universe started and the role of the DD in creating the very first two singularities.'

I stopped Abraham and asked why the current religions have not referred to the DD?

Abraham was pleased to hear this question as it gave him the chance to quote what has already been said and written regarding the DD under the title of the Holy Spirit. Then he continued with the following quotes from the existing holy books and literatures.

The Holy Spirit, rather than being a distinct person, is spoken of in the Bible as being God's divine power. Peter relates how "God anointed Jesus of Nazareth with the Holy Spirit and with power, [and Jesus] went about doing good and healing all who were oppressed by the devil, for God was with Him" (Acts 10:38). The Holy Spirit is the very presence of God's power actively working in His servants.

The scriptures reveal that God imparts His divine powers to His Prophets and servants through the Holy Spirit. Peter noted that "prophecy never came by the will of man, but holy men of

God spoke as they were moved by the Holy Spirit" (2 Peter 1:21).

I was so amazed at how religions can provide rational explanations if correctly interpreted. I looked at the Holy Men of God as described above, 'I understand, now, why you are making these clarifications based on current rational thinking. It is due to the scientific knowledge that has already been achieved. Without such knowledge your message will be seen as mysterious as many of the pronouncements of Jesus and other prophets.'

Abraham was pleased to see me absorbing the new ways of looking at ancient knowledge and continued to expand on the revised Genesis:

'A. God created the DD as nothing comes from vacuum.

'B. The DD is made of a substance that cannot be detected by physical instruments. It is the cradle for the physical dimension and the means by which God controls everything.

'C. The DD substance can be split to form photons in opposite directions.

'D. God, or some force at His disposal, must be able to split the substance in the DD to start the first two black holes.'

'Genesis 2) God said, "Let there be light and let time and space commence" and the two black holes collided creating the expanding universe.

'This means that God had a plan which included time and space. He has mapped out the whole creation process from the beginning of time for eternity as the Greatest Architect. God has ensured that He stays in full control and whatever happens in the physical dimension would not be detrimental to the DD. So this means:

'E) God has great vision and intelligence to put into action an eternal and stable plan.

'F) God has unlimited powers to implement this plan and to ensure its continuity.

'Genesis 3) God said, "Let there be atoms", and some of the photons started to bend and rotate around themselves in very small and stable radii and in so doing created the physical universe.

'This means that God's plan included the creation of the physical universe in addition to light. The universe shall have time and space. The universe will be in continuous motion and will continue to change. This includes continuous birth, maturity and death with a cycle of expansion and contraction. For the physical universe to exist, the basic constituents, i.e. the photons must obey strict laws and have very specific predetermined values. For God to be in control of the physical universe at all times, He must know what is happening to all the constituents of His creation. This means that He must have included in His creation the ability to track and record the location and frequency of every photon He created. This is done by giving every photon a unique bar code. The information generated by each photon, from the moment of its birth out of the black hole until its death when it is sucked by a blackhole, is not lost.'

'The DD laws are different from the laws of the physical dimension known to man. In the DD, space has no meaning and everything is recorded instantaneously no matter where the photon is in space. This makes God very close to His creation at all times. So this means:

'G) God is the greatest mathematician who determined the speed of light necessary for a stable universe. This decision was made at the time of splitting the substance of the DD into two black holes. By allocating such unique values, He has ensured the existence and eternal continuation of the changing universe.

'H) God is omnipresent since all the photons are moving in the DD and the latter is under his absolute control.

'I) God is all knowing, since He tracks and records the vibration and location of all the photons.

'J) God is infinite since the DD has no limitation of space, time, or speed.

'Remember in Genesis 4) God said "Let there be gravity" and all the physical universe, its atoms and blackholes, started to interact with the Divine Dimension.

'For the universe to exist, as we know it, photons must vibrate and atoms must have gravity. Therefore, the DD provides the substance for vibration and for gravity. So this means:

'K) The vibration and the gravity in the DD make the entire physical universe possible.

'Genesis 5) God said, "Let there be seeds of life" and the seeds of life were created and spread around the universe.'

'So God's master plan was to create life in the form of a genetic program placed in seeds ready to be distributed to various planets in the universe. So this means:

'L) God's overall plan included the creation of life with the genes or the program of life at the heart of this creation.' Here Abraham quoted from the Bible, Corinthians 15:38 "But God giveth it a body as it hath pleased him, and to every seed his own body".'

Abraham continues, 'You see Mac, God converts the seed through evolution to the human body as He has planned (hath pleased Him). Every genetic program will end up into its own body.'

'Genesis 6) God said, "Let the seeds evolve to create intelligent beings in my image as the Creator" and the genes' instructions started to evolve to create intelligent beings.

'M) God created the universe with stars and planets to support life and intelligence. Then He created a living organism with its own evolving mechanism to ensure the creation of intelligence.'

Darwin smiled, 'So there is no contradiction between evolution and creation. I will explain this tomorrow at some length.'

Abraham continued, 'So, this means that:

'N) God's purpose of creating the universe and all living intelligence over the entire universe was to create advanced beings to continue with creativity. This is similar to the creation of computers by Mankind to advance knowledge.

'Genesis 7) God said, "Let the living organisms have Soul" and the Divine Dimension started to interact with the vibrating genes.

'The ultimate objective of creation is for man to continue to advance knowledge, ending with the storage of such science and technology at the nano level in the seed of life. This doesn't mean that man is planned to evolve to look like God. It does mean, however, that man would be blessed with intelligence and creativity to expand further the useful application of photons and atoms making up the physical dimension. The giant leap will come when man achieves the ability to communicate with other intelligent beings in the universe and share knowledge and experiences with others.

'P) God's purpose of creating the Soul is to link intelligence with the DD, to reward man for his deeds, and to allow Souls to act as the Creator's agents to ensure eternity of the life in the universe.'

Abraham started quoting again from the Bible, Ecclesiastes 12:7 "And the dust returns to the Earth as it was, and the spirit returns to God who gave it". Ezekkiel 18:4 "Behold, all Souls are mine, the Soul of the father as well as the Soul of the son is mine: the Soul who sins shall die".

'You see, Mac, we are not saying anything new. Those who sin will not get their sole activated after their death. The Soul of the father means those who will become God's agents.'

Then Abraham continued with a quote from the Quran (Suraha Ghafer 15), to show that all religions with the correct interpretations are saying the same thing but in different words, "God the Highest Lord, Grants the Souls (activates the Soul) as He chooses on their death as a warning (that they may not get it)". The words in bracket have been added for illustration of our explanation.

Abraham, with some hesitation, continued with another quote, '"From light all livings things are made and to darkness they return, but the essence of life is from the spirit and in the spirit only the righteous will dwell".'

I looked at Abraham and said, 'Are you reading to me from your Gospel?'

All of them smiled and asked me if I had any difficulty in unlocking its meaning.

I replied, 'I think I get it. Our body is made from photons (light) and ultimately they will get vacuumed by a black hole (darkness), while our real humanity is our Soul and ultimately the virtuous will dwell in the DD.'

Plato, asking for permission from Abraham first, quoted, '"Those who seek evil will find, and when they find they will be condemned. Those who seek virtue and wisdom will find, and when they find they will not test death".'

Before they asked me to explain, I said 'I think I get it,' and winked at Abraham to continue.

He did so, 'Man is destined by the original designer to seek unity with the DD through spirituality or the search for the truth which makes humans comfortable with themselves and truly compassionate. This is why when a person is about to pass a harsh judgment, he is asked to be human. Humans are at their best when they do things out of love, at peace with themselves and with others, helpful, generous, ethical and knowledgeable. The opposite must also be true. Man is at his worst when he hates, is in a rage, selfish, immoral, etc. This is more likely to lead to a heart attack or other diseases as programmed by the Creator for the body to do so when it is in defiance with God's original plan.'

As the subject of the Soul has occupied human minds since their brain started to tick, I asked Abraham to expand on the subject.

Abraham obliged by saying, 'The combined vibrations of all the photons making up each cell give rise to the Soul in the DD. This is the same in which the photon vibrates and the atom creates gravity. I will expand on this important concept later.'

'Wow,' I exclaimed, 'you cannot be serious. In the Quran, in Al Isra, verse 85, it says "And they ask you (the Prophet) about the Soul, say the Soul is known by the command of my Lord, and you have been given but little knowledge".'

'Well done Mac, it is really the time to reveal this knowledge as it is now possible for humans to understand its meaning,' Abraham said.

I said excitedly, 'You are now really revealing the knowledge God had promised in the Quran that it will be revealed? Therefore, the Soul is the interaction between the atoms making our cells and the DD. It is a direct result of the vibrations of all the cells in our body. The combined cells' interaction with the DD forms the Soul of the individual. This is just like the combined electronic signals on a 3D TV screen forms the motion pictures.'

'Probably a better example is the way you are seeing us as holograms,' Darwin said, expanding on the concept. 'This is similar to the use of a wireless internet, linking a computer to a remote server for back-up storage. Therefore, the information recorded in the DD represents the Soul of the living organisms. The Souls of the virtuous individuals are energized at death by the properties of the DD. It stays linked to the living organism and it is only separated on death of the organism. The Soul acts as the link between the person and the DD through meditation, if the correct tuning is achieved. This is why when a human dies, the Soul continues as the eternal living records of the physical existence from cradle to grave. This is how we got you the tape of your history to date. This is how you can explain most supernatural human experiences, including telepathy and the mystic powers of some individuals.'

I was getting excited and confused at the same time. I said, 'This is how to explain the quote, 'When you are two you will become one, when you are one what you will do?" Therefore, when we are alive we are body and Soul. When we die we are only Soul and it is too late to do God's work.'

Abraham looked at me, 'There is a great debate between atheists and religious people regarding the existence of the Soul. Scientists see the mind and consciousness as nothing but brain waves. When a human dies, those electrical pulses stop and everything comes to an end. Simply put, if the scientists cannot see it, touch it, or observe it through some instruments, then it does not exist. The believers however, rely on the wealth of experiences humanity has recorded over many thousands of years and across all cultures to support the existence of the Soul. Some "out of body" experiences and many unexplained observations give them confidence that they are correct.'

Abraham then continued with another verse from their holy book and said, '"Don't let your mind deceive you, don't your rationalism blind you, the truth is in front of you and behind you, the truth is above you and below you. From this truth your essence has come and to it you will return".'

Plato continued with another verse, '"When man's eyes are opened he will marvel, and when he marvels he will become knowledgeable, and when he becomes knowledgeable he will be truly free to live in eternal wonders".'

Before I could open my mouth to ask for the meaning, Newton looked at me and said, 'You will work out the meaning without help from us.'

I wondered if the scientists in my lifetime would support the explanation given by Newton yesterday. Then I thought to myself if they accept the existence of the DD to explain gravity and photon vibrations, then they would not find the explanation given by Abraham regarding the Soul so outlandish?

Plato, trying to assist Abraham, said, 'The only impediment to true human liberation is the blind adherence to absolute rationalism. Let me now turn to the Soul that dwells in the DD (Holy Spirit) and this means:

'Q) God has structured the brain to search for the unknown and simulate abstract ideas. God will ultimately reward those who seek and are virtuous to dwell in the DD.

I interrupted by reciting from the Quran, Al Umran 133, "And hasten for the pardon of your Lord and for Heaven which is as wide as all the Skies and Earth, laid for those who take heed for themselves and fear God".

Newton confirmed that mathematically only the whole space in the universe i.e. the DD could have the width of all the skies. According to many holy books, Heaven will offer unending goodies. All these goodies will be in the form of converting whatever one wishes in Heaven to perceive as reality. He said:

'R) The Holy Spirit is the cradle for the whole universe with all its beauties, mysteries, and complexity.

'S) The Holy Spirit houses the Souls of all intelligent beings in the universe.

'T) God rewards Souls that have performed good deeds and creative achievements. On the other hand Souls of those who disobeyed God's teaching would not get activated.'

I shouted, 'Wow! Wow, you are effectively rewiring my brain and revising many things I know about human existence and faiths. You are telling me that God's powers are exercised through the Holy Spirit. The universe floats in the Holy Spirit. Our Souls are part of the Holy Spirit. A person ends up in Heaven or Hell depending on whether his Soul is selected or rejected by God's appointed Governor (Senior Angel). The scoring criteria are how one performs during the journey of life.'

They all noticed my internal struggle. I was not sure what to make of this explanation.

Darwin, being the one with knowledge of biology, was concerned about me, 'Mac, you need to have rest until you are comfortable and ready to come back.'

I lay down and hoped to get some sleep but couldn't. I reviewed what I had heard so far and realized that it has been presented in logical sequence that made more sense than current explanations. They had not introduced any supporting evidence to these claims except their presence and their request to wait until humanity discovers the accuracy of Newton's explanation. I wondered if what I was hearing was a mere exercise in logic. To accept this reasoning, I still needed a lot of faith until Mankind accepts the accuracy of what had been revealed. I suppose faith with logical explanations is better than faith without logical explanations. Would it have made a difference if I had seen some miracles to trust these people? Isn't the situation I am in a kind of miracle? Therefore, I should accept that whatever they were saying was worthy of further considerations and debate. What happens if I discover everything I am experiencing is a long dream? How would I feel then? If the miracle part of this encounter did not exist, would the whole experience become less convincing? I also realized that I had many questions to ask and I better stop and return to the shadows or, as they call themselves, "God's Agents".

I looked at Abraham and thanked him for expanding the explanation of Genesis revisited.

Abraham said, 'Let me comment on the subject of religion, spirituality, and passing Gods' test. I will try to be as structured in my approach as I can, but I do not promise I will succeed.'

As they mumbled, I understood that this is a long shot for Abraham to be logical, as the teaching of faith is never meant to be so.

Abraham asked if I would like to make any comments before he continued?

I replied, 'I don't know where to start. Let me ask one question at a time. I detected that you were unhappy about religion's rigidities. They have ended up, in some cases, as destructive by galvanizing actions that commit injustices. The original message must have been to focus on instilling ethical values and to ensure that they evolve with time to remain relevant and to give true joy derived from good deeds and spirituality.'

Abraham looked at his colleagues and said, 'Mac, you speak as if you were with us when the decision was made to organize this encounter. We are here exactly for this objective. We hope to call for less emphasis on what differentiates various religions and more on good deeds, creativity, and purity of spirit.

'Let me explain in some detail.

'Undoubtedly all Divine messengers focused on morality, spirituality, and virtues. This was necessary to build societies and provide the basis for acceptable human conduct. All new Divine messages emphasized the omnipotent aspect of God and the concept of rewards and punishments. Heaven and Hell were necessary to ensure adherence to ethical conduct within each human being. Some religions put greater emphasis on forgiveness and love. Others put greater emphasis on punishment, not only in this life but also beyond the grave. The different approaches have substantial differences on the behaviors of the followers of each religion. After all, without the perceived pain and pleasure associated with Hell and Heaven there would be no lasting faith.'

Abraham continued, 'At the very early stages of receiving a new Divine message, it was discovered that human beings abide by the moral codes for a while and then their adherence gets weakened. The human desire to dominate and indulge in the pursuit of worldly pleasures becomes stronger, and sticking to the straight and narrow path becomes more challenging. This has led to the need to send other messengers to correct the situation. To overcome this short-term adherence to the moral code, a new approach was borrowed from previous civilizations. This lead to the founding of formal religions with established institutions to ensure the continuous adherence to the original message. Moses, having been brought up in the house of the pharaohs, brought with him such experience. This combination of institutional structures to keep and protect Divine messages lies at the heart of religious rigidities. For thousands of years many successive dynasties of the pharaohs ruled Egypt by regarding their entire pronouncements as the words of the Lord. They had religious institutions to enforce that belief.

'Therefore, the stages to convert faith into formal religion are:

'1) Prophet: You must have a very strong, charismatic, and ethical messenger who comes with a new vision addressing the negative issues experienced by the society at that time. This is why the greater the death and destruction afflicting any society, the greater the need for a messenger to appear with a new moral code to act as their savior.

'2) Paradigm Shift: The new messenger would not usually be accepted or permitted to challenge existing beliefs unless there is a paradigm shift in the thinking of those being addressed. Sometimes, the use of real or perceived miracles assists in this paradigm shift. This is especially the case if the followers of the prevailing faith are drowned in the darkness of rigidity, ignorance and intolerance. They usually have no confidence in the superiority of their arguments and resort to force to stop the flow of ideas. In most cases, a civil war will erupt until one set of values prevail over the others.'

'The other reason for challenging new ideas of faith is the established religious institutions. For example, this is what happened during the inquisitions in Europe. Those were one of the darkest times for that continent. Today, some Muslim minorities are adopting similar tactics used by the inquisitionist during those difficult times to force many Muslim societies to adhere to their interpretation of the faith. I tell you Mac, wars and bloodshed will be widely prevalent in the next twenty years. This is why we feel it is time for a paradigm shift as humanity is fed up with religious excesses. The more people realize that the religious extremists are failing them the more likely it is that the new message of tolerance and compassion will be accepted. It is the duty of every freethinking person, no matter what belief system he holds, to reject the damage extremists from all faiths are doing to peaceful co-existence on this planet. Brave are those who fight injustices with the power of conviction and love.'

Plato interrupted, 'Those who live in moderation, choose life and those who choose luxury and extremism choose death and destruction.'

Abraham thanked Plato for his comment and continued,

'3) Vision. The messenger must come with great vision to ensure salvation of the whole world. Without a clear vision accompanied with a burning passion, the message will not get to the heart of the people. For example, the new visions we bring with us are: "for humans to live creatively in peace, for wisdom to accumulate throughout the generations and for love and prosperity to be shared with others". The righteous among humans would be rewarded by receiving eternal life. Through meditation and prayers, a channel of communicating with the DD will be established to achieve true spiritual experiences.

'4) Commandments: The visions must have principles or commandments to deliver true salvation. The vision and principles are in effect, the moral code or the "straight and narrow" path of every religion. More on this will follow.

'5) Disciples: For the messenger to succeed, he must have Disciples. In all established religions, it is the disciples who ensured the spread and success of the delivery of the message. This is especially true in the case of Christianity. This may be the reason why Christianity is nearest to meeting the needs of its followers. It was tailored by a group of theologians to ensure that what was included in the Gospel would be of practical use and easy to understand. Knowing that the Gospel has been put together by man has also made its interpretation more flexible so that it can evolve with time.

'6) Continuous Learning: For any faith to last the test of time there must be continuous learning to ensure that the message is not forgotten or diluted. To ensure that this is the case, a weekly sermon by trained men must be instituted. Synagogues, churches, mosques and other places of worship were built to ensure continuous learning. Preachers must continuously update their message to respond to the changing needs of their followers if they want to remain relevant to the need of the group. Religious edicts which are written in stone risk becoming irrelevant with the passage of time. This is especially the case when those who interpret the faith are inflexible and have drowned in ignorance, rigidity and intolerance. Unfortunately, over time, many of the existing religions have failed the test of continuous renewal; hence, the need for a new approach has become inevitable. This is why Jesus did not give humanity a written holy book but left it to his disciples and theologians to interpret his sayings and deeds to fit the need of the Christian community.

'7) Rituals: All religions develop rituals to support the faith. These rituals give the faith its unique identity and let the group create a sort of brotherhood. The greater the intolerance and the impatience at the time of delivering the Divine message, the more likely the religion will include demanding rituals. The objective is to spend more time rewiring their brains and to have less time for temptations. The rituals usually give rise to great social values in providing a platform for the interaction with other individuals of the same faith in addition to its spirituality. Therefore, in theory at least, prayers and pilgrimage are done in places of worship to get the followers of the faith closer together. In current commercial language, the rituals are the same as product branding.

'8) Culture: Traditions are added to the rituals. These are usually a combination of religious celebrations, practices associated with birth, marriage, death and legacy traditions. All these supplement the rituals and the commandments to give the followers of the religion their unique identity or branding. Most traditions are relics of the cultures before the messenger got his Divine message. It should be remembered that every religion is made of less than 10% from new Divine messages and the rest are adaptations taken from the prevailing culture or borrowed from other faiths. Some religions cover all aspects of human life and regulate their activities in minute details making adaptation and change rather difficult.

'9) Reward and Punishment: Humans need to be motivated to perform tasks. Religion has achieved this objective by creating a perceived reward and punishment stronger than any real ones. Fear of punishment is a strong barrier to committing bad deeds while Heavenly rewards are great motivation to be virtuous. There would be no religion or faith without this principle. It is often said the fear of God is at the heart of wisdom.

'10) Money: All religions encourage the act of giving to religious institutions and to the poor. This is a blessing when it is used as intended and a curse when it is abused. The powers of the religious institutions are derived from the moral hold they have on their followers. They often issue edicts or fatwa to influence behaviors.'

I looked at Abraham bewildered to hear that a religion has a road map and asked, 'Why did Abraham come up with a monolithic faith that did not call for the establishment of religious institutions and practices? He must have known what could go wrong once he introduced these earthly processes. I need you to expand on that, please.'

Plato replied, 'Mac, you are absolutely correct. Many things could go wrong with formal religious institutions. Abraham had known that Mankind would be poorer if he established a formal religion due to the rigidities and intolerance it would bring with it. On the positive side, without such institutions, faiths and beliefs would be fragmented and they will not serve as a unifying force in the society. This is a very vast subject and I will try to be very brief on the pros and cons of this matter.'

Abraham seemed animated as he explained the pros and cons of turning faith into structured religion.

'Let me first start with the common moral messages among all religions and their minor variations. Why do these variations exist? Why must the principle of evolution be applied to all religions, as is the case with all living organisms to survive? I will also explain the reasons why all religions need to evolve continuously to meet the needs of humanity at large and why discriminations based on faith must be condemned in the strongest terms

'By now you know Mac that humans have evolved as intelligent beings. It is not important to our teaching whether this intelligence had evolved gradually or if it was genetically engineered by visiting aliens to planet Earth. The human brain was completely redesigned to have the frontal lobe during the last 70,000 years. The purpose of the frontal lobe is to act as a simulator to deal with all the abstract matters whether likely or unlikely to happen. This is a very short period in comparison with the millions of years all living organisms have been evolving on this planet according to God's original plan.'

Darwin noticed the shock on my face on hearing that we may have been genetically upgraded by some visiting aliens. 'Mac, whether intelligence has evolved on Earth as planned in accordance to the original seeds of life, or due to visiting aliens is not important. What does matter is that Mankind has his frontal lobe.'

I jumped from my seat and said, 'This may be not important to you but it is very important to us humans.'

'Yes, I know,' he quickly replied. 'Humans are still struggling with this question. Are we alone in the universe? I trust that our presence here is good proof that humans are not alone in this vast universe.'

I said, 'So you are confirming that you are not angels but some sort of Chosen Souls, but...' They all laughed before I could complete my sentence.

Darwin continued, 'We are Souls of other intelligent beings that have passed God's test and are doing God's work. In human terminology we are God's Holy Men, doing God's work and reside in the DD and get our power from its characteristics.'

I did not really know how to react as the explanation advocated during this encounter seemed too easy to have been overlooked by humanity over thousands of years.

Abraham looked at Darwin, wanting to regain control of his lecture, and said, 'I am sure Mac can ask Darwin more questions tomorrow.'

They were all looking at me for a reaction, so I said, 'I see now how your explanation of God as the great designer, who does not get involved in the details and your explanation of the DD which has all the power over us and so on. These revised religious principles are compatible with rationalism without too much struggle. I see why you use the words "of God's power" when you mean the DD power, as they are ultimately Divine powers. This is the reason for the trinity concept in Christianity, although Abraham has not explained the role of Jesus yet. I am sure during the course of this encounter more details will be given to substantiate this doctrine. Please move on and explain the Universal Moral Codes.'

Abraham continued, 'The Creator's eternal plan is that the seeds on each planet, with the correct life supporting system, will end up as intelligent beings. The Divine objective is for a total galactic intelligence, to share knowledge and experiences, to widen the applications of photons to as many uses as possible. To do that effectively, humans must have the correct moral codes to supplement their genetic deficiencies. The objective is to enable them to act as a team, to preserve knowledge through peaceful co-existence and to be trusted.

'As you know Mac, humans spend billions of dollars, organizing hundreds of meetings and spending thousands of hours discussing how to win wars and satisfy their cravings for luxuries. Have you ever seen or heard, in the whole history of Mankind, such efforts to win peace? If the trillions of dollars being spent on wars were spent on peaceful programs, then humanity would have been nearer to being trusted with more knowledge and technologies necessary for their true liberation. We assure you that the current path, where the devil is allowed to roam within each human freely, will never lead to peace. It is very sad to see human intelligence being enslaved by evil tendencies to favour wealth and power over love and compassion.'

I could not let this opportunity go unanswered and so I said, 'If we are created by a powerful God then why does He need intelligent beings to continue with creativity? Some will say that God is man's invention to feel good and to avoid the terror of leaving this life without a purpose. Others will say it is just a game for God to entertain Himself by observing the wonder of His creation. Now you have come up with a new explanation. We have been created to meet God's curiosity by enhancing what can be done with the physical universe and ensuring the continuity of life in the universe. I suppose this is similar to humans creating intelligent computers and getting them to communicate with one another to advance human knowledge. I must say, somehow it makes more sense than we have just been created to worship God or just to be tested in this life. I suppose if by accepting this rational explanation, I upset God, then I have to blame Him for blessing me with the gift of preferring what is rational over what is blind faith.'

Abraham thanked me for the good humour and continued. 'It shows that we are making some progress. Why would God go to the trouble of creating the universe, including all intelligent beings just to worship Him? Where is the fun in that? Would human beings create intelligent robots just to pray or fast? It would make better sense if they are created to satisfy man's need or for his scientific curiosity. Why should atheists or others deny this right for God to have? You see, the physical universe is subject to strict laws of nature and God has limited power in influencing what is happening in this regard. On the other hand with the creation of Talents, God is in continuous control and observance through the DD.

'Now let's turn to the very important subject at the heart of our visit and that is: what is required of humans to meet the Lord's three original objectives? Of course I will be brief as this subject could take years to spell out in detail.

'1) To be Creative and Inquisitive in all Human Activities:

'Most religions play down the importance of this role. They are suspicious of scientific research as it may lead to some conclusions that may challenge the established religious doctrines. Until recently, it was a heresy to say that the Earth rotates around the Sun. Humans must accept the existence of God and the Divine Dimension. Without this belief, humans will not be sufficiently persuaded that there is a Divine Power that can be used to help them escape from Earth's gravity. Imagine the speed of scientific progress if Mankind can communicate with other intelligent beings and share experiences. Humans need the religious zeal to approach total peace on Earth and seek continuous advancement of scientific research for peaceful purposes. Creativity requires courage, imagination, and persistence. God has blessed humanity with an inquisitive mind, not just to search for him, but to also to leave no stone unturned until they understand His creation and fulfil His tasks.

'2) To be a Team Player i.e. Empathetic:

'Humans need to work as a group to advance knowledge. This is why humans are programmed to be social animals. If you appreciate the wonder of creation in your surroundings, you will feel for all living beings. This is a basic concept in Hinduism and hence the principle of incarnation. Most human needs can only be fulfilled with satisfaction if they are in the company of others. This means that they must have the necessary Universal Moral Codes (UMC) to live and flourish in a group setting and in the world at large. Humans need to communicate peacefully and respectfully within the group and with other groups. Only then can they demonstrate to God that it is safe to let them communicate easily with other intelligent beings. Terrorism, tribal jealousies and tendencies to favour the few must be abandoned to avoid continuous wars and conflicts.

'3) To Comply with the Universal Moral Code (UMC):

'For humans and other intelligent beings to live in harmony and peace with each other and with their environment, they must overcome the evils of their selfish worldly desires. They must adhere to the UMC. These moral codes are the true compass in all human activities as they interact with each other. Similar Divine moral codes are usually found in most religious teachings with some minor variations. This realization should be taken as a powerful force to true religious dialogue and understanding. It is usually poor interpretations based on lack of respect, rigidities, ignorance or half knowledge of the basics of those beliefs, which lie behind many conflicts.'

All of them looked at Abraham and appeared very excited, as they knew that the time had come for spelling out of the Universal Moral Codes (UMC).

Abraham appeared very relaxed as he said, 'I always enjoy this part of our mission.' Then he continued to list the UMC:

'A) Respect the sanctity of human life. Continuously seek to improve its quality and maximize inner peace and tranquility:

'All faiths share the commandment "Thou shall not kill". Without full adherence to such commandment, no society can flourish. No one can claim to believe in God and then proceed to kill a fellow human being. God will never forgive those who kill or those behind the scenes who create conflicts leading to bloodshed.'

I noticed Abraham was getting very angry as he spoke. He added, 'Those who commit such crimes appear in the eyes of the Lord not only as criminals but are also condemned for eternity irrespective of what other good deeds they have done. The Lord is very proud of his creation. Each human being must be given the opportunity to fulfil his role on Earth. For those who brainwash or manipulate, whether individuals, groups, or governments who give themselves the right to kill, directly or indirectly, or torture fellow human beings are never forgiven by God.'

Plato interrupted, 'By the way this also includes all those who instigate wars and mass killings in the name of winning the argument in a perceived clash of civilizations. In the eyes of the Lord it is of the utmost wickedness to manipulate groups or nations who have not reached political maturity into destructive civil wars.'

I jumped in and asked, 'Are you saying that all taking of human life is forbidden? In many cases you may have to take a life to save more lives.'

Plato continued, 'This is very true and it must be done with a proper process based on the UMC. When everyone develops his own code, without any regard to morality, they start to kill the innocent on the flimsiest excuses. This is very apparent by the actions of many extremists who are buried in ignorance of their faith.'

I looked at Abraham and said, 'You spoke about the quality of human life. How can you explain the action of those extremists who inhibit the most basic of the human spirit? How one could love and enjoy life within the boundaries of the UMC? To some who regard every act outside their tradition, become prohibited and punishable by God.'

Darwin could not help himself interrupting, 'There are some who have not yet evolved to control their animalistic instincts. They tend to measure everyone by their immature standard. The female of the human species is subjected to the harshest isolation in the name of morality.'

Abraham, not wanting to dwell on this subject, said with great sadness, 'You have to pray for those tormented Souls to see the light of the day. They dwell in darkness and ignorance and see only their shadows. All I know is that these people are a great burden to their seeds.'

He continued, 'You see, Mac, how many misconceptions have crept into religion? Those extremists are doomed to the dustbin of ignorance and irrelevance. They will be condemning their offspring to the same fate unless some external force breaks this cycle of indoctrination.'

Darwin, with the survival for the fittest principle in mind, added passionately 'Human prosperity is for those who pass the fittest virtues to their offspring and who are creative in accordance with the Creator's design.'

Abraham continued, 'The female of the human species is most precious in the eyes of the Lord. She is the one who bears all the pain to ensure continuity of the species and instils values in the young. Their education and liberalization is necessary for any society to see the light of wisdom and enlightenment. Any group of people who do not give equal rights to females are committing themselves to hardship and backwardness. God does not discriminate on the basis of sex, colour, race, or tribal origin.

'That brings me to B) Minimization of total conscious suffering of all living beings:

'This means that any action, which causes conscious pain or hardship to humans or other living organisms, should be minimized. This commandment also provides guidance to the way humans should deal with animals. If animals are used for medical research, they should first compare the expected total reduction of suffering among humans in comparison with the total conscious suffering experienced by the animal subjected to the experiments. If one can choose an animal with a lower level of consciousness to pain, then more animals can be used relative to those with a higher level of consciousness. This must mean that no research on animals should be permitted if the research is for cosmetic use only, as no or very little human suffering will be eliminated. All principles of Human Rights, Treatment of War Prisoners, Geneva Convention and Rules of War, Animal Experimentations, Treatment of Animals, etc could be derived from this principle and the previous one.

'C) Preserve biodiversity and maintain Earth's long-term capabilities of supporting it:

'All living entities share in the original Creator's genetic program. Therefore, humans must do their best to preserve the biodiversity as their genetic code contains valuable information essential to the advancement of knowledge, including genetic engineering and improvement of the quality of life. These genetic programs are irreplaceable.

'Humans should watch out for the damage they are inflicting on their planet, as this is the most dominant reason for the destruction of biodiversity. Human actions in this field could lead to tragic deaths far in excess of the forces of nature. Therefore, you can see that this principle along with the previous two should outlaw any human action that results in polluting the environment and destroying animal habitats among other things.

'D) Do not rush the evolutionary process through aggressive genetic engineering:

'Genetic engineering is part of the Divine plan to speed up the evolutionary process, provided that it is done with great care. Any error will have untold consequences and this is why utmost care should be exercised. While this human activity could save lives, it could also destroy lives in a massive way. The deeper the human knowledge in unlocking the secrets of the genes becomes, the more understanding and respect they would show the Great Designer.'

I asked with great concern, 'I have always thought that the boundaries of God and those of humans must not overlap due the catastrophic consequences which could result from the manipulation of the genes.'

They all looked at each other, as if a bomb has been thrown at them. Abraham came close to me confirmed that intelligent life on many planets was destroyed or did not make it to fulfilling their Divine role due the abuse of this power of

112

creation. He continued to say, 'This is why we are here in force to warn of the serious consequence facing Mankind if they do not upgrade their moral code universally. The rhythmic nature of all God's creation requires continuous change. Religion is not an exception. This is why the different speeds of evolving various faiths and traditions are the reason for most conflicts.'

I looked at Plato to expand on this serious warning, as it sounded very gloomy.

Plato obliged, 'At present human beings are on train journeys with different directions and speeds. There are those who are developing their scientific knowledge at relatively high speed without sufficient care about improving their moral codes. On the other extreme, there are those who are not only refusing to join the age of rationalism but also moving backwards in the name of adherence to rigid traditions. We can see on our cosmic simulator that those who have managed to master the power of the genome would have completely different cultural values to those who are burying themselves in the past. Then, in the mind of those who start to regard themselves as a superior race, the scientific knowledge could be used to design specific viruses to target those who would be classed as not worthy of sharing the planet with them. They will argue that these people are not adding value to human knowledge and they are a burden on the planet.'

I was almost in tears for the first time. I said, 'Of course according to how things work, if human beings do not change to create cultural proximity (reduce cultural gap), then the current momentum will continue for a major shake-up on the planet.' Then I looked at Adam and asked, 'Could you tell me whether the world economies will be affected by humans playing the role of God?'

Adam responded, 'At present the laws governing scientific progress associated with discovering the role of specific genes and the development of new ones are being patented to encourage private funding in this area of research. These discoveries will lead to controlling the prices of food and medicine that will enrich those with the know-how at the expense of the others who are left behind in this race. As international law favours the strong and the rich, no momentum at present is being created for a fairer world. This will be another factor in increasing the cultural and knowledge gap between those who have and those who do not.'

I interrupted and said, 'And these will lead to deepening of cultural differences and in the words of the supremacists "the super race would have to cleanse the world from the inferior race"? The appearance of the likes of Hitler will be in evidence all over again. Except this time it would be done in silence through tailor-made viruses.'

To avoid ending the discussion on such a gloomy note, Darwin said, 'Human beings have shown so far a very strong resilience in avoiding major annihilation of the race. We hope that our message for peace will awaken the human consciousness into action at the expense of the individual's selfish needs. In a world where the people are divided into classes of superiors and inferiors there will be no winners. There will be only losers. Let us move on for the sake of time.'

I tried to change the subject by saying, 'I suppose one can regard the empowerment of man to manipulate the genes is like humans creating intelligent computers capable of developing new software writing tools. By using this capability, it is expected that computers would develop exciting new apps.'

Newton commented, 'So, you should not be surprised if we say God created intelligent beings to find new applications out of the photons and atoms. By the way, we envisage that once intelligent robots are created an IT dimension will exist where robots will talk and interact with one another and with other devices in an intelligent way. The Internet will be the equivalent of the Divine Dimension if you like. Humans will have great pleasure in observing their interaction and progress in creating new applications and other activities. However, they will be completely at the mercy of their Creators, i.e. humans. These robots will be automated to seek sunlight for their energy but will not have the independence of birth and death.'

'And that brings me to E),' put in Abraham, 'To value human spiritual wellbeing ahead of excessive Luxuries.

'That means that Health and Education should be the top priority of any society, as excess material well-being has low marginal value and no permanency. Happiness can come from being creative and being in tune with nature. True human spirituality is to feel that he is part of the total Divine scheme of things and can tap into the Divine power. One way of doing this is through genuine prayers and deep meditations. All religions promote prayers and regard them as central to their faith. Mindful prayers to the Divine are not a question of physical exercise, or being a means of socializing with others but it is profound meditation and tuning into the Divine Dimension. For a prayer to be a truly spiritual experience, it must be done with absolute submission to, and a love of, the Creator. It is a means of tuning the conscious mind to the timeless and spaceless Holy Spirit.'

I stopped Abraham, 'Hundreds of books have been written on the subject of prayers and I am not sure you are going to teach humanity anything new here.'

Abraham said in agreement, 'When intense and submissive prayers are recited, the vibrations of the conscious and the subconscious mind get synchronized and become the wireless link to the DD substance. Only in such situations, prayers can be effective and, I say, may be answered. Not all prayers are answered as they may not fit the overall working of the universe.'

Abraham noticed my puzzlement said, 'Spell it out. What is bothering you?'

'I just can't work out how prayers can be answered. I know the DD has power over the physical dimension and things could just happen, as in the case of miracles or by the manner in which I am having my food in this cave. So, if we do pray and if we do get our prayers answered, then who is making these things happen? God does not get involved in such details as I have been told several times,' I answered.

Plato looked at Abraham, 'Let me deal with Mac's concerns.' Then he turned to me, 'If you do good deeds and help others in any way, then your virtuous actions will get noticed in the DD. Souls of the relatives or friends connected with those you have helped would return the favour and respond to your prayers. This is why one should be a Good Samaritan and volunteer to do all sorts of charitable work. Those who commit sins, truly repent their evil deeds, and then ask for forgiveness from those they have wronged, will also be noticed in the DD. It would be an act of insanity to have no good deeds and then expect your prayers to be answered.'

I was rather relaxed with this type of reasoning. The main condition for prayers to be answered is to be virtuous, do good deeds, and truly repent sins. The secondary condition is to be spiritual and in tune with the DD. This explanation reminded me of a Suraha in the Quran (Al Kaadir 4) "On (this night) the

116

Angels and the Souls descend by permission of the Lord to meet all requests". During this night, Muslims believe that their prayers will be answered. Those who make this happen are the Elites Souls (Angels) and the common Souls.

Abraham continued to explain some more common reasons for prayers. 'Regular heartfelt prayers assist people to focus on the tasks ahead and resist temptations. Heartfelt regular prayers could also help to achieve better results in adjusting behaviours in comparison with some other cognitive therapies. As we will see later, for the brain to be re-wired, one needs to be open-minded and reflective. True prayers achieve both if the person believes in the unlimited powers of the DD.'

I asked Abraham to explain how we could get those who strayed to become virtuous again.

He replied, 'We see the shortest route to adopting the UMC is not by asking people to abandon their faiths. On the contrary, we ask everyone to be comfortable with their religion, provided they support its true evolutionary nature to comply with the UMC. We agree that it will require great mobilization of all human efforts as if the Earth were being invaded by aliens.'

I exclaimed, 'Oh my God, it sounds very depressing. The task ahead is then very difficult. This is why humanity is struggling to achieve the right balance between religious indoctrinations and liberal thinking.'

'Don't be too gloomy,' answered Plato. 'The glass is always half full. You need to recognise the current speed with which ideas are passing around the globe. Many of today's youth can be mobilized for good causes. In order to mobilize people and then get the elite to focus on upgrading Mankind's moral codes, they need to start tackling the prevailing injustices, ignorance, and lack of tolerance all around the world. To solve any problem, break it down into smaller components, and prioritize.'

'That is why we have F) Seek moderation in all human endeavors and avoid excesses and extremism:

'This is a key principle and everyone must live a balanced life for healthy living. Religious excesses by well-meaning people can be regarded as matter of personal choice provided it were kept confined to themselves. Most deadly sins and neuroses are the results of excessive behaviours in one thing or another. Everyone should seek moderation to achieve true happiness and social acceptance. This principle is also very relevant for environmental survival. Excessive use of fossil fuels leads to global warming and the destruction of habitats of many species. All education systems must instil in children the virtues of moderation and rational thinking. Moderation is the meeting point of peace and harmony.'

Plato added, 'The combination of politics, ignorance and blind faith, with excessive energies, is an explosive cocktail in the hands of extremists and a trigger for most religious conflicts.

Plato looked at Abraham for permission and continued,

'G) Put community needs ahead of individual greed:

'For society to thrive, individuals must always put what is good for the community ahead of the need of the individual. No society or group can thrive without such altruistic behaviours. By the way, one of the greatest contributions of religions is the creation of missionaries to preach the right message. If it is done with the correct adherence to universal virtues, then the road to true salvation will be much shorter and Heaven on Earth will be within reach.

'This is why we have H) Do unto others as you have them do unto you:

118

'Love others as you love yourself. Treat others, as you like to be treated. This is the golden rule in most religions. This is truly an important principle. If this were put into practice then humans would have a serious chance of avoiding many wars and conflicts. In fact, this is one of the basic failures in the evolution of man. It is the role of the family and the society to ensure adherence to this doctrine. It is the devil or the genetic imperfection within each human, which stands as the barrier to compliance with the golden rule.

'I) Have the right views, thoughts, speech, action and livelihood:

'It is necessary to apply the correct set of virtues when views and thoughts are formed. If virtuous thoughts are formed, the rest will follow. One should consider all the facts and one should be in full possession of his faculties when important decisions are made. Continuous learning is essential to keep his knowledge and skills up-to-date. All earnings must be from honest, morally acceptable and decent sources. The ones who have wealth, or power, must not exploit those who do not.

'L) Have the right efforts and mindfulness:

'One should make time for one's spiritual well-being and practice meditation to achieve mindfulness. Only then can one feel true fulfilment and happiness. In doing so, one can have a true mystical experience that brings the person nearer to the Holy Spirit.'

I felt I was overwhelmed with this morality and spirituality exposure. I looked at Abraham and asked, 'How come there is no break during your teachings? Does religion have anything against relaxation and entertainment?'

All of them laughed. They looked at Abraham and said jokingly, 'Yes Abraham, give the young man a chance to rest.'

During the break, I said that all this looked too good to be true and rational.

Plato asked me. 'Is there a problem if our teachings fit all the observed human facts and experiences, even though they make sense according to human's rational thinking? Scientists always apply logic to the facts in order to adopt them as coherent principles.'

I replied, 'You are coming up with explanations to answer Mankind's search for the truth. Man has been trying to answer these questions over many thousands of years with limited success.'

Darwin interrupted, 'This is not correct. Human beings have made many observations and reported their experiences. We are only here to present them in a logical and comprehensive way as a total explanation or theory of everything. If we tried to give this explanation in any other period of human knowledge then they would not have been understood. You see Mac, first the unknown "unknown" has to become the known "unknown", then, and only then, an answer will be understood.'

Plato sat next to me and asked me to summarize my understanding so far from this encounter. I was rather taken aback as I was hoping for a rest. However, I thought it might be a good idea to be tested so that I could be corrected if I had got something wrong. I then summarized my understanding in a rather low voice to avoid embarrassment in case I made major mistakes or omissions:

'The physical universe was created and it did not start from nothing. God created processes and does not involve Himself in the details.

'The physical universe floats in the DD, or Holy Spirit. God and the DD represent the total Divine powers.

'Photons vibrate in the DD. In addition, atoms create gravity, and the living cells create Soul in the DD.

'God created seeds with a built-in evolutionary processes utilising the science and technology implanted in the seed.

'The living organisms ultimately evolve into intelligent beings.

'Life is very common in the universe and you are an example of Souls of intelligent beings from other planets and acting as agents of the Lord.

'The agents of God derive power by harnessing the DD characteristics.

'All religions have their positive contribution in instilling moral values. They are also the source of divisions and conflicts in the hands of the rigid and ignorant.

'Souls that are selected for service of the Lord become angels according to our current terminology.

'God does not create devils, as it does not make sense to create eternal processes and at the same time create elements of destruction. Devils are the imperfection in human behaviours due to the wrong genes and/or the wrong moral codes of the individual.

'The UMC is necessary to deal with the devil within every individual and to guide us to become decent human beings.

'Every religion has its own "straight and narrow" path. Some draw the boundaries too narrowly, making many normal human activities appear to contradict God's will. In doing so, they oppose the very reason why God entrusted man with intelligence. Others draw the boundaries too wide to render them ineffective in organizing the lives of individuals in the society.'

My companions were very pleased with this short summary. As nothing exciting happened during the break, we eventually reconvened.

I looked at Abraham and said, 'The most dangerous aspect of any religion is when the majority of the so-called spiritual leaders send their rational thinking into a deep slumber. They start to indoctrinate the young and poison their minds. As we have said before, mixing politics, ignorance and faith, becomes a very explosive cocktail if it gets planted in the minds of the young.'

Abraham came up next to me, 'Now, do you recognise how much could go wrong with structured religions? Yet everyone thinks it does not apply to them, as their religion is immune from such irrationalities. '

I nodded saying, 'This is very unfortunate. Once a set of instructions and beliefs are accepted as part of a faith, they are then treated as absolute Divine truth. Are we doomed forever to continuous conflicts and clashes instigated by extremists due to religious ignorance and bigotries?'

'Not necessarily,' replied Abraham. 'We hope that our call for religious dialogue will be taken seriously to enable a reawakening that would help to marginalize the few extremists. Only when man is freed from the bondage of blind faith can he truly fulfil the Divine message of creativity and wisdom. Only on Earth do we see great civilizations flourish and then get destroyed as if humanity never possessed such wisdom and knowledge before. The best examples would be to look at the lost civilizations of the Sumerians and Ancient Egypt.'

I agreed, 'This is very true. It is very scary. Do you think this could happen again with so many books and records in existence to pass knowledge to the future generations?'

Plato responded, 'It will be even worse. Yes, you do have all the records but you also have a much bigger destructive force to destroy the whole planet several times over. Unless human beings change their ways of dealing with one another, then wars and destruction will continue. It is irrational to expect different results if humans continue with their craving for wealth and power.'

'This is very depressing,' I said. 'Are humans doomed forever? They keep losing ancient knowledge due to continuous wars and conflicts. Humanity has received hundreds of prophets as if they were in an institution for delinquent beings. The messengers are usually abused as soon as they start to challenge those with privileges and powers. The new message then becomes a source for division and additional conflicts.'

It was agreed that we should have another break to allow me to digest the real risk facing humanity, as I appeared truly concerned about the fate awaiting Mankind.

As we were having a walk, Adam said, 'The same reasons that lead to wars or peace, lead to economic failures or prosperity. The individual is a product of his moral values and culture. A nation is the sum of the individuals. For any change to be effective, all the efforts must be focused on building virtues from childhood. This will require sustained efforts over several generations at individual, national and international levels.'

Plato turned to Adam, 'I think this is an excellent time to meet Mac's vision for religious coexistence. This will require dealing with human failings. Education based on internationally agreed virtues is the foundation for the new dream. Let us structure our callings on the same basis that formal religions are created to ensure quick results.'

'At last!' I shouted, 'I will hear some answers to getting the human race out of their misery and continuous failings. Please go ahead.'

Plato continued:

'1) The New Vision: "Prosperous Humanity and a Just World Order" based on Wisdom, Courage, Moderation, and Political Activism.

'2) The Principles supporting the Vision are:

'a) Respect: All religious beliefs, including atheism to be respected, as they are a matter of individual choice. Those who preach hate or demand special privileges from the Lord are to be treated for "Blind Faith Intoxication" or at least isolated to be rendered harmless.

'b) Education: All formal education must encourage the value of virtues and ethical conduct. All elements of indoctrinations, religious or otherwise must be eliminated. When the devil that dwells within us is well managed or cast away, the Divine Souls will surface to give the Lord's children hope during this life and for all eternity in the next.

'c) "Religious Openness and Tolerance" to replace the insistence of "Absolute Truth" claims: All acts of injustices committed in the name of religions or God's promises and covenants are to be condemned and isolated. The Lord created all men equal. Those who claim otherwise are at war with God the Almighty and the rest of humanity.

'd) "Natural Law of Justice": Justice is unbiased in the eye of the Lord and cannot be compromised. It applies to all with equal vigour. The Lord is swift with his anger against those who break this fundamental Divine Law.'

Plato, trying not to spend too much time in this respect, said, 'I am sure it is well within human intellect to spell out these principles in a more precise way than anything we can say in this brief encounter.' Then Plato continued,

'3) Disciples for Peaceful Co-existence: Every decent individual is invited to be a disciple for the "Just World Order". Strong popular movements are required at grass-roots levels, accompanied with the wide use of social media to counter the current lobbies of domination, misinformation, and money politics.

'4) Continuous Mobilization of the Masses: To get the message of love to drown the message of hate, continuous reminders and activism are necessary. The enemy of the Just World Order will try to wear you out and will get their way unless the mass movements follow this route with persistence and continuous renewals.

'5) Cultural Bonding: The world should celebrate these virtues annually: e.g. "Love Day" and "Peace Day" and so on.'

Abraham turned to me, 'I am sure you think Plato is dreaming or has no idea what obstacles exist to convert this road map, or any variation of it, to reality. Just keep in mind that it took more than 300 years for Christianity to be formalized and be widely accepted.'

Plato looked at Abraham and responded, 'I am not naïve to think it will be easy. At the heart of the problem is the awakening of the human spirit to care about what they believe in, and to do something about their beliefs. The ultimate enemy to world peace and good governance is apathy. Bloodsucking insects thrive on those who are too weak to dispel them. This is also the case with political apathy. People should stop moaning and start tweeting, writing, organizing if they want a government that represents them. I will cover this matter tomorrow at some length.'

I looked at Plato, 'I see that you are still very passionate about politics and you are building hope for the masses to be awakened. I think this is a good time for a rest.'

We broke for dinner and apparently, Abraham had prepared a surprise for me. I was amazed to see a huge 3D TV screen. The scenes were out of this world.

They all looked at me and Newton said, 'What do you think we are showing you?'

'I can only imagine it to be Heaven. Everyone appears to be happy, thoughtful, content and overflowing with love surrounded by beautiful bright colours.'

They looked at one another and Abraham said, 'Interesting. You see Mac, in Heaven, reality and perception are the same? What you are seeing is nothing but a figment of your imagination. Humans have this wrong belief that the physical body will re-materialize and continue in Heaven. This belief is a perpetuation of the pharaohs' fascination with the afterlife in its physical form. This is why they devoted so much energy on mummification. You must be able to see from Newton's lecture yesterday that the universe is in continuous renewal and does not reconstitute itself exactly. Only what is made of the Spirit is eternal.'

After some reflection I said, 'I think I can see what you are telling me. All the wonders of Heaven spoken of in the holy books are nothing but perceived reality. In Heaven, there will be no physical brain for the photon or atom to interact with. This does not make Heaven less appealing. On the contrary, it makes the potential of good feeling limitless. '

Abraham, realized that it was getting late and continued, 'When an individual dies, the brain goes into hyperactivity just before death to break the link between the Soul and the body. Many near-death experiences are often described as a deep tunnel of bright light indicating the disconnection of the Soul from the physical body. The light noticed is the energy used to power the Soul for its independent existence. So if you like, the Soul is nothing but the energized records of the deeds, actions, thoughts, experiences and achievements of the individuals. Those who fail the test are regarded as defective talents and left to experience the pain of isolation and rejection.'

I looked at Abraham and said, 'Can you tell me more about the religions on your planet and how they differ from the way you see them on Earth?'

They looked at Darwin and said, 'I think you have to answer that.'

'Yes,' said Darwin reluctantly. 'I think one needs to look at the way humans have evolved compared to us. At the last stage of human evolution, the animal instincts for possession and domination should have been replaced by stronger altruistic instincts of sharing and cooperation. Having realized that this evolutionary transformation has not taken place yet, greater emphasis was given on sending Divine Agents like us to correct the situation. This is why Earth has been visited regularly by messengers of the Lord. Only when human beings become tolerant, compassionate and creative, then there will be no need for further visitations to instil virtues. You see virtuous people wire their brains to control the chemical imperfections. Creativity and knowledge accumulation would have been much faster in a peaceful world. Humans are failing God in a big way and the result is war and destruction. The sooner humanity realizes the need to accept Universal Virtues the quicker lasting peace will be achieved.'

It was almost time for Abraham to call it a day and to conclude. They looked at me and asked if I had any comments.

I looked at Abraham and asked, 'Could you explain the role of Jesus? Is he really the son of God?'

After some reflection, Abraham said, 'Let me see how this belief has been established, and became part of the Gospel. There are almost thirty years of missing records of the life of Jesus. The Christians support their belief that Jesus is the son of God, because at the age of eight he said to his parents, in the Temple of Solomon in Jerusalem, "Why are you looking for me? Don't you know I am in my Father's House?" After his death, there was a big debate as to who Jesus really was. How did he perform all those miracles? The act of resurrection was inexplicable in human terms and therefore must be Divine.'

Abraham continued, 'The use of the word "Father" meant that God is the giver of all human talents. Jesus got his Divine powers in the same way we are showing Divine powers. The difference is that Jesus was dedicated to serve humanity and dwelled on this planet. Jesus was sent and tasked to get the Israelites to repent for abandoning their role as "God's Chosen People". Jesus kept referring to the "Kingdom of Heaven". The use of the word "Kingdom" meant the existence of a structure. The use of "Heaven" meant the DD. In the Kingdom of Heaven, Jesus was appointed as "God's Senior Agent" responsible for seeing human beings on planet Earth fulfil God's plan. Therefore, I hope that you can see why Jesus is different from other earthly messengers. I am not sure what Jesus will tell you during the last day of this encounter.'

'Stop please. Are you saying that the Israelites are no longer "God's Chosen People"? If this is the case, then please explain what that means. Why did God make them his chosen people in the first place and why did he change his mind?' I asked.

Abraham said, 'I promise that I will respond to these questions later. Let me continue with the role of Jesus first.

'Jesus appeared through his physical body and known to the Jews as the son of Joseph the carpenter. At the same time, from inception, a Divine Soul came to dwell in the womb of his mother due to his virgin birth. This is why Jesus is half-human and half Divine. The fact that Jesus is not the Son of God but half-Divine being would not make his message or powers any less relevant. One of the key new principles Jesus came up with was the role of the Holy Spirit (the DD) and the powers it could offer. In addition, he tried to get the Israelites to return to their roles of doing God's work as preachers of Morality.

'Let me now explain the term "God's Chosen People". This does not mean that God discriminates. For humanity to overcome their shortcomings, God chose the decedents of Noah to have easy access to the DD so that they could provide guidance to and direct Mankind to the path of virtues and wisdom. They continued with that task for many thousands of years and thcy were blessed for that role. Many messagers appeared and they were tolerated to some extent. This continued until Moses came and introduced formal religious institutions borrowed from the Ancient Egyptians. Jesus was sent to see if he could persuade the Jews to resume their role to provide virtuous examples and role models to the rest of humanity through full adherence an evolutionary moral code. He came empowered with all sorts of miracles derived from the Holy Spirit. Yet, not only did they reject his message, but they also conspired with the Romans to get him crucified. With the act of crucifixion, the Lord made all virtuous people "God's Chosen People" to spread the message of love and compassion.'

I asked Abraham to explain the resurrection.

Abraham explained briefly that Jesus's physical body was crucified and buried, while Jesus the Divine Soul could not be buried and stayed behind in a hologram form for forty days to complete his message.

I said, 'But doubtful Thomas wanted to see him and touch him?'

'Yes he did see him and probably tried to touch him but the reported details are left to historians to verify, as not everything that you read in books of faith represent 100% of what actually happened. In fact, the Gospel of Thomas, which was found some seventy years ago, did not mention anything regarding this incident. This Gospel was banned from the approved New Testament.'

I made the comment that many people will be offended when their core faith is challenged in such a direct way.

Abraham responded, 'Mac, the principle of Trinity is intact. There is God the Great Designer, there is the Holy Spirit (the DD) and there is Jesus who is appointed by God as Earth's Governor in the Kingdom of Heaven. Jesus is looking after Earth's Moral Codes after the Israelites abandoned this role. It is not our objective to dwell on the current interpretations or the rights and wrongs of any faith, as long as they are in line with the overall objective of adopting UNIVERSAL VIRTUES.'

Newton broke his silence, 'We can tell you with absolute certainty that all faiths have something which is not correct and cannot pass the simplest scientific scrutiny. This will always be the case as religions differ in some aspects of their teaching, especially in the non-core elements. They cannot all be a record of the absolute truth. Yet, if the believers of every faith are to insist that their faith is superior or more accurate than the others are, then we are back to square one. We hope that every human will be gracious enough to accept that his faith is nothing more than a set of codes and traditions passed onto him by accident of his birth. They should be seen as different roads leading to the same God.'

Abraham continued, 'Most current religious upheavals are between the followers of Abrahamic faiths, although they all affirm the oneness of God and He is behind all that exists. Christianity came to update Judaism and not to overrule its teaching. This is why the Bible includes the Old Testament. Islam came after both faiths. The Quran clearly says that it believes in the previous two holy books and it came to supplement them. This is why the Quran did not repeat all the moral teachings found in the Old and the New Testaments. The Quran lays more emphasis on spirituality due to the decadence of the people of Arabia and beyond at the time. Most current Muslim preachers have missed this point and focus on the rituals instead of the true value of the moral codes in the three holy books.'

Plato noted that it was getting late and said, 'Mac, please be brief and raise only a few important final questions for the day.'

I obliged with some comments and questions, 'Dreams have challenged the human mind, and we still do not know how to interpret dreams. Religions believe in revelations through dreams. Could you expand on that?'

Darwin explained that ancient humans saw dreams as a method of receiving signals from God. Currently some may interpret dreams as the free floatation of the personal ego, (sense of self-esteem), between the conscious mind, the unconscious mind (which deals with emotions and the selfish pursuit of pleasure) and the subconscious mind. He explained that the majority of dreams, however, are those that reflect everyday experiences of humans. Some dreams are messages from the DD to provide a glimpse of the future. Only a few are tuned to receive such messages.

Abraham continued with a practical clarification of how the future can be foretold. 'If you plan to take a trip by air from London to New York to visit your brother who has the full flight schedule, then he will know the future when he says, "Mac will arrive at six p.m. from London at John Kennedy Airport". If your brother is in full control of all the variables to ensure the arrival on time, then his prediction will be 100% correct. As he is not in control of the forces of nature or in control of human failures, he cannot predict with certainty. On the other hand, Divine predictions can be made with certainty as the speed and direction of all the moving parts governing all events in the universe are fully observable and predictable.'

I was rather puzzled with this explanation, 'You are implying that human thoughts and actions are also predictable. If this is the case then how can we say that man has freewill?'

Darwin responded, 'This is a very good question Mac. I will cover it in more detail tomorrow. For our purpose today, I can assure you that at the time of making the decision, man is governed by the structure and wiring of his brain, the chemicals flowing in his body and how they interact with his value system at the instant the decision is being made.'

'You cannot be serious,' I responded. 'You are basically telling me that humans are blessed with consciousness, intelligence and apparent freewill, yet they end up making predetermined decisions based on their value system and other components.'

Darwin replied, 'If we believed that man had no power to direct his destiny then we would not be here. Man has the power to reflect and guide himself and influence others to change what is stored in the brain for the next decision to be different. I promised that I will cover this tomorrow.'

All of them noticed my disappointment to know that man's apparent freewill is in reality nothing but the way his brain is being wired. He has the fortunes and the desires to seek virtues or the misfortunes and/ or the desire to be exposed to wickedness, through his upbringing, surroundings, education, and reflection. To help me have a better understanding, they added the following comment to put my mind at ease.

'In a religious cult for example,' Darwin emphasised, 'you see the followers of the cult make their decision in a very predictable manner, because one knows what that faith dictates they should do. If their beliefs are exact and with the same passion, then any variation in their response will be due to their genetic differences like the threshold of pain, level of relaxation, proneness to emotional fluctuation and so on.'

I followed with another question. 'What is meant by the saying in the Old Testament that God punished Mankind for the sin of Eve eating the apple, leading to her being kicked out of Heaven?'

Abraham replied, 'As I said before, the animalistic traits of selfishness and aggression are still prevalent among human beings. Therefore, the concept of the Devil whispering in Eve's ear is simply saying that the devil within humans is still strong. Most of the stories in Genesis have been taken from an ancient folklore. The recently discovered Sumerian Tablets here in Nineveh tells the same stories. "Sin of Eve" means that man has not managed to control the evil within him. By saying that Adam and Eve had been kicked out Heaven means that it is no longer certain that the Souls of all humans will dwell in the DD. As humans have refused to follow the path laid down by the Lord, humans are to be judged individually according to their deeds.'

'There is widespread belief in most religions about Doomsday scenarios,' I said. 'It is claimed that such events will force Jesus to come and save his few followers and the rest are condemned forever.'

Abraham responded, 'I think you know that some religions had to create a stick to whip their followers with, in order to keep them on the straight and narrow path. Many liberal religious leaders started to differentiate between what is acceptable in today's well-informed societies and what is not. If they didn't, they will be swept into irrelevance.'

'So are you telling me that Jesus is not coming back?' I asked. 'Yet there are five of you here who are not tasked to look after Earth's moral codes.'

'I am not saying that Jesus will not come back,' Abraham said. 'You will have the chance during the last day of this encounter to hear for yourself from our Holy Visitors what they think about the way religions have shaped human social fabrics and where these religions have gone wrong.'

Darwin then stood up and recited:

O Man! Wake up and be effective
Just peace needs you to be reflective

You are blessed you with talent to be used
Your fears and hesitations will not be excused

They were all concerned at the late hour of the completion of the lecture. They walked me to my bed and then wished me goodnight.

Chapter 5

Darwin
Evolution and Creation

It was Tuesday morning and I was looking forward to hearing what Darwin had to say. After all, no one had shaken the established faiths as much as Darwin did. He came up with the theory of evolution and survival of the fittest. After the usual breakfast niceties, we sat down quickly to hear Darwin.

'Let me start with what has been said during this encounter so far, which has relevance to my teaching today,' he began. 'Let me repeat the three relevant geneses with some comments.'

'At Genesis 5) God said, "Let there be seeds of life", and the seeds were created and spread around the universe.'

I stopped Darwin, 'What evidence exists in the holy books regarding God creating the seeds and not, as we are told, Adam's creation from Clay and Eve from his ribs?'

Abraham responded with a quote from the Bible. "He (God) has made everything beautiful in its time. He has also set eternity in the hearts of men; yet they cannot fathom what God has done from beginning to end. (Ecclesiastes 3:11)".

I looked at Darwin and said, 'I do not understand, please clarify.'

Darwin replied, 'This can only make sense if man is familiar with current scientific knowledge. "God has made everything beautiful in its time" means that as living organisms evolve, beauty appears in the new species as intended by the

136

Creator. "God also set eternity in the heart of man" means that God has planted in the heart of man the desire for eternal life and the urge to recreate the seeds of life. As physical life cannot be eternal, he must seek it in the spirit. For humanity to be eternal in the physical form, it must be through recreating the seeds of life. "Yet they cannot fathom what God has done from beginning to end" means that humans have not yet worked out the secret of creation and how it began and how it will end up. This is why the time has come for us to give this knowledge to humanity.'

Abraham continued with a quote from the Quran, Noah 17: "God produced you (human beings) from earth like a vegetable growth". You see Mac, only plants grow from seeds. This is a clear message that all living beings have grown from seeds since man is at the top of the animal kingdom.'

Newton looked at Darwin for permission and said, 'According to THE THEORY OF EVERYTHING, we confirm that life in its physical form can exist only in regions of space-time in which the three known dimensions and the time dimension are not curled up into a singularity. Souls, on the other hand, can only exist in the DD.'

Darwin thanked Newton and continued with his lecture, 'After God created the physical universe processes, steps were taken to make things more exciting by adding living organisms to the physical universe. God's master plan was to create processes to ensure the continuity of life in the cosmos. As the universe is constantly undergoing birth, maturity and death, the creation of life must take into account this reality. God's processes are eternal. Therefore, the seeds of life must have the built-in science, technology and mechanisms to enable it to create the appropriate DNA and RNA for the evolutionary processes compatible with its environments. The seed must also have the technology to pass the impulse to the ultimate intelligence to recreate the seeds with no intervention from the Creator. The science and technology in the seeds took into account the properties of atoms making up the physical universe. It is time for man to examine all type of living beings and find the science and technology behind various systems and activities undertaken by all type of living beings. For example how could some species change the colour of their skin as a part of their defensive mechanism to hide from predators? What is the technology used by some insects to conduct a chemical warfare to confuse the target specie for a temporary period to enable the former to plant its eggs in the lavre of the target?

Darwin expanded by saying, 'Carbon-based seeds were created and dispatched using comets as delivery systems to reside in various planets until the minimum correct atmosphere and environment were formed. As water is the source of all life in the universe, a precondition for the activation of the seed is the existence of water in liquid form.

'The seeds then start to divide as single cell organisms. Then they adapt to the changing atmosphere and source of light or energy. The cells are equipped with their own sensors to assess the direction of how it will evolve in accordance with the road map implanted in the original seeds. In doing so, they take into account the regularly changing ecosystem they find themselves in.

As the living organisms multiply very fast and grow in numbers, their by-products start to change gradually the atmosphere and climate of the planet. This in turn requires the living organisms to adapt to these changes. With time and after millions of generations, cells start, not only to evolve as single cells, but also to combine together creating multi-cellular living organisms. This allows the cells to specialize and communicate with each other for the survival of that organism. This must mean that cells have their own processes of decision-making and an overall built-in objective to create complex life. This alone must be a strong indicator of the existence of an intelligent DNA codes' writing capabilities driving single cells to unite in a single organism. It is highly unlikely for a single cell to start life as a matter of chance. For these cells to take the next step of communicating with each other and specialize to form a complex organism, requires an "Original Designer". A fair-minded rationalist would choose the existence of a designer over random chaos as the probable answer for how life has started in the universe.

'By the way, more than 99% of all species on Earth have ceased to exist in this continuous evolutionary process, as these species were not the ultimate objective. They are a stepping-stone in creating the ultimate talent in humans.

'Let me make some comments on Newton's lecture that has relevance for our study today. The cells are nothing but a cluster of atoms made from photons locked in a circular radius. What gives the cell its living characteristics including birth, maturity and death, is the DNA that is located at the core of the cell. Each cell is a complete biochemical unit with its moving parts at a nano level. The moving parts perform their duties at relatively high speed, joining atoms at the instruction of the DNA to produce various proteins. Since the DNA is permanently residing in the nucleus of the cell, the messengers, called the RNA, get their orders from the DNA and pass them onto the mechanical parts of the cell to do their jobs with no questions asked. This is like a managing director sitting in a boardroom issuing instructions, via messengers to his factory workers. Let us assume that the RNA is similar to an Internet-enabled message. Computer users are well aware of the big risk of someone tampering with the Internet communications. Therefore, for securing the accuracy of the messages, the Great Designer has introduced a security process in this tiny cell. This is like a pre-implementation audit to ensure that the information carried by the RNA is in line with the original DNA instructions. The pre-implementation inspector is called RNAi.'

I interrupted, 'This sounds like a really well thought-out plan. How does the RNAi know what the correct message should be? Does it get its information from a backup source? Alternatively, as in some bank account numbers, are they issued in a specific way to include a check digit? By applying the check digit one can tell if they have entered the account number correctly or not?'

'These are very good comments Mac. You are almost spot on,' clarified Darwin.

Realizing that they were not too keen on being more specific regarding RNAi, I continued with my observations. 'In the case of the Internet, there are computer hackers who create viruses. Please tell me who the cell hackers are, who interferes with the RNA? Do the hackers reside within the cell?'

Newton was quick to respond. 'Mac, although this is a good question, I thought you would work out the answer by yourself. The cells perform their duties in a continuously changing environment and sometimes in a hostile environment. The cells are surrounded by background radiation. Infinite numbers of photons are continuously bombarding the cells. These external factors could interfere with the RNA's photocopying of instructions. Viruses also exist and may enter the body of the cell to issue its own instructions to the cell. All these and more may lead to corruption of the message contained in the RNA.'

'So what happens if an instruction is rejected by the RNAi?' I asked.

Darwin responded, 'The message will be destroyed, and that specific protein will not be produced. This will lead to an imperfection in the cell. For example, if there is an RNA carrying the instructions to produce the protein for the skin colour is rejected, then that skin cell will have no colour. The cell will be white. If the malfunction is serious enough to the overall cell objective then that cell is programmed to commit suicide. This means that the cell has the intelligence to know its supposed duties in the living organism. It also has the capability of assessing these facts and makes a decision on whether to continue with its existence or to end its life. The normal cell is unselfish and lives to support the survival of the whole organism. The cell is not just there to do specific tasks and reproduce itself, it also communicates with other cells. It has predetermined objectives. It is altruistic in nature and very efficient in performing its duties.'

Newton could not hold himself any longer. 'You see Mac, if the cell was created by chance and started to divide, then why would it need an RNAi? In fact, without the RNAi you would have a chaotic variation of living cells without an overall plan. If from chaos, the first cell was produced, then to chaos it must be destined. We know that the ultimate destiny of the cell was not to produce chaos but intelligence and multi-cellular beautiful resilient creatures. By using this fact alone, i.e. getting the RNA to destroy itself, scientists could manipulate each gene. They would then see what would be the resultant consequence to that living organism if a specific set of instructions were altered. This process would enable humans to work out the specific function of each gene.'

Newton continued with a big smile, 'Ask any statistician to work out the probability of a cell created by chance and without RNAi to evolve randomly into having this capability. I think you will find him in a monastery praying for God before he finds the answer!'

Plato could not see himself left out. 'If man could only learn from the working and behaviours of the cell in a living organism, then our trip would not have been necessary and the road to tranquil and harmonious living would have been guaranteed. The DNA, RNA and RNAi are equivalent to the moral and ethical codes (UMC) of society and also similar to how these should be communicated and applied. The UMC of the society is its DNA. The RNA of the society is the media and the education system. The speed of communication is improving by the day through faster mobiles and Internet. The current world order lacks a good RNAi that should ensure that the media is not used to manipulate the masses, is not used to indoctrinate the young minds, and is not used to insult and abuse others. The new Just World Order needs to establish a code to ensure that human communications are compatible with a virtuous order.'

Adam also had to say something, 'The world economy would be in a better situation if the individual in the society becomes selfless as the cell is. If the individual remembers to put the community's needs ahead of his own then that community will flourish in every respect.'

I looked at Adam and said, 'I hope that you will explain later how this can be achieved as this is in complete contradiction to the teachings of the real father of capitalism. His economic theory was based on the principle that what is good for the individual is good for the society at large, subject to some guidelines.'

They all joked with Adam and said, 'We told you to be careful when you make comments in a science lecture.'

Darwin then proceeded to address how cancerous cells are formed. Why does the RNAi seem not to work and why the malfunctioning cell doesn't commit suicide?

'Cells are continuously adapting by referring to the stored knowledge in the cell to deal with various chemicals and environments it faces over millions of years. The meddling of humans with the environment, new chemicals entering the food chains or additional radiation exposures are the main sources of damage to the functioning of the cell. As a general rule, anything that is not found in nature could create a risk to the functioning of the cell. You see, if a cell starts to reproduce selfishly then what is good for one cell is no longer good for the body. You could say the cancerous cells have lost their moral code and no longer care about the rest of the organism. If you have too many cells misbehaving then you have an early death on your hands. This is also true if you have too many individuals with defective moral codes in a society. That society will certainly fail.'

Adam interrupted, 'This is similar to a monopolist who finds himself in a situation which allows him to exploit others without any consideration for the principles of fairness.'

Darwin continued, 'To put it simply, humans should not allow foreign substances to enter their lungs nor their bloodstreams which did not originate from nature. Living cells needs a long time to adapt to such substances. All new synthetic chemicals that manage to enter the body need to be soluble in water so that the body can get rid of it. If this cannot be done, then the immune system will try to discover an alternative way of dealing with this unrecognized substance. It may create a cyst to isolate it. In many cases, the continuing friction of the foreign substance with the adjacent cells may damage the cell. It then starts to grow selfishly without any regard to the needs of the rest of the body. Therefore, it is necessary to reject genetically altered food until it is well tested. The likelihood of genetically altered foods causing damage to health is much smaller compared to non-organic materials produced by man all the time. This is why one of the UMC is "Do not rush into genetic engineering". In short, for healthy living man should seek what is natural and reject what is made of newly produced chemicals.'

Abraham added, 'The adaptation of each living organism is a key feature of the original designer. Any seed of life created without the ability to adapt or change does not deserve the name "seed of life" as it will not survive the continuous change in the environment to achieve the original plan. Religions and cultures that do not adapt to the needs of time will lead their followers to relative poverty and ignorance. They will ultimately be swept away by superior cultures just as it occurs in the animal kingdom. After all, the moral code of any society is its DNA. Property to those who comply with the UMC will certainly apply'

'I understand now,' I said. 'You think humans are heading back to the jungle. Survival of the fittest will be the rule in international politics, as cultural differences keep widening. You are here to shake humanity into action. We must avoid sleepwalking into the worst wars. Those with the military might may start to equate their might with progress and civilization. Combine this military power differentials with the defective moral codes of those with religious ignorance and the wealthy arrogant and you have a toxic combination which will definitely lead to clash of civilizations.'

Darwin continued, 'Human genes have many switches which are inactive in addition to the monitoring gene. These switches could be activated to enhance survival of the species over a relatively short period of time. For example, if a woman in her very early weeks of pregnancy is subjected to severe malnutrition then some switches in the genes of the fetus could be turned on to assist in the storage of food at a later stage in life. During the life of identical twins, those who are subjected to severe anxiety develop differently, as some of the switches are activated or switched off. You see, without the genetic knowledge, scientists would have said, 'This is random mutation'. In fact, it is pre-planned switches that guide the survival of the species.'

I appealed to Darwin to summarize what has been said so far as the lecture had not followed a specific structure. Darwin obliged as follows:

'1) The cell acts as a single living unit with its own moral code and strictly follows the constitution of the living organism as written in the DNA.

'2) The cell's RNA is the communication system that passes the information to the mechanical parts of the cell.

'3) The cell's RNAi acts as an inspector that ensures that all the instructions passed by RNA are in line with the overall objectives of the organism before implementation. If they are tampered with, they are destroyed and the job is not done.

'4) The cell is selfless, putting the interest of the whole organism ahead of its own interest. In fact, it is ready to sacrifice itself if it ceases to be useful for the total good of the entire biological unit.

'5) The cell is at the mercy of the total ecosystem in which the organism lives. The cell tries to do its best to keep the unit functioning and replicates itself in the long run. If it needs to adapt for a better chance of survival in the future, it sends messages to the monitoring gene in addition to adjusting some switches.

'6) The cell communicates with neighbouring cells to collect information and then passes it on for the efficient functioning of the whole organism.

'7) The cell continuously regenerates itself to stay fresh and to function efficiently. The brain cells are an exception to this rule as their loss will affect the wiring of the brain, and the stored data will be wiped out. The result of replacing the brain cells will lead to continuous dementia and non-functioning of the entire unit. The Great Designer has put in the place of brain cell renewal, multiple endings to each neuron cell of the brain. The objective is to allow multiple brain circuitries for continuous learning and changing one's moral code. Again, you need a designer to make this differentiation into which cells should or should not regenerate themselves.

'8) If the cells become selfish and start to replicate in violation of the normal DNA's instruction, then those cells will be regarded as greedy rebels and they need to be recognized as such. The body will reject them as foreign bodies if it has the correctly evolved immune system.

'9) For a giant leap in human medical advancement, steps will be taken to encourage the body to release regular scout cells to identify defective body parts. Once they are located, stem cells will be directed through the bloodstream to the defective parts to bring about the necessary repair. Man will also find ways to slow the biological clock and to inject into the blood stream naturally-produced chemicals to help man stay young for much longer.'

'Wow,' I shouted. 'Are you saying that science will find the way to get our body to self-repair damaged parts? Would that make humans immortal?'

'No!' came the answer quickly from Darwin. 'Human brain cells cannot renew themselves and man will be destined to death in his physical form. However, not in the too-distant future, man will live for more than few centuries healthily.

'10) The evolutionary process on Earth did not unfold in a uniform manner all through time. First, the soft-bodied primitive organisms had to evolve to provide the infrastructure or food chain for more complex organisms that would evolve much later. The early processes had to deal with major environmental changes to ensure that life is possible for the more complex species that would follow. It took about 580 million years for this to happen. In the following seventy to eighty million years, most of the advanced species evolved. The rate of evolution was estimated to be three times faster than the earlier period. This is known as the Cumbrian Explosion. This is similar to humans undertaking a major land reclamation project from a nuclear waste site. It will take thousands of years to prepare the site for normal habitation. Once it is ready, then it will be much faster to add the remaining building blocks of the project.

'11) The cell has a monitoring gene for the planned evolution and adaptation of the species. Mice are a good example of organisms being blessed with an active monitoring gene that enables them to adapt and survive in various environments. The sooner the operation of that gene is understood the quicker humans will be able to adapt to their changing needs and environments. This may lead humans to specialize into mathematicians, artists, musicians, athletes and so on. The 'Just World Order' needs to be built on a model of the selfless cells devoted to serve the whole organism. Imagine a society where people put the group ahead of the individual. This is doable and it is not a Utopian dream. This is exactly what the Creator expects for the true salvation of humanity.'

I noticed that everyone was nodding with strong approval as if this were the main purpose of the encounter.

Darwin continued, 'Let me now turn to the question of intelligence. At Genesis 6) God said, "Let the seeds of life evolve to create intelligent beings in my image" and the genetic codes started to evolve to create intelligent beings.

'This process, which is called evolution, is not really completely random but it is pre-planned. Recently humans have just started to understand why there are a high percentage of genes that appear to have no purpose. They used to call them redundant genes. They are, in fact, key instructions to guide the evolutionary process over time. The next leap forward will come when man will start to speed up his evolution through genetic engineering. This does not mean that survival of the fittest principles have no value. It is actually part of the program of life to create species that can adapt and flourish in the new environment. Just as you cannot build a tower on a weak foundation, you cannot sustain a flourishing intelligent organism in a non-compatible environment.

'The same seeds of life on different planets will produce a different variety of living organisms, depending on the environments of those planets. This does not mean that intelligence will not ultimately evolve if the underlying seed is correctly designed. There is one type of ultimate intelligence in the universe, with some variations in the supporting bodies. In order to ensure that the evolutionary process is speeded up, the males and females had to evolve first. Without this step, species would have continued to replicate themselves with minor environmental adaptation. I tell you Mac, it is the male of the species that carries the monitoring gene. This gene gets its information from all the cells of the body so that it can be assessed and passed to the next generation. The information contains what the cells have found out to be useful for survival. The more a given tissue in the body is used, the more importance will be given to that tissue in the future. This information is not acted upon except after several generations of re-enforcing the same message. If this is not the case, then there will be frequent mutations and this would destabilize the evolutionary process. This is like the older generation teaching the younger generation how to improve their moral codes for better harmony in the community.'

'Isn't that incredible?' said Plato. 'Cells learn from experience and pass that knowledge onto the next generation via the monitoring gene.'

Abraham added, 'Once this is accepted and the relevant gene is identified by scientists, then they should stop their scepticism of God. They should admit that a cell created by chance would not have all these mechanisms to evolve in an orderly manner. The existence of a Great Designer would be the only rational conclusion.

'This is like the Google search engine gathering information at the user level. They use that information to give recommendations for some future searches,' I commented. I then asked, 'Darwin, is this another case of discrimination against women by giving the male of the species the glory of holding the monitoring gene?'

They all laughed and Darwin said confidently, 'I am sure you know that when the female conceives, the bundle of eggs is already there. This means that the mother's genetic footprint and environmental information are already in the eggs from birth. This is not the case in the males. The sperms are continuously created after puberty. Therefore, we can confirm that the monitoring gene sits on the Y chromosome. It is easy to test this on mice by subjecting males to specific chemicals, and then the females to the same chemical. As the cells are used, a record is passed onto the monitoring gene, to indicate what tissues need to be given more dominance than others are. This information is passed onto the offspring. After a several generations, if the same message is re-enforced, then the gene starts to adapt by giving a bigger role to those tissues needed to improve survival. Here again, we see scientists explaining things as being the result of random variation or chance rather than inherent design. "Randomness", "Out of nothing" or "It has always existed", etc, has become the atheists' equivalent of the "God Gap" to avoid answering the big questions.'

They were all expecting me to make a comment.

I obliged, 'Darwin is then confirming that man will acquire the knowledge to play the role of God. For instance, man could play God by altering the program of life to speed up the evolutionary process, to produce new species, to improve biodiversity and the quality of life and to ultimately reproduce the seeds of life.'

Abraham said with a frown, 'Those are your words, and not ours, that man will play the role of God. It is God's original design that man will have the talent to do so.

'Remember, at Genesis 7) God said, "Let living organisms have Soul" and the DD started to interact with the vibrating genes.'

Darwin stared at his colleagues and said, 'This is the most difficult subject to teach. Thanks to Abraham, a lot has already been said regarding this matter. Let me recap. God created the seeds of life with the objective of creating intelligence. The purpose of intelligence is to maintain the living dimension in the cosmos and to provide further advancements in knowledge. You see Mac, the stars and planets are recreating themselves through repeated Big Bangs. There is no need for intelligent beings to interfere in this process as it is beyond their capabilities to influence such cosmic events. In the case of living organisms, as planets die – Earth also will ultimately do so – new seeds need to be reproduced and passed on to start life on the newly born planets. If intelligent species do not master this process, life will ultimately cease to exist in the universe.'

I looked at everyone in amazement and asked, 'If this is the case, then why have the existing religions not spelled this out?'

Abraham smiled as he had the answer ready. 'Jesus revealed to his disciples this fact. However, humanity regarded it as one of his mysterious sayings and it was thus ignored. This confirms that one should continuously update the way holy books and mysterious sayings are interpreted and one should not stick to historical explanations. Let me recite to you Jesus's saying number 18 in the Gospel of Thomas.

"The disciples said to Jesus, '*Tell us, how will our end come?*' Jesus said, '*Have you found the beginning, then, that you are looking for the end? You see, the end will be where the beginning is. Congratulations to the one who stands at the beginning: that one will know the end and will not taste death.*'"

Abraham continued while his eyes locked onto mine, 'Relying on what you have just heard from Darwin, let me explain. "Have you found the beginning": means have you found the fact that life has begun from seeds? When you do find this out, and you know how to recreate the seeds, then this is when man has fulfilled "The Lord's Plan" of the renewal of life in the universe. You see, God will congratulate the one who recreates the beginning, the seeds. The one who reaches that level of wisdom will ultimately possess the knowledge of how

151

life will end on Earth and will learn that life will continue somewhere else in the universe.'

I could see that everyone was excited each time they confirmed that their teachings were nothing more than an attempt to bring science and religion together to find the truth.

This encouraged me to ask Darwin the next question, 'Since we are discussing cells and living organisms, can they exist without a Soul?'

He obliged, 'In fact, it is a misconception to believe that a cell needs a Soul to divide and communicate with other cells. The cell gets its energy from the food consumed. The mystery of the living organism is not in its movement or division but in the total science behind its creation and the orderly manner in which it evolves into intelligent beings. The Soul of every cell exists just as the vibration of the photon and the gravity of the atom exists. You see, without Souls intelligent beings based on DNA alone will not guarantee their evolution in the image of the Creator. The Souls enable the Lord, through the DD, to have full knowledge of what every individual is doing and thinking. Virtuous Souls released from the physical body also serve as agents of the ultimate Creator.'

'Why is this important if God does not get involved in the details?' I asked.

Darwin responded, 'God would not leave things to chance. He wants to be in full control of his creation. This is also to provide Him with the comfort of knowing what is going on in the Cosmos. Not doing so would be like man creating robots to occupy other planets without knowing what those robots are doing nor being able to correct their actions. Would anyone fund such a project? Sending robots to the unknown to be destroyed once the planet ceases to exist and without any communication at all would be an act of insanity. By the way, you cannot have faith unless you have Heaven and Hell as Abraham explained yesterday. Man will have no motivation to use his talent and to be virtuous if there is no promise of Heaven. Heaven on Earth will not exist if there is no purpose to life and there is no eternity to look for. The DD will have no Angels and Souls to assist the living. God's plan for eternity of life in the universe through the recreation of seeds will not take place. So God's plan for eternal processes will not work without the creation of the Soul by the Original Designer.'

I stood up with a spark in my eyes, 'Wow, this really makes sense to me. However, I am sure many atheists will ask for physical evidence. They are stuck in their narrow logic. If they cannot see it, touch it or measure it by some instruments made from photons and atoms they will not accept it. They regard all reported supernatural observations made by Mankind throughout history as superstitions, due to the mostly exaggerated and probably erroneous reporting of those events. They probably would ignore the logic of these presentations as just fancy words of science fiction.'

'Well, that is OK. That is OK with us, provided that this encounter becomes the trigger for man to be inquisitive and challenges the current sets of beliefs,' Darwin replied calmly.

Plato wondered if I could explain how man would create the seeds of life.

I replied, 'As man will master the understanding of the genome and nanotechnology, he will start to create new species and ultimately the seeds of life. He will surely carry out many experiments to ensure that he has it right. Once he has done that with perfection he will start to look for the nearest comet to be used as a delivery vehicle. This however will be a long way away and may require help from other intelligent beings.'

I then asked Darwin to clarify his understanding of freewill as a biologist. He obliged immediately, as if he was waiting for my question.

'Abraham has argued rationally why humans do not have freewill at the instant that decisions are being made. He also correctly confirmed current earthly research which shows that decisions are made in the brain before the conscious mind knows those decisions have been made by a second or more. This does not mean that it is useless to do anything about human behaviours since all their decisions are pre-determined. We have said that humans have a simulator in their frontal lobe. With it, they can simulate events that could happen and reflect on the possible outcomes. Therefore, the key elements for the existence of human freewill are the mechanisms he must develop to be open-minded and reflective. Without these mechanisms, man will be at the mercy of what others plant in his memory through parenting, the opinions formers, and other experiences.'

Darwin continued, 'Humans are genetically programmed to achieve pleasure and avoid pain. As they reflect on observations, ideas and actions, those that lead to pleasure are tagged with positive or green markers and those that lead to pain, real or potential, are tagged with negative or red markers. You also need to remember that each neuron has tens of thousands of endings to allow multiple paths to retrieve data. It is the creation of these multiple paths with the relevant stored mental scores that determine which path in the brain circuitry will be given priority the next time a decision is to be made. When a man says, "I have made a decision based on my gut feeling", he means that his subconscious brain has processed all the stored information and has arrived at the decision without him really knowing how or why.'

'You see Mac,' Plato interjected, 'if we thought that man had no freewill in choosing the correct path for programming his brain, then it would be meaningless for us to be here. This is of the utmost importance to our message.

Darwin thanked Plato and said, 'Let me expand. Most of Mankind's problems are the result of his inability to get the correct and balanced value system, the right moral codes, stored in the brain with the correct ranking or scorecard. Let us consider the important routes of learning in order to get our message conveyed more effectively.

'1) People must have an open mind to receive new ideas.

'These filters in the brain should not be shut completely due to strong beliefs or any other reasons. Ideas cannot be transmitted to a shut mind nor can it be generated by such people. One should always be inquisitive and ready to accept that the absolute truth of today may not be the case tomorrow. The higher the pain and pleasure score the individual attaches to his belief, the more difficult for the individual to be open-minded when it comes to those beliefs. Such strong faith should not lead to religious intolerance or worse, to action against other faiths. This is why the most important action to follow from our visit is to create religious tolerance. A complete open heart and mind is needed to debate the virtues spelt out by Abraham. There is no such thing as absolute truth when it comes to religions, no matter what most people think.

'All holy books are regarded by their believers as God's spoken words. In reality, they are ideas communicated to prophets expressed in man-made words. It is during this process of converting thoughts to words that inaccuracies start to creep in. By the way, the first step in creating religious harmony is to equate intelligence with open-mindedness or readiness to change and to understand others. Since God has created man in

155

his image, that is to have intelligence, then it must be a great sin to kill this attribute by being intolerant and closed-minded. Those who are not ready to consider other opinions, openly and reflectively, will end up unable to change anything. Using Darwinian language, human knowledge and cultures are continuously evolving and those who encompass change will flourish and survive. Those who reject change will end up in misery and rejection. Culture, including religious survival, comes with adaptation. The brain is like an umbrella, if it is not open, it will not give you protection from ignorance and bigotry.

'2) One should learn the art of deep reflection.

'The Individual must have the ability to absorb and to assess profoundly the new information against the existing beliefs he holds. The great thinker Confucius once said, "One may learn wisdom by reflection, which is noblest, by imitation, which is easiest or by experience, which is bitterest".'

'We have our own saying,' Plato continued. 'With an open mind and heart I reflect, therefore I will be.'

Abraham added that all religions have the concept of remorse and repentance that are the result of deep reflection. 'If someone shows genuine remorse then the likelihood of his repeating the crime is nonexistent and further punishment ceases to be necessary.

'3) One should assess the pain and pleasure associated with new ideas.

'To allow the new information and experiences to affect future behaviours, a third element is required in addition to being open-minded and reflective. It is the assessment that will lead to ranking and placing the thoughts, ideas and experiences correctly in the mental compartment. The score given differs from person to person.

'If one is visiting a country where possession of the smallest quantity of an illicit drug will lead to capital punishment, the reaction of those who take drugs will be either not to visit that country or not to take the drug while there. In assessing the risk, a much higher score is given compared to visiting a more tolerant country. If one thinks that the mere questioning of his faith will cause him great harm – if, say, a high negative score has been given to doubting the existence of God – then that person is unlikely to engage in the debate calmly. Therefore, the correct assessment is important to the ranking we place on the new knowledge or suggestions. It is this ranking that prioritizes the action or inaction that will follow. Correct assessment = Correct prioritization = Desired future reaction. Each person has the right and the duty to assess correctly and realistically what already has been stored to allow change and to transform new scores to new ideas in order to make a more appropriate decision.

'By the way, those religions which inform their followers of how immense the pain will be if you do "A" and how fantastic the pleasure will be if you do "B", are training their followers for blind obedience, just as cult followers are subjected to. It is clear that different societies require different penal codes to achieve the same level of compliance. This is required to counter balance what is already being stored in the mind of the individual. A society where violence is prevalent and widely accepted requires much harsher penal codes than a more civilized society. Advocates of human rights have to consider these facts before they advocate "One Treatment Fits All Approach". The religious extremists who advocate violence and isolate the moderate believers are in reality making decent observers associate that faith with pain and misery. The result

157

will be a mass rejection of the faith in search of better moral codes, to provide the society with peace and prosperity.

'4) Reinforcements and practices are essential to establish the newly acquired knowledge.

'To rewire the brain, repetition is required until habits are formed. Without practicing, habits will not be formed. Humans are the slaves of their habits. If they don't like some of them, they should work persistently and in a structured way to change them. If someone dear to your heart gets into bad habits then it is your duty to work, with their approval, on a road map to help that person change those habits. Reinforcement is the key to achieve lasting change. Humans know well that practice and repetition leads to perfection.'

Plato said with a smile, 'You know Mac; the most difficult part is to get someone to admit that he needs to be open-minded, reflective and that he needs to re-assess his beliefs. As humans often say, "You can take a horse to water but you cannot make him drink". When a person has some chemical imbalances in his brain, he may act neurotically. In this case, one is ready to say that this person has no freewill to escape the effects of his chemical imbalance. It is up to other humans to treat him accordingly so that his behaviour changes. This does not mean that once he is treated he will have freewill. It will just mean that his behaviour is now in accordance to what the majority regard as rational and that he is ready to listen and reflect on the consequences of his actions.

'By the same logic, a person who commits a crime is in reality wrongly wired and needs help just like those with the wrong chemicals in their brain. This approach would put more emphasis on the society to do two things. Firstly, to re-examine these crimes to see if they have a pattern, to reflect on the moral compass of the society and assess the actions needed to improve the level of compliance with virtues and moralities. Secondly, if the crime is due to an individual's shortcoming, then reforming the individual in prison must be the priority.'

I winked at Plato for taking control of the lecture and said to Darwin, 'I presume that you have finished for the day.'

They all giggled and after a short silence Darwin recommenced, 'Man will continue to discover the wonders of the genes. When he unravels its full meaning, his knowledge will be multiplied several times. He will be in a position to engineer bacteria genetically to do various specific tasks to enhance his quality of life and, probably, his survival on this planet. By the way, there is one thing all galactic intelligent beings agree upon. That is, God is the greatest artist. You only have to look at the various flowers and colours of some species and you will realize the message God is trying pass onto man.'

I could not help asking Darwin a question when he said humans have imperfections. 'Why did God not hardwire us through the evolutionary process to be perfect?'

Darwin looked at me and said, 'We are often asked this question when we visit civilizations requiring corrective cognitive action. As you know, human babies are the weakest and cannot survive without their parents. This means that the human brain is not hardwired in advance in order to give the individual the maximum flexibility to adapt and cope with the various environments. Without this flexibility, humans could not have spread all over this planet with its multiple environments. This ability to adapt is also required as the planet warms up or cools down. It will give humanity the widest spread on the planet and the longest time to recreate the seeds for the next generation of intelligence. Therefore, by design, humans are not supposed to be hardwired.

'However, your question should be why God has not planned for humans to evolve with perfection to have the right chemicals: to be less selfish and more compassionate, to show more love and less anger and hate, and so on? We admit that this imperfection is not uncommon in the universe due to what could go wrong in the evolutionary process. The good news is that if humanity applies universal virtues for several generations, the chemical imbalances will disappear, as the monitoring gene will correct the situation automatically. Unfortunately humans have not adopted the high moral codes for long enough to evolve correctly. Usually aggressive societies driven by their selfish genes invade peace-loving groups before they can complete the evolutionary process.'

'This sounds rather disappointing,' I said. 'It leads to the conclusion that peace-loving societies must use military force to defeat those warmongers in order to allow humans to complete their evolutionary road map. I trust that Plato will have more to say on this subject.'

Darwin continued, 'Each neuron has thousands of endings to allow each one to have multiple paths. In such a structure, one path could be ignored and a new path established with every new acquisition of knowledge. If this is not the case then all those who are unlucky to be wrongly wired will be condemned forever due to the brain's faulty wiring. We are very hopeful that by opening the debate resulting from this encounter a momentum for true human awakening will start. This is the only road humans must follow to avoid wars and destruction at an unprecedented level.'

'I am unable to work out why so many species have been created if the objective was just to create intelligent life?' I asked, trying to widen the conversation.

Darwin responded, 'This is a very good observation. The Great Designer did not want to create only intelligent beings from the seeds. He also allowed for some genetic diversification to ensure greater variations of species to cope with the greatly varying planetary environments. This sideway evolutionary process allowed humans to observe the wonders of God's creation. This variation in species has also become a great source of knowledge and rich a supply of medicine.'

I asked Darwin if he could give a rational explanation of how woman is created from the rib of a man according to the Old Testament. And why is biology symbolized by a snake in accordance with ancient wisdom?

'Well Mac,' he started, 'If you were born 100 years ago, let alone many thousands of years ago, and were shown the DNA structure would you have not described it as having the shape of a snake or a serpent? After all, that was the period of symbolism. Can a female genetic structure create a male? The answer is definitely no. This is the case with all species. On the other hand, when chromosomes of the male are split, you can create a female from the male. So here again with a slight effort, and not to take every word in the holy books as literal, science and religion can co-exist and supplement each other provided that both scientists and religious people approach discussions with an open mind and with mutual respect. So when the Old Testament says from the "rib of man" it means from "splitting the genetic material of man".

'Since we are talking about the creation of Mankind, can you tell me if man has been partly created by aliens? There are increasing numbers of people who quote Sumerian Ancient Tablets discovered here in Nineveh that supports this theory and speaks of "Those from Heaven Came",' I said.

Darwin responded, 'Whether it happened or not, this does not make you any less human than other intelligent beings, provided that humans correct their ways as explained before. We are aware of the existence of aliens who have mastered interplanetary travel within your galaxy and they may well have visited planet Earth. They have mastered genetic engineering but not yet the full creation of the seed of life. Let me ask you this, Mac. Humans are doing their utmost to visit other planets in their solar system. If you start with putting bacteria there to make the atmosphere support life, would that make humans God? Of course, it wouldn't. They are only using some knowledge acquired to expand human habitats as they are programmed to do. If they do find ape-like creatures that are genetically similar to various forms of life on Earth doesn't that mean all the programs of life have the same original Creator? Would you feel it is beyond human capabilities to implement such genetic engineering in the not too distant future if humans survive their moral imperfections? This does not mean that early prehistoric man would not have evolved to support intelligence. All it means is that the process was speeded up.'

Plato could not hold himself, 'You see Mac, it doesn't really matter whether the evolutionary process took its course or whether humans received a helping hand from aliens. However, it does mean that humans and aliens share the same genetic origin. This is the best proof of the existence of the Great Designer.'

After some hesitation, I said, 'So the discovery that we are not alone in the universe should strengthen human belief in God and not weaken it?'

'Of course this is so, provided religions are ready to move away from the dogma of literal interpretations of their holy books. A philosophical approach to religions with true

162

understanding of the role of God and the Holy Spirit should strengthen beliefs and not weaken them,' Abraham said with excitement.

During the break I asked Darwin to expand on the bar coding of cells.

He responded by saying, 'The main objective of the bar-coding and tracing of data is not different from having a continuous recording of events on a computer server. The data can be retrieved at any time. God is more sophisticated in nanotechnologies. He records things at the photon level and not just at the cellular or atomic level. So you see Mac, at the cosmic level, we can observe which planet needs visitation and assistance and which are beyond redemption. We don't think planet Earth is beyond redemption yet and this is why there will be regular visitations by God's Agents.'

'Oh yes,' I said half-heartedly. 'As long as there are too many evil people around, those who try to be good all the time will come to ruin. We see countries starting with great ideals and those hungry for power and money corrupt the system with manipulation and deceit. Religious movements fall in the same manner.'

Abraham responded, 'Don't be so gloomy Mac. You have to wait until you hear from Plato and Adam. With education, with the correct use of the social media and with increased activism there will be a new dawn of enlightenment. This will scare the hell out of the deceitful clites. It is time to ensure that all education systems teach their students how to think and find the facts for themselves. This is the only way to escape the slavery of blind obedience.'

Darwin returned to the mystery of the seeds and of how they could hold so much information to guide the entire evolutionary process.

'Not all the genetic code of the modern human being is stored in the original seeds. The mystery of creation is to hold the science and technology that allow new sets of genes to be formed and added. These new genes should be compatible with the environment of the planet and in line with the ultimate objective of creation. This is similar to technologists and computer programmers are being tasked to monitor, specify and develop new computer programme codes based on the supplied working manuals available at their disposal to solve any persistent problem.

To move on I asked Darwin to explain the mystery of the stem cells and the manner in which they could help humanity repair damaged body parts. They all looked at him to see how much he will reveal, as though this was part of forbidden knowledge.

'You know Mac,' Darwin said, 'if knowledge is given at the wrong time it could turn into a curse. Look at what humans did with the knowledge of nuclear physics. The first act was to develop thousands of nuclear bombs sufficient to annihilate life on Earth. This is due to the imperfection of their belief system. Yes, stem cells will lead to a revolution in improving human health, the quality of life, and longevity. This will be an irresistible progress for man to pursue. For our purpose today, let me just say that humans will harness the automatic release of stem cells into their bloodstream. Those genetically manipulated stem cells will recognise damaged cells in any organ and try to replace them. If you combine this with the improvement in the immune system, you will have a real revolution in body repair and maintenance on one hand and fighting infections on the other hand. The new immunity system will improve the recognition of all defective cells including cancerous ones while stem cells will replace damaged cells in faulty organs.

Sustainability of a youthful healthy life will become a reality. Society has to find a way to adapt their moral code first, before such knowledge can be applied, otherwise overpopulation and wars will be widespread.'

'Darwin, I think you heard Abraham mentioning the preservation of biodiversity as a key virtue. Most species have limited life-spans. They are then replaced by others. What is going on?' I asked.

Darwin answered, 'Well, in the whole universe only one thing is certain and that is change. This applies to the entire physical universe as explained by Newton. Over billions of years planet Earth is continuously changing. This will require the species to adapt in order to survive. Therefore, the disappearance of species and the appearance of others is part of the overall process of creation. This is why the monitoring gene has been implanted. It is to guide the evolutionary process and to ensure compatibility of the species with the changing environments. The evolutionary process within the genes has been organized so that one biological foundation is built at a time. The unfortunate thing for planet Earth is that human knowledge is progressing at a faster pace than the evolution of his moral codes. This is leading to greater emphasis on advancing knowledge and technology for wars and destruction instead of peace and for the sustainability of the planet. Destruction of the environment and the collapse of biodiversity at such great pace is something humans will regret forever. Genetic banks need to be developed. These banks must have genes from not only the current species, but also from fossilized remains of species that have become extinct in order to examine possible reactivation at some point in the future.' Darwin then looked at everyone and continued, 'I suggest that we discuss the action needed to preserve biodiversity on this planet over lunch, as this matter is dear to my heart.'

We were late for lunch. I kept quiet as they were whispering to each other. Apparently, they communicated through some sort of telepathy and rapid data transmission. I could not help asking them if they could share whatever was being discussed with me. They told me the amount of data they handle is beyond the current human mind to take in. They were discussing their next assignment where a planet is about to be destroyed and the aliens there are asking for help.

Plato said, 'Mac, take my advice and play down the information you have just heard. You need to focus on earthly issues and not make this encounter sound like an exercise in futility.'

I wasn't sure what to say. I couldn't really see how else to see this encounter unless the information given was shown to be true while these messages were being debated.

'Mac, we think that our teachings here will start as a nice fictional story. Then as it is digested, it will appear as a logical explanation of current human observations. I am sure that what is being said here will make sense in time to many fair-minded people as a theory of everything. Like any theory, we are confident that it will be supported by subsequent scientific findings. Once that happens, this encounter will be taken more seriously due to the wealth of revelations being made.'

While we were having lunch, I asked Darwin about the great concerns human beings have over the fate of the planet and the speed at which its resources are being depleted.

Darwin replied, 'Let me mention a few doctrines that need to be adopted by Mankind to maintain the only planet they have:

'1) Maintain the Earth's capability of supporting biodiversity.

'We note with great alarm the pace at which the planet's environment is being damaged beyond repair. Most of the planet's resources are used, not to meet life-sustaining needs, but to keep people employed by pushing for unnecessary consumptions. I am sure Adam will expand on that in the coming days. The higher human productivity, the lower the need for labour would be. To keep the expanding population employed, societies push for creating needs for luxuries that deplete the Earth's resources and pollute the environment further. Therefore, as the number of people and their lifespans expand, they need to take positive action to ensure Earth's biodiversity and sustainability. It is not sufficient to be passive. It is already too late for thousands of species unless a gene bank is created for later activation.

'2) Improve water utilization and distribute it more evenly around the planet.

'Water is the source of all life on Earth. If not properly utilized and fairly distributed, many wars will be fought over the dwindling reserves of fresh water. Many species will die due to lack of water. Initially more dams need to be built to collect water in arid regions of the world. This should be followed by more research to master some control over the direction of the wind. This could be utilized to drive more clouds to dry land. It is not a dreamer's vision, but a visionary's dream. It is something that can be achieved within a few generations, if humans focus on this task rather than on wars and destruction. Man will also succeed not in the distant future to genetically engineer plants which get their water from the atmosphere allowing them to survive and grow in a humid, rainless environment.'

I asked Darwin, 'Please give me some idea as to how better water distribution can be achieved.'

He obliged, 'Some giant mirrors could be placed in space to deflect the sun. They need to be placed in the right places and in sufficient numbers to have an effect on redirecting the light for maximum effect and in reducing global warming.

'That brings me to 3) Minimize the consequences of Earth's destructive forces.

'The easiest way for humans to minimize the destruction of the environment is by reducing the burning of fossil fuels that lead to global warming. The suggestion I have just made to cool the planet and redirect the rain will serve this objective, as more plants will be growing on Earth. As for the other destructive earthly forces like earthquakes, they have little effect on biodiversity but more on the loss of human lives. Great progress can be done to predict earthquakes and improve construction methods.

'4) Minimize human destructive activities and improve Earth's sustainability.

'This is the most vitally important requirement for maintaining biodiversity. Destruction of habitats and depletion of resources at a rate faster than the planet can replenish, accounts for the extinction of many species. The new substances introduced into the environment, including nuclear waste and other mindless meddling with Earth's precious environment, are good examples of that.'

Plato looked at Darwin and said, 'Let us take it easy and allow Mac to raise any questions he may have.'

'Thanks Plato,' I replied quickly in my attempt to change the subject. 'I do have a few questions. I understand that by observing the growth of a human fetus, from the first cell division to birth, one can notice the various stages of evolution that have led to the conclusion that man has evolved from fish. How does this stack up with what you are telling us regarding humans being the product of intelligent design?'

'Mac, you have answered your own question,' Darwin started. 'The traces of legacy genes in the evolutionary processes are aimed to guide Mankind's future endeavours to create the seeds of life.'

Time was passing in general conversation. I looked at them and asked what memorable experiences they have had from other visitations. As usual, Plato jumped in and explained the fun they had had from the last visit to a nearby planet (by their measurements).

'The intelligent aliens on that planet have perfected bionic body parts to such a degree that they were about to replace a biological brain with artificial intelligence. They have not developed the software with sufficient protection mechanisms to make the unit immune from random interferences. This had led to a very dangerous situation where a faulty bionic machine was about to destroy its Creators and end all biological intelligent life on that planet.'

'Did you re-write the software for them?' I asked.

'No,' said Darwin. 'We only asked them to remember that they cannot succeed outside God's plan by fully replacing their biological brain. They can use the machines as a support system for it.'

I looked at them and all of them noticed my agony. They asked whether I liked the food or not.

'No, that's not it at all,' I responded. 'I am rather struggling to pluck up the courage to ask a very disturbing question.'

Plato said, 'Mac, it sounds serious. Please go ahead and we will be very understanding in our response.'

I said, 'Thanks Plato. Darwin had explained earlier that for humans to survive they need to put the well-being of the society as a whole ahead of individual needs. The functioning of the cell and the entire organism is similar to the individual "being the cell" and the organism "being the society". Once the cell ceases to be useful or if it becomes faulty, it commits suicide to allow for the efficient functioning of the unit.'

Plato quickly picked up the point I was trying to make and continued to save me the embarrassment of having to spell out what was bothering me. 'Mac, you are struggling with our implied contradictions. As we mentioned, the first commandment is about the sanctity of human life. Yet Darwin said that one should take guidance from the cell that ceases to exist voluntarily if it is no longer useful to the whole organism or if it is damaged. So you want to know if we are suggesting that humans should put themselves to death once they reach a stage where they are too sick to be useful, or too old to add any value to society at large.'

'Yes, this is bothering me a great deal indeed. I have come from a culture where the family unit is regarded as the foundation for any well-functioning society,' I responded.

Plato smiling said, 'I am glad to hear that. I will emphasize the role of the family tomorrow and show you how serious damage has already been inflicted due to the erosion of family values in some cultures. Well, the answer is neither easy nor straightforward. It requires developing a very well thought out strategy to avoid any misinterpretation or wrong conclusion due to its sensitivity. The advancement in technology to lengthen life expectancy is leading to big changes in the fabric of many societies. Ratio of old to young will continue to increase. Sustaining a reasonable quality of life during old age is at present a serious problem. It is true the first commandment was the "sanctity of human life". The second one is "to minimize conscious suffering and improve quality of life". The balancing act lies with these two principles. Let us start with the less debatable situation and assume that there is a person in extreme pain and his brain is totally damaged beyond repair due to a major stroke or accident. Do you let nature take its course and switch off the life support systems? Whose decision should this be? These considerations are debatable. They need to be done in agreement with the majority views by passing appropriate laws. What is acceptable, changes with time. One must keep in mind the overall happiness of the community at large.'

'Thank you for that Plato. I do understand that it is a valid ethical call and many variables need to be taken into account. All you are saying is that such a question should be regularly debated to ensure that a correct balance is reached between the need of the community and the sensitivity of the near and dear,' I said.

'It seems whenever humans interfere with natural processes they create more problems than they solve,' said Darwin. 'Could a heart attack at old age be a blessing compared to a sustained life of misery? This is nature's way of removing inefficient biological units swiftly and humanely.'

Abraham laughed and said, 'Darwin being a scientist, always talks in a matter-of-fact way and lacks sensitivity.'

They all looked at Darwin, 'Let us enjoy lunch as we are sure Mac has many questions for later.'

After lunch, Darwin returned to the subject of how the human brain is wired. 'When a child is still in the womb, it hears noises. Those neurons that deal with sound start to connect and continue to do so after birth. Then the sight connectivity starts. For the first few weeks after birth, the child is practically blind, as the neurons linking the eyes to the visual part of the brain are not connected. Once the neurons are ready, the light passing through the left eye creates a connection to the right part of the brain and from the right eye to the left part of the brain. If for any reason the right eye is not letting light through, then the light coming from the left eye will create additional neurons to connect to the left part of the brain in addition to right one.

'Therefore, you see Mac, this feature of connectivity of the neurons after birth is fundamental to human versatility. After sight comes the facial expression formation. Once the child starts to see, it will observe the face of its mother as it suckles milk. Therefore, a relaxed mother with relaxed facial expressions will be copied by the infant. Facial expressions, language and sounds are hard wired during the early age of a child. Learning at a young age will become the solid foundation for future development. This is why we strongly advocate the education of women and children for harmonious living in any society.'

I enquired about the significance of this neuron connectivity as I had heard this repeatedly.

Darwin answered, 'The connectivity is similar to fibre optics, connecting different parts of the brain where memories are stored. For example, a girl who is excessively attached to her mother means that she has more connections that lead to where the data relevant to her mother is stored. Therefore, when she observes or hears something, she is more likely to be reminded of her mother, rather than say an absent father where very few neuron connections exist. This is why when someone has a tragic accident and does not receive support, they may become withdrawn, as every little event will lead to a connection ending with the memory of the accident. The advice usually given is to go on a holiday to forget it. That is, get on with life to create new connections and do not dwell on the accident and by doing so you will only reinforce those negative memories. You also need to know that hormones lead to the strengthening of connectivity. This is why events accompanied with strong emotions become memorable. Those who experience miracles, real or perceived, are unlikely to forget them. Most people remember their first kiss as a lot of hormones are released showing pleasure of the event or a high positive score.

'The human mind is continuously stimulated by sight and other human senses. It may also get stimulated by mere ideas generated randomly by the brain. These stimulated thoughts, whether induced or due to retrieval of data already stored in the brain, are not usually acted upon. Only those ideas that pass the test, i.e. the individual value system, with its associated rewards and pleasure scores are acted upon. In reality programming of the human brain is not different from training an animal by associating pain and pleasure to various actions. The difference with humans is their ability to reflect and therefore create their own perceived pain and pleasure. The result is the same, i.e. self-induced reprogramming.

'It is of vital importance to achieve peace and tranquillity on Earth to instil the correct perceived pain and pleasure resulting from simulated thoughts. A person who is planning to commit a crime will not go ahead if he knows that more pain will be the result compared to any potential gain from the crime. If there is great injustice with no hope of eliminating it, a person may see violence as the only way of defending his perceived rights. The tragedy is magnified if, those committing the acts of injustice, and those reacting to them are driven by blind faith. The task becomes much harder to resolve unless a bigger impartial force deals with the causes of injustice and at the same time deals with religious extremism and ignorance.'

Darwin continued with a more relevant example of newly married people. 'Let us take the example of two people getting married. If they didn't see each other before marriage, then each comes with their own value system and brain connectivity. If they are not related or if they are from different cultures, then their reaction to various events would be very different. If the man tries to impose his will, irrespective of the woman's preferences and she regularly accepts that as the norm in that relationship, then one of two things may happen. Either he has a decent moral code and treats his partner with respect, or he has a poor moral code and tries to abuse her. The woman on her part may sense the difference in sexual drive and if she sees that abstaining from sex will get her what she wants then she will start using this as a tool to weaken his resolve or aggression. They will go through this tug of war relationship testing each other until they establish a workable understanding. If this cannot be reached then permanent misery or divorce will follow.

'By the way, this is another feature of the Great Designer's beauty. The physical strength of the male of the species is balanced with his strong need from the female to achieve sexual pleasure. This makes him more accommodating and supportive in order to satisfy his sexual needs.'

I looked at Darwin and wondered, 'You have spoken about the importance of being open-minded and reflective in order to acquire new knowledge and rewire the brain. You also spoke that this is part of the Creator's greatest design geniuses to give the cell multiple ending for establishing new connections. Please spell out the science behind these claims?'

Darwin was pleased with this request. He looked at me and said, 'This is known as neuroplasticity or if you prefer to call it the incredible, flexible brain. The wonderful brain has the innate ability to change itself physically when faced with new beliefs and challenging experiences.

'The brain has billions of neurons. These neurons are the cellular building blocks that interact with one another in complex ways. Signals travel from one neuron to another down intricate neural pathways whose structures determine your thoughts, impulses, emotions, insights, and more. If one becomes clogged up then it will create a mental rigidity. This will stop new neuron connections from being formed. The thought process will then pass, over and over again through the existing connections. In so doing he reinforces established beliefs and deepens the brainwashing. In case of children, as their brains develop, these neural pathways are established more readily. Less used pathways are pruned away while pathways that are used regularly grow stronger. Every task one does relies on a different neural pathway.

'Neuroplasticity is the brain's ability to create new neural pathways and reshape existing ones. This happens even in adults. The brain makes these small changes naturally throughout a person's lifetime. But when neuroplasticity's potential is thoughtfully and methodically explored, this physical reorganization can make the brain faster and more efficient at performing all manner of tasks, no matter how large or small these tasks may be.

'Unfortunately in people where mental rigidities and ignorance of all types come together, the best gift of the Lord to man, that is the neuroplasticity process, is kept under lock and key waiting to be opened up.

Darwin realized my fascination for the functioning of the human brain, looked at me for comment. I smiled and said, 'I get it. I cannot make the excuse that I am too old to learn new teachings. I have to believe in change, get engaged in people's issues and problems, and become an activist for a just cause.'

Abraham did not want to miss this opportunity to say something that he had left unsaid the previous day, 'You know Mac, there is nothing more upsetting to the Lord than man's actions in interfering with the normal functioning of his brain. This includes taking of drugs for recreational purposes, excessive consumption of alcohol, insisting on traditions not compatible with the age of reason and refusing to train the brain to be creative. Continuous acquisition of knowledge is what pleases the Lord most.'

I interrupted Abraham and asked, 'Why did the Greatest Designer not make the interference with the functioning of the brain painful? This would have automated the process of avoiding harmful interference with the human brain.'

Darwin took control of the dialogue and responded, 'If you think carefully, this is exactly what the Lord has done. Those who continuously abuse their brains by using drugs or alcohol are punished through poor performance or early death. In the meantime, they always have the chance to repent. Those with rigid brains are too lazy mentally to upgrade their creativity. They get left behind in the race for a better life to their seeds.'

Plato added, 'The wicked plant seeds for cultural diversion to give them the excuses to speak about the inevitable clash of civilisation so that they can rule supreme. Those with virtues work tirelessly to create cultural proximity for a better tomorrow with a universal brotherhood of man as an objective.'

After a long silence, I thought Darwin had finished for the day. Then I saw them whisper into Darwin's ear.

He said, 'Mac, I hope you do not mind if I continue. Let us tell you about the urgency of our message. We see a great danger facing humanity as science has progressed to create bionic man. This combination of man, machine and artificial intelligence will speed up scientific progress manifold.'

'I am all ears,' I replied with excitement.

'Not in the too distant future, man will reduce mobile phones to a size of a small chip implanted in the human body. This implant will be strong enough to pick up brain signals and communicate with others through an advanced mobile network. It will enable humans to access the vast data stored on the Internet.'

'What is scary about that?' I asked.

Darwin responded, 'Mobiles are getting smaller and smarter by the day. If every individual is fitted with these chips and they have GPS connectivity then those in control will be able to trace every movement and thought of the subscribers. In this case, the chip will also be able to get videos transmitted to the visual part of the brain bypassing the need to use the human eyes and ears. It will also make humans telepathic, as they will be able to read the thoughts of the selected people without the effort to ring them. This ability to access vast amount of data will enable creativity to be multiplied.'

'Now you are losing me. How could interrogation of data affect creativity?' I asked.

Plato turned to Darwin, 'Mac is right. You need to explain what creativity is first in order for Mac to understand.'

'Yes, sure,' replied Darwin. 'Creativity is the ability of a person to fire several brain pulses simultaneously to retrieve data and then try to simulate the outcome. A physicist, for example, has stored in his memory the accepted theories of physics and the potential challenges and shortcomings of those theories. Creativity or a moment of genius is when the brain simulator comes up with a new explanation addressing the existing shortcomings, or even gives a completely new approach to the observations in question. Therefore, knowledge evolves. Every new idea must have had some preceding trigger in the creative mind. The more one is trained to deal with several variables at the same time, the more creative he will become. The brain can be exercised just like any other part of the body, by dealing with several issues simultaneously or by regular exercise in solving puzzles. Therefore, if a man has access to a large store of data outside his biological memory and he tries to use his brain to search for a logical answer, then the possibility of enhanced creativity is multiplied. The data may be stored in a similar way as the human brain does, so that it can be retrieved in similar fashion.

'The next step in human advancement will come with a more bionic application of body parts to enhance human performance. The time will then come to create artificial intelligence. This will mean that the brains of robots will be built on the same principles as the working of the human brain. The key elements in any artificial intelligence will have to include parts similar to the following components:

'1) A silicon chip with multiple endings to allow different paths for writing and retrieval of data

'2) An indexing system to record and retrieve data from various compartments for specialization and ease of access

'3) Multiple layers of data-writing capabilities to keep the storage size manageable.

'4) Recognition of the relative importance of data so that some information could be overwritten

'5) A sensor to register what is equivalent to the level of pleasure or pain associated with each stored data of the artificial intelligence moral code.

'6) The artificial intelligence should have the ability of self-learning and reflection to update continuously those scores.

'7) A simulator with the ability to check if what is simulated is rational. The accumulation of accepted logical activities forms the basis for future rational decisions.'

What I heard sounded very realistic. I needed to move on. I asked Darwin to explain how the evolutionary process can explain morality. 'Can Morality exist without religions? Why do we need a new set of moral codes if evolution is capable of delivering the desired result?'

Darwin responded, 'Many of the animal species, especially at the insect level, are creating very successful societies based on putting survival of the colony ahead of the single biological unit. There is specialization in these insect kingdoms and they are selfless. This makes them very successful survivors but not creative. Imagine if humans learn from their examples without losing their love to be inquisitive. The bottom line is that nature can hardwire the instincts for love and compassion. This is not well developed in humans yet.'

I asked, 'Why are some rationalists still using the theory of evolution to conclude that there is no God?'

Darwin replied, 'A great atheist has recently said, "Since Darwin explained beautifully how life on Earth has evolved from a single cell then it is very unlikely there is a Creator for the original cell". He goes on to say, "We need another Darwin to explain how the Cosmos has evolved and then we will have a total scientific explanation of everything without the need to use the "God Gap principle". We fail to understand how explaining a process replaces the need to have an agent for that process. Someone must have designed the process and triggered it to start in the first place.

'A prominent biologist was so overwhelmed with the beauty of the evolutionary evidence and the strength of the logic behind it. His argument went like this: "So much of life's complexities have been simply explained by evolution. Why do I need to wonder about the small cell that is left unexplained? I am sure there is a simpler explanation than the existence of God. Therefore, I concluded that God's existence is improbable. Many millions did and still do believe that man has not evolved from fish but created by God as a complete biological unit. We now know they are wrong. So why should I continue to believe in God just because of a measly cell?"'

Plato commented, "The atheist's strong argument against religion has some rationale behind it. Religions jail the best gift God has given to humanity, which is the impulse to investigate and seek the truth. Atheism claims that they do not have that dogma or fear. They are confident that current scientific methods would not find anything supernatural.

'This is what religions should move towards. Religions should encourage people to have inquisitive minds and not conduct inquisitions. On the other hand, atheists should not dismiss Divine explanations just because they cannot prove it scientifically with their current atom-based concepts. Civility requires both groups to be open-minded to the approach of each other in their search for the truth. Atheists' dismissal of all unexplainable supernatural human observations and miracles as fairy stories or mushroom-induced experiences, are at best irrational; and at worst, are denial of the remote possibility of forces beyond human perceptions.'

'I see,' I responded. 'This reminds me of a Bedouin who needed a computer for his son. He was ready to pay a higher price for the computer cover because it can be seen and touched but not for the important software which is invisible. We need to get some atheists to be the first disciple of the new message.'

Plato, being the next lecturer, stood up and recited:

O Man, wake up and ask
How, from heaven I shouldn't be sacked?
The truth is out there for me to seek.
Sure, in poverty I don't want to be parked.

I sensed that it was getting late and they all wished me goodnight. As I got to bed, I saw a sign in the ceiling saying, "Power and greed are the hallmark of most politicians". I assumed that this must have something to do with Plato's lecture tomorrow.

Chapter 6

Plato's Day
Politics and Sociology

I woke up to another brilliant morning. We had breakfast in the gardens of perpetual bliss. Amused, I asked, 'Are you trying to spoil me with all these wonders?'

Plato laughed and said, 'We are reminding you that not everything you see is in fact reality. It is all in your mind. If you are going to regard this as a Divine experience then you will probably say, "God showed me Heaven". We are telling you that we are not here to create Divine experiences. We would like to correct many of the misconceptions about what various religions have reported as miracles. Various holy books differ in the way they describe many places and events. All prophets received their own revelations and reported them as Divine experiences. They were tasked to guide their tribes or people to follow a "Straight and Narrow" path. To help them achieve that, they needed the full set of tools of miracles and "Heaven and Hell" – or as Darwin explained, perceived Pleasure and Pain – to assist in instilling those values and get individuals to observe them. Not all that you read in scriptures should be taken literally. Usually their reported experiences are out of the ordinary. They then report what they have observed in obscure wordings that are open to multiple interpretations. Some rationalists claim that those who suffer from epilepsy or take psychedelic drugs could have similar experiences to those reported by religious people. From these observations, they conclude that all religious experiences are nothing but tricks of the mind and they should be treated as such. I think, by the end of this encounter, you will have a better set of tools to help you judge the shortcoming of these arguments.'

As we were walking in the colourful garden with plenty of ponds and waterfalls, the scenes changed to reveal Classical Athens in all its glorious splendour, and many of its philosophers. We walked into a public area where Socrates was in his usual rags and barefooted. He was surrounded by the youths who were listening and challenging him. He was a man of great intellect and virtue. He wanted nothing from life except to inform and encourage the youth to seek the truth. Socrates proposed that only through dialogue and debates could one do that. By applying rational reasoning and reflection, one can create intellectual heroes who would master these processes. He advocated that Philosophy should be encouraged to question all aspects of human life including religions, in order to arrive at conventional wisdom. In a healthy social and political structure, one should constantly challenge commonly held views to arrive at what is just and virtuous. Socrates proposed a few steps to seek the truth. First, find a common statement to fit the facts being discussed. For example, "wealth reduces stress". Second, think of a situation that is an exception to this rule. Some wealthy people commit suicide. Third, adjust the statement to incorporate the exceptions. So the statement could be revised to read, "Rich people experience less stress than poor people". Forth, continue with the process of refinement until the statement fits all the observed facts. The great philosopher Plato was one of those youth listening and participating in the discussion.

Then Aristotle, who was a student of Plato, appeared on the scene with his extensive writings. He emphasized the need for a rational approach to every aspect of human life. He argued that the universe is not controlled by blind chance, by magic, but it is subject to natural laws that require investigation.

Reflecting on ancient political wisdom Plato said, 'Citizens, especially in failing states, need to be guided by well meaning philosophers to get them out of their chaos. Once people moved away from being hunter-gatherers and started to live in communities, guardians of virtues with some enforcers were needed to be put in charge. This is in reality the role of government. It is to protect lives, liberties and properties from those morally defective individuals, where the family and the society have failed to instil in them the correct moral codes. The true wealth of any nation is the accumulated virtues of the people residing in that country relative to the total number of its citizens. A country where the majority of people are honourable will need a very small government to fill the gap that the individuals and other voluntary institutions cannot fill. On the other hand, where intolerance and corruptions are widespread, where greed and selfishness is prevalent and where there is a lack of open-mindedness, the state will become a weak or a failed state.'

With rising interest, I commented, 'Now I see why there is great emphasis during this encounter on virtues. It is to remind Mankind to control the evil within each individual. It is to remind humanity to correct the moral codes through continuous assistance and nurturing from those who are blessed to do so. I once read that Confucius said that the superior mind manages his conducts by two principles, *jen* and *li*. *Jen* is defined as the "benevolent concern for one's fellow men" while *li* consist of a combination of virtues, rituals, custom, etiquette and propriety.'

Plato was very pleased with my comment and continued, 'I think by now you have an idea about how things were in the times of Ancient Greece. It was a superb period in the history of this planet. It was the time when the youth challenged their elders and established beliefs. They practically questioned everything and everyone including those who were referred to as the "Elites and Opinion Formers".'

I interrupted with some delight, 'This also reminds me of the sixties when we thought that true happiness came from exhibiting love, embracing simplicity, rejecting selfishness, challenging the status quo and being in tune with nature. The youth effectively revolted en masse against the war in Vietnam and demanded peace and a new value system to govern the conduct of people in society.'

All of them noticed my excitement. Plato continued his comments on Ancient Greece, 'In the case of Socrates, he paid with his life for the virtues he was instilling in the young. You see Mac, for more than 3500 years nothing has changed. If at all, it has got worse. Those who have powers and privileges will do everything to resist sharing them with others. The real problem with humanity, as we have said before, is the worship of wealth and privileges. All religions try to instil the merits of living with moderation and contentment. Those who are born with good mental capacity and abundant energy but without virtues are the ones to fear most. Some of the worst such individuals are those who foment disorder in some communities and mass murderers like Hitler and Stalin. In genetics, if you have a defective gene, you could have a monster on your hands. In the same way, if you have a defective moral code (defective

185

social DNA), and then you will have real sociopaths or maniacs on the loose.'

Abraham looked at Plato and quoted from the Bible. Ephesians 6:12 – "For we wrestle not against flesh and blood, but against principalities, against powers, against the rulers of the darkness of this world, against spiritual wickedness in high [places]."

I asked Plato if he had any structure to his lecture for the day. Philosophy, politics and sociology are very wide subjects and thousand of theories and books have been written in this respect.

They all nodded in full agreement and Plato asked me if I had any preferences?

He actually put me on the spot. They were all expecting an answer. I explained that in the previous three days, each teacher had started with a brief explanation of the current situation and then touched on the gaps facing Mankind within that discipline. This was then followed with some new basic principles to be instilled that would lead to the establishment of a 'Just World Order' based on creativity, love and respect.

Although I am not a student of political sciences, I do notice the great injustices in the world. This gets very serious when those with absolute power try to justify the unjustifiable by peddling lies and half-truths. The invasion of Iraq for example, was built on the greatest lie ever told in recent history. We all know of the falsified "Yellow Cake (Uranium from Niger)" documents, Tony Blair's dodgy documents to the British parliament and the nonexistent Weapons of Mass Destruction.

'Yes of course,' Plato responded, 'and I will assure you that you will never find out who falsified those documents or pedalled those lies. Those who commit the crimes of deceit, manipulate those in power. It is a shame that democracy has been sacrificed so cheaply to satisfy the few.'

Plato continued, 'Let me now turn to ancient Plato's description of human nature and his political theory. I will touch on man's fundamental weaknesses that have led to the failure of most political systems. I will then discuss how a 'Just World Order' could be established to deal with these shortcomings.'

'Why do you think you will succeed when others have failed, including Jesus who was empowered to perform many miracles and came with the greatest message of love and forgiveness?' I asked.

Plato responded, 'With passion for action by the youth of the day nothing is impossible. With the latest tools of social media, the hearts and minds of billions can be reached in practically no time. Many are undoubtedly dissatisfied with the current political and economic systems and they need a trigger to be galvanized into action. You see, this is not the time to ask for adherence to blind faith. It is the time to offer rational explanations and a road map for dialogue and action. If the youth of the world are united, they will become a potent force to change everything. Eradicating ignorance, corruption, greed and nepotism are tasks that appeal to every healthy young mind. Those who think that they have Divine rights to wealth and power will be swept away by the tsunami of the virtuous, seeking change.'

Plato saw that drivers of action among humans are made up of three elements:

1) The rational or reasoning driver (top part of the body or the brain)

2) The passion or spirit driver (middle part of the body or the immunity system and the muscles)

3) The big appetite or worldly driver (the lower part of the body or organs and emotions)

'Each of these three drivers needs to be managed by exercising the relevant virtue to censor excesses. A rational person or a philosopher should be blessed with wisdom. A passionate person or a soldier should be blessed with courage to do the right thing. A person dominated by his appetite (the ordinary common man in the streets) needs to be blessed with moderation. All of these human problems over recorded history are the results of not applying the correct level of virtues to deal with these drivers. Let me expand on that and then apply these individual drivers to the state or government. Then I will discuss the various failings of each political system. Only after correctly diagnosing the problems of the day, will we move to prescribe the correct treatment.

'1) The Rational Thinking Driver

'A rational decision of one person may differ from that of another, as each may distort the evidence or rely on something perceived to be true when in fact it is mere blind faith. The atrocities of Hitler and Stalin must have appeared to them and their followers as rational decisions. So rational thinking needs to be censored with a lot of wisdom. To be wise is to be virtuous. Those who are blessed with virtues are blessed with plenty of wisdom. Those who manage to live by those qualities will be truly wise men and women. They should lead the rest of Mankind's salvation. Hence, the famous quote from Plato, "only philosophers deserve to be kings" is absolutely true. To instil the correct moral codes in individuals, you need a very well thought out education system. You also need much more from the family, the media and from other civil institutions.

'In failed states, some international bodies should take control of this task. Religious institutions can provide help only if men of the cloth are themselves enlightened. For a state to function and flourish, the total virtues of all its citizens must exceed a certain critical mass. Only then can that country achieve escape velocity from darkness to light. This is why widespread immigration of individuals with deficiencies in moral codes to a well functioning country will corrupt the society and this must be guarded against. The existence of strong emphasis on education, philosopher lodges, charities and liberal teachers of faith will enrich the lives of the whole society. Due to tribal legacies in most countries in the Middle East, such cultural traditions need extensive examination and probably some change.

'2) Now, let me expand on the Spirit and Passion driver.

'Spirit is what animates humans and gives them the power to act. Passion is the intensity, determination and love with which one acts. Therefore, this driver is very important for an individual to achieve anything. This "anything" could be a good or a bad action depending on the first driver, i.e. the rational driver.'

Plato continued, 'Athletes, military personnel, adventurers, etc have this drive in abundance. True leaders need plenty of the first drivers (rationalism and wisdom) and a reasonable quantum of the second driver, expressed as charisma, to differentiate themselves from the rest. The use of courage to do the right thing will drive people with strong spirit to excellence. A person with high spirit but without wisdom would abuse power. This is what lies behind most dictatorships. The best scenario is for a person to be strong enough to defend himself and at the same time moderate his behaviour with virtues. This also applies to the state. If the state has to use force, then it should be at an appropriate level, so that the natural law of justice is not violated and the innocents are protected. Very often, when you have an act of political violence, search deeply and you will find that the true reasons behind that is the breach of natural law of justice. A prolonged period of injustices and cruelty often leads to revolts and revolutions. Justice is the compromise between having the power for assured defence and respecting the full rights of those who do not have it.

'3) The Appetite driver

'This is what all humans exhibit to satisfy their needs to a varying degree such as food, shelter, sex, etc. Too much of this driver would lead to greed and corruption. This driver is the true evil behind many failing states and pressure groups who seek personal or tribal gain. Many wars have been fought and will be fought due to excesses in applying the appetite driver. To safeguard against that, one must apply a lot of moderation. A state where those in power possess little wisdom, strong spirits and unstoppable appetite will end up controlling the state as oligarchs (e.g. Russia under Yeltsin). The same principle applies in some major Western governments where the politicians are dictated to by a few pressure groups with similar defective moral codes (i.e. with strong appetite drivers). In such countries, many well-meaning politicians are bullied into submission, for fear of not getting a second term or worse, for fear of being politically assassinated if they stand against the interest of the rich and the powerful elite.'

I looked at Plato and said, 'I understand that every nation gets the government it deserves. It all depends on understanding what good virtues are and getting them adopted by the majority of the citizens while irresponsible behaviours are eradicated. Therefore, what you are saying makes a lot of sense. Could you tell me why Plato was against democracy and called for an autocratic system of government? Is there any country now or in the past that has applied Plato's prescription to politics? What are the conditions that must prevail so that democracy can truly serve the people and deal with all the concerns Plato raised? Could you also link that to Darwin's teaching yesterday? He confirmed that those who run the state have a lot to learn from the way a biological multi-cellular organism works.'

Darwin loved the last question as he noticed that I was paying attention to his lecture. Plato looked at his colleagues and then said, 'I will touch on the most common type of political systems according to Plato and try to answer the questions you have raised.

'Let me start with monarchy, the oldest form of government. The true reasons why we have monarchy in the first place is one of the following two reasons.

'Divine or Tribal Monarchy:

'This is where the people feel that the ruler or his family has Divine or special rights and should be trusted to lead. A prominent example from history is that of the pharaohs in Ancient Egypt. Ancient Egypt was governed by the pharaohs for thousands of years until it was defeated by external forces. This has exposed the great risk arising from blind faith and obedience to everything labelled "Divine". In most Arabic countries, tribal culture still prevails as a substitute to the concept of the states. Blind loyalty to the tribe makes loyalty to the state rather difficult to realize. This also applies to the Israelites who have maintained a greater loyalty to their tribal origin, the twelve tribes of Israel, being the descendants of Abraham, Isaac and Jacob. Over time, this has become a force for good to retain their culture identity and also a force for being questioned by the community where they have settled. This challenge is usually expressed in the form of anti-Semitism.

'If God sends a Divine person to dwell on Earth, would that be OK to let him rule the world?' I asked.

They all were puzzled by what appeared to be an irrational question when the whole emphasis was on rational thinking. I quickly clarified my question.

'Christians are waiting for the coming of Christ and Shiite Muslims for the coming of the Mehdi Al Muntathar, a descendant of the Prophet Muhammad.'

Due to the sensitivities of dealing with issues of faiths, Abraham replied. 'We can assure you that Mankind will always be ruled by earthly people. We leave it to you to raise these questions during the conference call with Jesus and Mohammed since they are implicated in your questions.'

'Monarchies are a system wherein a Great Warrior retains power and then passes it on,' Plato resumed. 'This is unfortunately the most common type of government system across human history. Under such rules, one can include presidential monarchies like North Korea, Cuba and Syria. The greatest damage inflicted on the Islamic world started during Omayyads' rule in Syria, when the Khalifa moved from being an autocratic system of government to a monarchy. The Khalifa should have been selected, as in Plato's ideal system, by and from the enlightened few, whether Shura Majlis or a house of senior Holy men.

'As most Middle Eastern countries are governed by rigid monarchies or presidential monarchies, you will see violent change unless they act fast to allow embryonic democracies to establish strong roots. This should include raising the total virtuous scale of the nation through liberal education, civil institutions, etc. to support the rulers due to their philosophical deficiencies.'

'Why does the overthrow of a tyrant leader usually lead to anarchy instead of democracy?' I asked.

Plato obliged with a very pessimistic answer. 'Non benevolent dictators do not usually know how to build virtuous functioning civil institutions. They apply politics of fear to control the masses. Once you remove this fear, a septic tank will be opened. At best, struggle for power will take many years to establish a new functioning order, provided outside help is given. At worst, civil wars and a failing state would be the outcome. This will continue until one group dominates the others after a heavy loss of life and major destruction.'

'What is the solution?' I asked, 'Since most poor countries are under such systems of governments?'

Plato replied, 'There is no quick solution as you are dealing with political maturity of the majority of the citizens. International pressure should be exercised to guide the rulers to increase the number of virtuous citizens through education and other civil institutions. Such demands and the speed of the move should be steady and continuous. Those rulers who fail to comply should be tried as committing crimes against acceptable norms, just like committing a crime against humanity. After all, most deaths and suffering are experienced due to lack of virtues of the political elite. This does not mean that we are advocating regime change from outside powers. However, help is needed from well meaning international organizations to achieve a smooth transition.'

Darwin jokingly said in support of change from within, 'If you break an egg from the outside, no lasting good thing will come out of that. However, if it is broken from the inside and at the right time, then a hopeful new beginning will be the result.'

They all nodded as if they knew the level of destruction that would follow from the invasion of Iraq. I said with a serious tone, 'Having fled Iraq due to Saddam's atrocities, how could you imply that Iraqis would be better off without this invasion?'

Plato responded, 'You see Mac, many like you are naïve when it comes to politics. Do you think those who where guiding Bush to invade Iraq would like to see a strong, democratic and vibrant Iraq? Few religious drivers were at work behind the scenes like the building of the Temple of Solomon in Jerusalem. This cannot take place until the resilience of all those who are likely to resist this project are silenced through infighting and collapse of the moral fabrics of those societies.'

'Oh my God,' I exclaimed. 'This is very disheartening. Tell me what you think will happen then.'

Plato obliged, 'First they will dissolve all the apparatus of power within the country to create a vacuum for anarchy to be unleashed. They will introduce what appear as a system, based on Western values, rules of law and human rights.'

'What is wrong with that?' I asked.

'Nothing,' Plato replied quickly, 'provided that the average Iraqi respects the law and understands democracy as the average Westerner does. Laws have to evolve to match the moral and emotional compass of the people. The new system of government will deepen the divisions in the society. It will bring about the complete break-up and eventually the complete collapse of what is left of the moral code of the nation. Civil wars will rage for decades. Return to tribalism and various religious groupings would be the only means of protection left for the individual. These conflicts will spill over to adjacent countries. Widespread corruption and destruction of life and properties will be the order of the day.'

'Please don't tell me that the region is doomed for a generation or two,' I said.

'Nothing should surprise you as long as the people in the area are buried in their cultural and religious ignorance. The outside world that controls the levers of power, including the media, have hidden agendas driven by pressure groups who believe in their Divine rights to fulfil various religious revelations. In this context, Richard Dawkins is absolutely correct when he said that religion could be a source of great evil. It drives believers to commit atrocities based on blind faith, irrational revelations and out of context interpretations of the various holy books.'

Adam looked at us and said, 'Although all this is very interesting stuff, Plato needs to move faster to be on time to finish his lecture.'

Plato nodded in approval.

I knew that this remark was rather directed at me and that I needed to ask fewer questions. However, being very interested in the subject I asked, 'Please tell me what the solution would be then?'

Plato looked at his colleagues and said, 'For Iraq or any failed state to escape from its political immaturity, it requires a clear road map which should include among other things the following: 1) All young men of military age should be conscripted to provide employment, education, loyalty to the state, instead of the tribe or sect, to instil virtues. This of course implies the presence of some wise men in charge of such a state. 2) Provide courses and training to all politically-active individuals, head of tribes and religious leaders on the way modern states are governed and on the art of compromise. 3) The media to be effective for installing virtues instead of pedalling lies and seeds of divisions. 4) Strict compliance with laws against corruption, preachers of hate, etc 5) Seeking help from international bodies for educating the young and installing long-term values in line with universal virtues.'

Plato continued, 'In the short-term sometimes you may have to take life to save greater number of lives. We are not abandoning the "Sanctity of life and its quality" doctrine. One needs to use special powers to assassinate and imprison, without trials, those who are very likely to be behind the atrocities. Once the most dangerous individuals have been isolated, a gradual return to the rule of law can be re-established. You see, this is a good example of how to apply the principle of selecting the route of least evil. Nation building cannot be done without great sufferings and scarifies, and at a great cost to the international community. As various nations are getting closer together in a shrinking world, the international community should not sit idle to avoid a malfunctioning world order.

'An example of using assassination outside the norm is already in use by America and Israel, as part of their war on terror. They are resorting primarily to assassination in dealing with people who have abandoned the rules of welfare in an imbalanced world. They definitely need to make greater efforts to deal with the causes of terrorism, if they are to occupy the high moral ground. Injustice in any part of the world would lead to wider conflicts and this should be addressed with wisdom and not by more conflicts.

'You see, Mac, systems of governments and international laws are nothing more than "rules of the game" which govern how players interact with each other at various levels. Once these rules are agreed upon, then they must be implemented with equal rigour, whether they are broken by the weak or by the powerful. For example, Israel's non-compliance with most UN resolutions dealing with its occupation of Palestinian lands is not helping to achieve a more peaceful world. It is a great fallacy to think that by making a good argument to your supporters, you have a new and acceptable definition of justice. Justice is truly Divine and universal. Over time, justice cuts cross all cultures and boundaries. Only by applying the natural law of justice a more peaceful world would be possible.'

Abraham commented, 'The claim of the "Promised Land" cannot override the "Law of Natural Justice". The Israelites cannot come back 600 years after leaving Palestine voluntarily to join the good fortunes of Joseph in Egypt and try to claim it back through military superiority. I think more on that will be covered by Moses.'

Plato looked at his colleagues before continuing, 'Take Syria for example. It is a presidential monarchy. This is the worst type of government, where the ruling class lives in real delusion. They claim to be an elected government with a normal rule of law when in fact; it is nothing but blind tribalism. The whole wealth of the nation is put at the service of the few.'

I said, 'You have not compared this system to the working of the living organism?'

'Yes, let me get to that,' Darwin responded. 'These rulers who come from a military background are supposed to be guardians of the state. They get to power by a military coup d'état. The new rulers, with their military apparatus, are similar to a body's immune system getting out of control. It starts to regard healthy cells as foreign bodies and attacks them. The body will be a very sick entity and will suffer from a terrible death.

'Oligarchy is a government controlled by and run to enrich the few

'This is what happened recently in Russia. The transformation from dictatorship to democracy is never smooth. Those who took control of the regime ran the country to enrich themselves under the name of democracy. This is why Plato in his book *The Republic* explained at length why democracy cannot work unless the population is a true participant and enlightened to understand the issues discussed and the choices they have to make. Here, again, the appetite drivers were unchecked by moderations. This has led to sudden appearance of many billionaires. Wealth of the country systematically transferred to the few in the name of democracy and a free market economy. In the case of the biological unit, this is similar to the enlargement of an organ like the heart or the liver, leading to the ultimate death of the individual.'

'I am struggling to see how you have equated pressure groups in the USA with oligarchs in Russia,' I said.

Plato responded, 'Mac, behind every pressure group there are a few very strong individuals with lots of power and money. They don't want to lose their privileges. They will spend any amount of money to get the candidate of their choice elected. In return, they get from the elected politicians the passing of the laws to facilitate their objectives.

'That brings me to D) Democracy

'A lot has already been said in this regard. The masses, who are driven by their appetite, will vote for those who make the wildest promises.'

'This sounds very familiar,' I commented. 'Tony Blair, the UK prime minister, came to power on the promise of making a true change from what he termed the "Nasty Conservatives" and he ended up with nastier policies and furthermore, introduced unethical foreign policies to promote wars and destruction.'

I asked Plato to touch briefly on the conditions for democracy to work.

Plato obliged, 'For democracy to work the following fundamentals must be met:

'1) There should be strict laws to prevent the concentration of the media in the hands of few groups, influential tribes, or pressure groups.

'2) Contributions to political parties must be limited so that individuals, groups, religious entities, tribes, financial institutions or any other entity under the control of the few would not have an unfair advantage. Limit on expenses for election campaigns must be imposed to diminish the role of money in elections.

'3) Definition of political bullying should be widened to protect against intimidating the politicians. We see how various politicians may lose their chances of being elected if they apply their true virtues to solve the Middle Eastern problems in accordance with international law. They will be exposed to some scandals or some stories from the past will be brought to the surface to defame them.

'The whole world remembers what happened to President Clinton during his second term in Office. A young woman intern was implanted to influence the president's foreign policy. With the advice of her elders, she kept her dress with his semen on it as a means of political bullying.'

I asked Plato to highlight the doctrines within the Universal Virtues listed by Abraham, which have relevance to strengthening democracy. He listed the following:

'F) Seek moderation in all human endeavours and avoid excesses and extremism of all sorts.

'G) Put community needs ahead of individual needs. What you do not want to be done to yourself, do not do it to others.

'I) Have the right views, speech and action.

'These doctrines are important to deal with greed and craving for power. They also require all citizens to care by being politically engaged.'

Plato continued, 'Democracy seems to work only when the majority of the citizens have managed to introduce wisdom into their rational thinking, courage to their aspiration and moderation to their appetite. By these measures, the Scandinavian countries and Japan may rank at the top.

'Let me conclude by saying that a healthy human body could be seen as a truly functioning democracy. For a healthy body, the brain is open, reflective, rational and wise. The immune system is strong enough to recognize true enemies and not perceived ones. The rest of the body works without enlarged organs or cancerous cells. Therefore, you see, Darwin was right. Humans could learn from a healthy body to run their societies.'

Then Plato moved to explain his favourite form of government.

'D) Autocracy

'This is the system where there is true specialization to serve the state. Those at the top, i.e. the political leaders, go through a long process of selection after extensive education to ensure that only rational and virtuous people are selected. From among the philosophers, the politicians are selected as they can judge who would be the best to serve the community at large. The one condition to ensure that they do not turn against the state, once they become powerful, is to remunerate them modestly.

'Aristocracy in its most just form has been advocated in Plato's *Republic*. In this case, the regime is headed by a philosopher king, and thus it is grounded on wisdom and reason. Unfortunately, due to human failures, aristocracy degenerates over time due to miscalculation on the part of its governing class. The next generation of guardians and auxiliaries would be dominated by persons of poorer characters. Under this distorted aristocracy, the chosen leaders will tend to be more high-spirited and simple-minded types who are better suited for war. They value power and they seek to attain it primarily by means of military conquest and the acquisition of honours, instead of by intellectual means.

'Currently the nearest autocratic regime is the Vatican in Rome. Another example is the spiritual leader of Iran, who holds the true power, is also elected in this way. The difference between Plato's autocratic government and the present system in Iran is that the former relies on philosophy and rational thinking while the latter relies on blind faith and complete obedience. The Supreme Religious Ruler of Iran is the head of the Supreme Religious Council of Iran. He regards everything he says as Divine instructions and it cannot be challenged by any human being. This shows the importance of incorporating philosophy into the training of mullahs and imams in areas where religion plays a major role in the life of the people.

'The selection of the Khilafa under Islamic law is supposed to follow a similar process to that of the Iranian system.'

Abraham looked at me and said, 'Mac, I assure you that all governments or states based on religions will cease to exist before the middle of this century as they are the source of all conflicts in the world today. People in the West will be awakened to the cost and dangers of supporting one religious state while opposing another. By definition, creating a state based on religion is a great contradiction to American and Western values. It is a great contradiction to see them support any state based on religion. Would they support the mass expulsion of population of different faiths to keep the religious identity of the state?'

Before Plato could move on to the next subject, I said, 'In the last few days, I have heard of many claims about the need to awaken the human spirit to swap darkness for light by applying universal virtues. You also mentioned the need for all human beings to live in peace and harmony on this planet. Are you actually proposing a New World Order? This has become a buzz word on the lips of many politicians who feel that they have the intellect to reshape the world.'

Yet Abraham suggested that we rest while Plato organized his thoughts, as this was a very complex subject. One needs to work on the individuals in the various countries before such an order can be established, they said.

During the break, I was left alone. They had a long discussion on how best to handle this subject. They indicated that this is a very difficult and sensitive subject. They were informed that some, who are already advocating that supranational sovereignty of an intellectual elite, and world bankers, are surely preferable to the national auto-determination practiced in past centuries. This is why the mere mention of creating a new world order makes everyone shiver with fear.

They fear domination by the few who think they have monopoly to the truth and wisdom.

Plato led the team and spoke with some authority, 'I think we will call it a "Just World Order". I will cover the subject in three elements:

'A) Why this noble objective has eluded humanity for thousands of years.

'B) The preconditions which must exist for such world order to be attempted, and

'C) The recommended road map, with some basic test, which must be satisfied for various nations to be ready to join the Just World Order.'

I commented half-heartedly, 'Wow, are you serious? You think it can be done? '

Plato responded with a passion that I hadn't noticed on his face before, 'If it is not done, then Mankind will be consigned to the flames of perpetual wars, and pain. Neither God nor Angels will do it for the human race. Only Mankind, through international cooperation and the widespread of virtuous cultures can do it. However due to the great cultural variations between nations, ranging from those buried in complete darkness of blind faith and ignorance to those who are rational and virtuous, the task will be onerous and lengthy.

'Humanity needs to deal with his deadly sins of greed and his evil drive for domination. Most importantly, great attention must be paid by all men of virtue and the enlightened youth to the "Arrogant Elites and Bankers" who hide the ambition to dominate the world through the most powerful countries in the West.'

Abraham quoted from the Bible again: 1 Peter 5:8 – "Be sober, be vigilant; because your adversary the devil, as a roaring lion, walketh about, seeking whom he may devour:"

Plato continued to tell me how countries could lose centuries in their march to progress and said, 'For example, since the military coup d'état in Iraq in 1958, the country has been in continuous decline in all aspects of life. Today it is a completely dismantled country. It will not survive as a normally functioning country without being managed for at least few generations by an international body. Most Arab countries claim that by adopting Sharia laws, they would achieve the desired political maturity. Unfortunately, those who interpret these laws need to pass the test of free thinkers, in order to guide others correctly.

'Political and social maturity league tables need to be published just like other international league tables to name and shame those countries into positive political action.'

I asked if there is an easy test to apply to whether a country is morally and politically mature and ready.

Darwin laughed and said that the easiest test he is aware of is the "Loo Test".

I looked at Darwin to see if I had heard him right and asked, 'Did you say *loo*? Please expand. It sounds very interesting.'

'You see, a nation can be judged as virtuous when the golden rule is widely applied "do unto others as you would have them do unto you". When you visit a public toilet in a crowded area, and you find it always clean, you know that the golden rule is at work,' Darwin explained.

After some reflection I said, 'Oh my God, you are absolutely right. I have travelled widely around the world and I have always dreaded going to a public toilet in some countries!'

Plato was keen to come back to the lecture and said, 'I am sure you have heard of the "Tebbit or Sport Test" before.'

'No, please explain.' I replied.

He did. 'For testing the loyalty of citizens to their place of residence, one needs to check if they support the country of their citizenship, or whether they support the country of their origin? This is called the "Loyalty Test". For truly harmonious communities, one should support his country of residence even when it plays against his country of origin or against his tribal upbringing. This a true test of integration.'

'Very interesting,' I said, 'I see how complex the subject of creating a Just World Order would be. Please move to the roadmap for achieving that.'

Plato continued, "To create a Just World Order, one needs to create an international body to head the convergence of all nations to acceptable international norms. This will require an international agreement on the constitution of such a body and on the international norms to be applied. Financial support will be provided through an internationally agreed tax system. Adam will expand on that tomorrow.

'Countries need to be classified according to their political maturity and the moral compass of the average individual within that society by creating relevant league tables.

'There would be a need for effective peace. Marshal plans would be required to be drawn up to assist those countries who submit to the guidance of the international organizations. Corruption by politicians is to be regarded as a crime against good social order and treated as equivalent to crimes against humanity. Corruption is the worst enemy of the fabric of any community and must be treated as a serious political cancer. All religious leaders who preach hatred are to be monitored and prosecuted by an international court. All faiths are to be respected and freedom of speech need to be mindful of faiths sensitivities.'

I interrupted Plato, 'I think I get the message and I can see the difficulties. The first problem is that those currently in power in all the major countries would see their unchecked authority diluted. They are enjoying their dominance of the world. Why would they care about upgrading the moral codes of other less fortunate countries so that they can enjoy a better life?

'The weaker countries would also be suspicious as they are usually governed by corrupt or ignorant politicians. They would not cooperate unless forced to do so by some international pressure. We also need to deal with the suspicion that some major countries will use the international bodies as tools to further their domination when it suits them to do so. When it does not suit them, they will ignore those organizations as it happened in the case of the invasion of Iraq.'

Plato sensed my doubt and said, 'You are right. No progress can be made unless the politicians are forced to act. Therefore, the true drivers will be the youth of the powerful and freethinking nations. They will have to make a difficult choice between:

'1) To close their borders to economic migrants and thus prevent a continuous clash of civilizations.

'2) To have true globalization where they can travel freely and enjoy cultural variations that enrich Mankind as a whole.

'I tell you Mac, Western countries have already made great sacrifices in the last decade or two under globalization by allowing the export of jobs to the poorer countries. In the long run, they will be reaping the fruits of dealing with richer and less hostile neighbours. The peace that would prevail from true world harmony cannot be measured by the fortunes of the few who may lose some of their current privileges. It is time for the 99% of the world population to speak out and shout, "We are united to give peace a chance".'

I asked Plato if he could think of a scenario where some of the Ambitious Intellectual Elites could collude and organize themselves over few centuries to manipulate major world events in their favour.

Plato responded, 'Don't be surprised if I tell you that they are already busy in doing just that right now. In the absence of effective international organizations to create the Just World Order, the few organised ambitious intellectual will continue carrying the mantle for achieving a world political system to satisfy their greed for privileges and wealth. Sometimes they employ great cunning and deceit in statecraft and in general conduct. I will spell out for you their potentially deadly cunning schemes in some detail. We hope that by shedding some light on their tactics, the awakened majority can stop them from achieving their desired domination. I can assure you that any political system relegating the majority to relative poverty will ultimately be rejected. This is why the world needs all rational thinkers to become reflective activists in all political matters, if the Just World Order is to serve the many and not the few.

Plato, after some hesitation and discussion with his colleagues said, 'Let me tread carefully here, as we don't want to point the finger at any minority group. Some elites usually bring up their children on the understanding that they are superior to others and that they must protect their identity by striving for excellence in every field of human endeavours.'

'I am struggling to see what is wrong with that. Isn't the aim of every parent to give their children the best education and to prepare them for a very competitive world?' I asked.

Plato thanked me for this clarification and confirmed that they are supportive of the role of families in pushing their children towards excellence.

Plato continued, 'The unacceptable part is when those with the intellect start to collude, using easily gained money through speculation to control the media for the purpose of gaining unfair privileges and political domination. They drop the principle of fairness and they are blinded by greed at the expense of the majority.

'Any region of the world where it becomes part of their plan to dominate or to weaken will experience chaos, ethnic and religious divisions, extremisms and civil wars over many decades. They will not hesitate to create regional wars and they will most certainly push for the arming of both sides to guarantee a balanced power of incompetence, to ensure that self-destruction is the result. They may also subject those nations to severe economic boycott under false pretences where millions could die through malnutrition and lack of adequate medication. Let me expand below how they see the world. Let me also explain a little about some of their tactics and possible approaches.

'1) The call for freedom is to be used as bait, to attract the masses to crush those in authority outside their influence. This is based on the assumption that the immature electorate does not know how to use freedom in moderation. They will use simple logic that seems to meet the aspiration of the people, and other means to create dissent and anarchy. They base their plans on the well-tested experience that the power unleashed by the mob is a blind, senseless, unreasoning force and always at the mercy of suggestions from others. It is not possible for the masses to deal with the affairs of the country calmly and without petty jealousies. It is not possible for the masses to do this without getting them mixed with their personal interests. Corruption will be widespread, creating a downward spiral leading to great hardship.

'2) Every major change in any government system passes through several stages. The first stage is anarchy, where the raging mob takes centre stage. Freedom turns to violence and anarchy in the hands of the mob. The second stage is the struggle for gaining power and popularity by arousing emotions, passions, and prejudices of the people. The third stage is dictatorship and tyranny. This is often led by a person or persons planted by the privileged elite or who can be manipulated by them.

'3) The few justify their acts by claiming that destroying the moral structure of the society they want to dominate, is similar to a secretive military attack to achieve a quick and decisive victory.

'4) Their triumph becomes easier by the fact that their relations with the men serving their cause are guided by money, cupidity, and their insatiable greed for material wealth. Each one of these human weaknesses, taken alone, is sufficient to paralyze initiatives and it hands over the will of free men to the disposition of the paymasters.

'5) In the name of the supreme interest of the state, they propose emergency laws, and even suspend temporarily the working of the constitution. Any checks and balances that may exist are eroded little by little; they award themselves with greater freedom of action within the purview of the law.

'6) Their intermediate aim is to turn a few major governments to become sympathetic to their cause. They call for passing laws in line with their long-term objectives. They define freedom and justice as compliance with the law. This interpretation of the word "Law" will, at the proper time, be of service to them.

'7) The various platforms of the media under their control will be of all possible affiliations: liberal, republican, socialist, revolutionary, even Salafist (strictly orthodox Sunni Muslim). They will have a hundred hands, and every one of them will have a finger on any one of the public opinions as required. When the need arises, these invisible hands will lead opinions in the direction of their aims. As soon as the new social media start to offer a real alternative to the established media, they will go into overdrive to minimize its effect. They will start to spy on all electronic communications under the pretext of the war on terror. They are also creating millions of false identities to overwhelm the social media electronically. This is done with opinions that appear to be coming from ordinary individuals when in fact it is pure electronic manipulation.

'Many well-meaning citizens will start to lose their powers of making independent judgment and they would easily yield to their suggestions. Unfortunately, unwary citizens starts to think that they are repeating the opinion of a newspaper or a tweet of their own camp by repeating the opinion of the scheming few. In doing so, they are killing the courage within most individuals to think for themselves, leading to the creation of zombie-like parrots.

'8) They create "Opinion Formulation Lodges" in the most important countries and then get into those lodges all who are prominent in public life. These lodges usually become excellent platforms for genuine debate to raise the cultural heritage of the community. However, in these lodges, they shall find their principal agents and means of influence. All these lodges are then brought quietly under the purview of one central authority. Many of those serving in the lodges are completely unaware that may become part of a bigger plan to ultimately benefit the few.

'9) They have publicists, cheerleaders, administrators, diplomats and economists as supporters. They also have the support of highly educated people who understand human nature and how the worst in people can be unleashed to serve their purposes. Their plan is to assume a mask of honesty, of a free market economy, liberty and of legal compliance. They infiltrate all major institutions which shape government policies, especially in the realms of their immediate interest.'

'10) They adopt a formless and a flexible approach to deal with all events that may derail their plans. The greatest risk to their plans is to find a politician escaping their clutches by winning an election through mobilizing the masses. In this case, they will use all their powers to undermine the economy and the smooth working of the government to create a wedge between that politician and the people.'

I was out of breath after this gloomy explanation by Plato about some of the approaches being used by the few who are determined to elevate themselves unfairly at the expense of others. I didn't know if he was describing the situation on a different planet or, essentially, telling me what is actually happening on Earth today to avoid paying the price of just peace. The injustice in the Middle East is an attack on justice everywhere. Yet the world is silent. For those paying the price of domination, it looks as if every step toward peace is going to be filled with risk, pain, struggle and a terrible cost in human lives.

The road to peace seems to be slipping away in the short term, as the majority of the people in the Middle East are buried in ignorance and drunk by the various interpretations of their faiths. A mere rumour at a remote corner of the Earth could lead to violence and ugly uprising. People of the Middle East truly need to wake up to the dangers of their own ignorance. They need to immunize themselves with deep understanding of how the world around them works. They need to practice openness, tolerance and rational thinking. They have only themselves to blame if their adversaries make use of their weaknesses and mob like mentality.

Plato then resumed his lecture, 'Mac, I think your concern is that our call for the Just World Order could be seen as similar to that adopted by the privileged few, deserves some further clarification.'

I said with a wide grin on my face, 'How could one provide an intelligent answer to such an accusation? Isn't this how the world works? There are the few, under the guidance of their elders, who care enough from a very young age to devote their lives to serve their cause, while the masses follow their insatiable needs. Isn't it in the interest of the Just World Order to get these brilliant minds to be invited to lead the march to human salvation?'

Plato responded with confidence saying that the majority of the so-called elites are decent people and that they are like the rest of humanity; misinformed by the few. 'It is quite possible, with the strength of appropriate arguments, to get their young to join the march for peace. After all, not many decent people would support nasty and often barbaric upheavals worldwide for hidden political agendas.'

Abraham stood up and said, 'Blessed are those who can see what is hidden, as what is apparent is often not real. When you know what is hidden, then you know what needs to be done.'

Plato smiled at Abraham's quote and continued passionately 'Mac, the world needs political giants who are ready to pay the political price by marginalizing the extremists to establish a just and lasting peace. All militarily imbalanced conflicts to suppress justice would feed into a bigger cauldron of resentment that will end up in rivers of tears and regrets for all. The wise politicians are those who lead their people to live in harmony and mutual respect with their neighbours and not to isolate themselves behind concrete walls. Walls of hate, no matter how high and strongly built, will end up imprisoning both sides. Love and justice flourishes in the hearts of people and removes the need for walls that segregate.

'The history of Andalusia in Spain tells us how the Muslims and the Jews lived in complete harmony. Isn't it time for the descendants of Abraham to live under one flag instead of continuing to pay the price of Sarah's jealousy from the young boy Ishmael?'

For the first time, I could not help applauding with joy and said, 'Bravo! If you were not a shadow, you would have deserved a nomination for the Nobel Prize for Peace.'

Abraham was encouraged by my excitement and continued in the same vein. 'You know Mac, there is no difference between the Jewish settlers in Israel, and the Taliban, as both seem to be guided by blind faith and driven by religious fervour. The settlers are resorting to illegal activities according to international law and in complete breach of the universal law of justice, yet the international community seems to be powerless to address the issue. The Taliban are violating many of the moral codes that should govern human behaviour. They are destroying their society from within and promoting widespread terror. The settlers are destroying the possibility of establishing a viable Palestinian state and insulting Jewish intellect by claiming that they are adhering to some moral rights and legalities.'

Abraham continued, 'For those who are born to live in darkness and see shadows will start to believe that the shadows are the real things. When true light is revealed to them, they will feel blinded and will close their eyes for fear of the truth. It is the job of all decent people in the world to fight the darkness in all faiths. Our call is a genuine message to every individual to care seriously about raising himself from "the comfort of inactivity" and "nothing to do with me attitude". Life has no room for those who keep sulking and blaming others for their misfortunes. The only way to challenge darkness is by shining a powerful torch for the masses to join the march to wisdom and peaceful action. Only in so doing, will they be able to isolate and marginalize the destructive efforts of the deluded few.'

I asked Plato if they had any bold suggestions to solve the Middle East Problem that has defied many well-meaning politicians for generations.

Plato was rather excited to unroll his plans. He said. 'The solution is staring humanity in the face but they are failing to see. Let us remove the dark glasses of mistrust and blind faith. What we see at the heart of the disputes are religious drivers. We see those who want to have their Temple rebuilt as a symbol of their faith and those who don't want to give up their temple. Both want to worship and have access to the land of their ancestors. Well, we have seen in "The Kingdom of Heaven" a drawing of the "New Jerusalem". At the heart of the city is an area called the "Abrahamic Holy Mile". In the centre of this area is a great Whitehouse as a museum for Abraham and his descendents from Ishmael and Isaac. Around this museum, are located the Temple of Solomon, Al-Aqsa Mosque, and the United Church of Christ. All these sanctum sanctorum receive their faithful in peace and harmony from all around the world. Under this plan, Jerusalem would grow into a financial and cultural hub for all of the Middle East. It will link the cultures of the East and the West and act as the bridge for rational spirituality. It will be designated as the capital for the Just World Order. Its international financial institutions will be recommended by Adam. In the Abrahamic Holy Mile a "Multi Faith Flag" will be raised which will have a white background with the Symbols of the Holy Cross, the Crescent and the Star of David in equal dimensions. God will bless the Holy Mile with the presence of Angels and Souls to answer the prayers of all the devotees of the Lord who visit the city with love and spirituality in mind and forgiveness in their hearts.'

'Wow, wow!' I screamed. 'Why didn't you say that before? I do understand that all the other alternatives are so bleak. All sides need to look beyond their immediate prejudices for the sake of their future generations.'

With such a wonderful end to the day, I asked Plato to give me a brief philosophical summary of what had been said so far to ensure that I hadn't missed anything.

Plato responded, 'All our teachings are targeted towards re-building individual character and rewiring the brain to become a positive force for peace and prosperity. I will summarize below "Seven Individual Initiatives" to achieve that.

'1) Shape your Destiny, Chose your Direction.

'Human conduct is the product of every thought, feeling, contact, and experience they have during their lifetime. They are in a continuous state of becoming. A person never stays the same but continuously changes as a result of daily contact with his surroundings. If one directs his attention in the direction of what he wants to be, then that is what he will become. If on the other hand, he allows circumstances to determine randomly his actions and contacts, then he becomes a prisoner of a lottery outcome. Those who are afraid of change will stay unchanged. Those who meet the same people, and do the same things will stay as they are. As Einstein once said famously, "It is an act of insanity to do the same thing and expect different results".

'2) Generate the Correct Emotions to Pursue Your Vision.

'Beliefs and feelings are fundamental for shaping personality, and hence reality. The desired goals can only be achieved if the correct aspiration and emotions drive the individual into action. All humans have the capacity to generate correct emotions provided that they have been trained to do so. Train yourself to smile and love instead of to sulk and to hate. Life is too short and you may not have another chance.

'With the right thoughts, feelings, decisions and actions, the desired goals can be achieved. You cannot become a good gardener if you don't love plants or believe that you can do it well. The unengaged mind becomes a fertile ground for boredom and depression. The best gift you can give to a child or a friend is to show him how he can train his mind to be engaged fruitfully.

'3) Have Realistic Expectations.

'Whatever you dream about passionately and pursue with diligence, persistence and confidence, would become your reality. You are what you strongly think and feel you are. So Mac, you cannot say, "it is impossible to create a Just World Order" and at the same time to say that you want to become a positive force for a just world. You need to build a road map of realistic and deliverable small steps. Plan well, execute with speed and even out the workload. Leaders should always find the facts for themselves and create the correct processes and habits.

'4) Engage the Power of Attraction.

'People attract into their lives those who share their feelings and beliefs. Just as "birds of the same feathers flock together", people of the same cultural values seek one another. This is very important in parenting. Guide your children away from bad company. Involve your parents and grandparents to pass on their heritage but be wary of negative traits or tribal values that are not compatible with Universal virtues.

'5) Engage the Subconscious Mind.

'The conscious mind can deal with one issue at a time. To get assistance from the large information stored in your subconscious, define your goal clearly. Your "gut feeling" or instinctive decisions are usually your best decisions as they come from your subconscious mind. This are called "eureka moments" i.e. when one suddenly gets an inspiration from out of the blue.

'6) Practice, Practice, Practice.

'To be a leader in any field you must practice long and hard. Through repetition, children's brains are wired at a faster speed than those of adults are. The best way to spend your time and money is on building the contents of your children's character through good parenting and education. It takes great foresight and wisdom to spend less on luxuries and more on education of the young. To practice for any goal you need determination. To stop smoking, for example, you should start with the belief, "Yes I can do it" followed by the strong desire to stop smoking. Fill your mind with positive thoughts to continue. Do not get weakened by temptations. Use meditation to achieve self-hypnosis and a feeling of calm. Try with all your might to change yourself, but if you can't, then seek help to avoid abandoning the goal. In short, you must create habits of what you want to become. If you want to become a positive person, you need to practice during every minute of your consciousness and in all situations. If you are not doing that, then you are allowing doubts and negativities to creep back into your mind. Form good and virtuous habits and make them your master.

'7) Learn to Relax.

'The mental world is opposite to the physical world. The more one is relaxed about what he wants to achieve, the more likely he will get it to happen. To re-wire your brain, you need to relax and to release those positive hormones which come with positive beliefs.'

I sensed Plato was coming to the end of his lecture. I asked him if he had any guiding principles that could be used to enable us to formulate our thoughts and actions.

Plato listed a few of these principles with pleasure:

Promote tolerance, justice, compassion and honesty

Promote moderation, courage and moral activism

Promote family values as the building block for a functioning society.

Respect cultural, racial and religious diversity.

Respect the rule of the majority without oppressing the minority.

Promote freedom of thought and speech with responsibility and respect.

Guard against all politics based on religious Absolute Truth.

Protect democracy from the corruption of money and controlled media.

Deal firmly with failing states through international efforts.

Addressing my teachers I said, 'I am really impressed with Plato's confirmation that the roots of most of Mankind's problems lie in the absence of the probing mind. It teaches us that the unexamined life is not worth living. One should stand up for one's beliefs and challenge the prevailing maxims if one truly seeks peace and justice for all.

Human awakening will begin when we start to quell the silence and fear about the things that matters most. An inquisitive mind is the light while blind faith is the darkness. One should always choose light over darkness. It is obvious by now, that accepting evil in silence is sinful in the eyes of all rational thinkers. One should always put defeat in a just cause ahead of evil becoming victorious. Real change starts when the individual takes the first step, even if he doesn't see what is around the corner. Only by changing the individual can the world change?'

I noticed that they were all pleased with my summary. Plato said to his colleagues, 'Didn't I bet you that anyone who passes our well tested program gets librated from his existing dogmas and fears?'

As was routine, the speaker for the next day stood up next to me to recite some poem to reflect upon the subject of his lecture.

Oh Man! Wake up to be free
With your actions, from poverty, from ignorance flee
Engage your mind, reject fear, and reject surrender
Doing nothing, saying nothing is the real blunder

I got the hint from this recital what to expect next. Looking at my guest, I smiled and said, 'I know that it is getting very late and that I must wish you all goodnight.'

Chapter 7

Adam Smith
The Economy

It was seven a.m. on Thursday. I woke up rather tired as the previous day's lecture by Plato started to touch on the difficult task ahead. I could not help thinking that behind the chaos in the Middle East there are those who are exploiting the emotional poverty and ignorance of the people in the area. The instruments for implementations are often the dictators in the region. They usually have many personal defects. Their behaviour is predictable and ideal for manipulation by their enemies.

Adam noticed my hesitation to get out of bed. He came and sat next to me and stroked my hair. He asked me to take a good shower to freshen up. I quickly realized that there would be no escape from starting early. The economy is very important to fund the new awakening of the human spirit. Human salvation needs to cash the cheque of equal opportunities God has signed with the human race.

We had a quick breakfast and Adam swung into action so that no time was lost. He said that he would follow the same style that had been used during the previous days.

He continued, 'Let me first explain what I will cover during the day. I am sure you will have many questions as you have considerable knowledge of economics.'

I looked at him and smiled.

'As you know, we are not here to teach you economics. There are enough theories and studies since Adam Smith came up with his theories on capitalism and the invisible forces of supply and demand. Since our themes are on implanting virtues and ethics, I will try to show how economic theories succeed or fail mainly because they don't take into account the changing nature of human behaviour. I will emphasize the role of education, faiths and the role of upbringing in creating cultural values and work ethics. I will touch on the negative effects of greed and "get rich quickly attitude" on the whole economy. I will touch on the role of business leaders and social responsibility in creating a better tomorrow. I will try to cover the various aspects below, by commenting on few of the current economic events and link them to the underlying human behaviour:

'• Micro economics and the role of individual and culture

'• The role of banks and the evil of speculation

'• Economic cycles as reflection of human swings in mood

'• The welfare states and the role of the Family and the Community

'• Micro Finance and the role of Charities and Entrepreneurs

'• Funding international organizations'

Adam looked at me and realized I was not as engaged as I had been in the previous days. He asked me if I had any preference as to how he should approach the subject.

I quickly took up the offer and said. 'Can we do it as a question and answer session? You can always fill any gap not covered in this process.'

'Whatever you like, Mac,' said Adam. 'Let us then have the first question.'

'How is America going to fund its wars on terror? The economy is already suffering from major structural imbalances. Who is lending to the USA and why?'

Adam responded, 'America is not only a military superpower but also an economic one. It is the most creative and dynamic nation on Earth. They inherited a system of government that led to unleashing human energies from the dogmas of religions and fears. The mighty dollar is used as a reserve currency by most countries. Therefore, you can say its economic success is the result of its great liberal system of government. In recent times however, some unethical politicians started to commit their nation to huge debts and leave it to future generations to deal with the deficit. Things may get out of control leading to hyperinflation that will penalize the whole society. The other alternative is to go through a long period of economic stagnation and the resultant widening the gap between the rich and the poor.

'When politics was more ethical, wars were fought to defend liberties. They were funded by increasing taxes. This can happen when wars are a matter of national necessity and they get the full support of the nation. In the case of this war, there is no such consensus if we remove the lies and deceits of the opinion formers. This is why President Bush reduced taxes and went on a military spending spree at the same time. It is an act of economic lunacy. By reducing taxes, he is effectively bribing the electorate. When the voters wake up to the human cost and financial ruin, then one should not be surprised if there is a massive reaction against the politicians and the groups which have led the country to economic ruin.'

Adam continued to explain who is lending to the USA. 'The lenders like China, Japan and the Gulf countries are always happy to purchase US assets to keep their export surpluses. The Federal Reserve is participating in creating the feel good factor by keeping interest rates near zero while the economy is creating a property bubble. Politicians and bankers colluded to create the feeling of invincibility. The people are stuffed with credit cards. Property prices are rising as if nothing could go wrong. Well, I tell you now Mac, something very big will happen to the world economy triggered by the burst of the property bubble or some other speculative excesses. Take it from us, bubbles always burst. The bigger they become the greater the subsequent pain.

'Every extreme economic human behaviour must be corrected through successive economic downturns. This is how economic cycles work. When the consumers and the state indulge in overspending with structural imbalances, then corrective action will ultimately follow. If this is not done at an early stage and in an orderly manner, then the market forces will find a way to make it happen more painfully. The longer the politicians and bankers mismanage the economy and bury their heads in the sand, the greater the panic when it comes. Those indulging in the excessive behaviour need to be deeply shaken up from time to time so that they revert to reality.'

Adam continued, 'Those who manage the central banks and the politicians need to have under their disposal multiple tools to deal with economic imbalances rather than relying only on the blunt instrument of adjusting interest rate. So far, it appears that the Chinese have adopted a more balanced form of capitalism by applying guidelines to banks and other economic participants to deal with excesses at early stages. In the case of over-borrowing by individuals for example, a minimum deposit could be introduced, or no lending for second home buyers and so on. This will deal with the specific problems of a housing bubble and nip it in the bud. The speculators will fight tooth and nail any such regulations, as it will limit the swing in assets prices. Without this swing, they cannot suck the money out of everyone else. The bankers usually fuel the situation by their race for bigger bonuses unless they are forced to moderate their behaviours.'

I asked, 'Why don't the clever politicians, the central bankers, and the regulators have multiple corrective tools since they make sense and the evil of speculation is so obvious?"

Adam responded, 'This is a very good question. I think you know the answer from what Plato was saying yesterday. The greedy few speak with simple persuasive arguments. They advocate that full banking liberalization and forces of the market are better than intervention by the state. The truth behind this argument is "trust us, the unelected few, instead of your poorly informed elected politicians".'

I asked if by the greedy few, he was referring to those in charge of 'Casino banking'.

Adam explained, 'Let me go back to the 1970s and early 80s when the trade unions exceeded their expectations and wanted more than their share of the economic wealth. That was a good example of mob mentality. The excessive wage demands and restrictive practices led to major economic difficulties. With no virtuous and philosophical leaders to mentor the various labour movements into moderation, their demands started to multiply. They demanded unhealthy industries to be kept alive against all economic reality. They shut down the operation of public utility services to blackmail the society into submission. These excesses stemmed from not "putting the community needs ahead of individual greed". Regan and Thatcher used all the necessary means to smash the trade union movements with the support of public opinion. They passed laws to restrict the abuse of the unelected trade unions leaders. They also opened up trade with low wages countries like China and other Far Eastern countries to keep wages down in their countries. At the same time, all those countries that joined globalization were brought within the clutches of the financiers in 1986 when the banking big bang legislations were passed.

'Under these legislations, the bankers were given almost complete freedom to wheel and deal in any asset, real or structured, with the sole purpose of making a quick profit at the expense of the hard-working people. The financial products started to get more exotic. Scientists and mathematicians were employed to devise even more complicated methods to unlock the psychology of the savers and investors. Once they are hooked into the banking casinos with their hard-earned money, the smart money gets out and reaps huge profits without adding one grain of food to meet the real human needs. The Internet bubble is a good example of how millions of people lost their savings.'

'Wow!' I shouted. 'Plato beautifully explained yesterday how money can corrupt and how speculation is employed by the few to get to the toils of the real producers in the economy. I suppose if what Plato said yesterday about the power-craving politicians is correct, then no strong action will be taken to control the bankers similar to that taken to smash the trade unions. Could you expand on the psychology of those who run these banking casinos and the psychology of the target victims?'

'Yes,' Adam replied. 'Let me start with the bankers. To devise intricate and appealing games, they attract top university brains. They use the lure of very attractive pay packages including mouth-watering bonuses to reward short-term performance. They employ the fastest computers for a truly global banking lottery. Top sales people pedal various financial products in the wealthiest countries. They are usually managed by "too big to fail financial institutions". The world's wealth is now within their grasp through speculation under the pretext of liberalization of the banks. They have become the true Masters of the Financial Universe. With the might of the untold wealth, they are now untouchable. They exercise undue influence on many politicians or even on political parties through legitimate unlimited political funding. Very few, if any, politicians dare to recommend reining them back with effective regulations. The bankers who are pulling the strings have lost almost all morality. Easy money started to weaken business ethics. Leaders of other businesses started to copy the bankers by seeking high bonuses for short-term performance. They see no shame in making huge profits at the expense of the rest of the population as long as it is legal.'

Adam continued, 'You remember what Plato said yesterday. The selfish few will convince the masses that what is legal is moral, as these laws are the expression of the free will of the people. A herd instinct develops among all business elites. New financial institutions are established completely outside the weakened regulatory system of the banks. They argue that the players or gamblers are mature enough to know what they are doing. Hedge funds, private equity funds, fund management, private banking, investment banking, fund of funds and so on join in the act. Most of their activities are barely regulated or at best lightly regulated. They usually ask the average investor to sign reams of paper as disclosure; documents that are not intelligible even to the expert. Some of these unregulated financial institutions get too big. They involve indirectly deposit-taking banks so that if they fail, they would bring down with them the entire financial system. Taxpayers' money then rushes in to save the day without imposing the real pain of bankrupting them. Politicians are usually lenient with the conditions of such bailouts. They argue that the banks are at the heart of the economic system and cannot be allowed to fail to avoid economic depression.'

Abraham looked at me and said, 'Mac, the real message is to get rid of greed and to get rid of being enslaved by money. This is the real challenge. If man loves his fellow men more than he does loves money, then he will be truly Divine and librated from bondage. Those who worship money are usually the ones behind all excesses and all evils. It was Jesus who said, "It is easier for a camel to pass through the eye of a needle than the greedy to get to Heaven." The true damage from the Thatcher and Regan era was the opening of the doors of Hell through the serious worship of materialism. It must be remembered that the fear of losing power leads to corruption. Money is the main tool for obtaining and keeping power. Human salvation will start only by reversing these trends.'

Looking at Abraham I said, 'How can we eliminate greed and at the same time keep the economy functioning efficiently and fairly? Such rewards are necessary to get people with magic powers. Magical abilities are very rare. However, I am deeply concerned with mixing money gained through speculations with politics. A well-known banker has recently been quoted as saying "My thanks to the directors of many influential publications in America, who have attended our 'Elites' Meetings' and respected their promises of discretion for almost forty years". In his statement, he continued to say that it would have been impossible for the elites to develop their plans for the world if they had been subjected to the glare of publicity during those years. He then concluded by saying, "The world is now more sophisticated and prepared to march towards a world government. The supranational sovereignty of an intellectual elite and world banker is surely preferable to the national auto-determination practiced in past centuries".'

I continued, 'For politics to serve the people, it should not be reduced to tinkering with fringes. It should pay attention to the deep philosophical and cultural issues such as the role of money in politics. Governments should also find ways to immunize the masses from the control of the few and so on. It is unfortunate that we've been indoctrinated for so long. We are no longer able to differentiate between light and darkness as if we have been blinded by our masters. It is not easy to admit that we have been deceived and fooled all this time. We must remember that once power is given to those who worship money, they will never give it back voluntarily.'

Plato was pleased with this analysis and made the following comment, 'You see, there is a way out... To build a fair economic system, the society needs "Just Elites", whose decisions will be based on being fair to the many, and not just to a few. In doing so, they will expand the middle class at the expense of wealth concentration. Just Elites will call for creativity, religious tolerance and a true democracy that serves the majority. Economic rewards will be based on respecting merits, not privileges, and rewarding real economic benefit. Humanity will only thrive through openness and sharing of ideas and through cultural exchanges based on mutual respect. Humanity requires greater honesty among business leaders by inviting experts to examine their thoughts and deeds to enrich the community at large. Those who think they have a monopoly on wisdom are a curse to themselves and to others around them.'

After a long pause to absorb what Plato had just said, I looked at Abraham and asked, 'How many doctrines of the Universal Moral Codes are being broken by the "Greedy Elites and Bankers", in order to dominate world affairs?'

Abraham obliged, 'They have broken the golden rule "Do to others as you would have them do unto you" or "Don't do to others what you don't want to be done unto you". The second is to "Put the community needs ahead of the individual greed". When such excessive behaviour leads to the destruction of the economy, then obviously this rule is broken with little regard to the consequences. The third is to "Put spiritual well-being ahead of materialism". Most existing religious codes outlaw gambling especially if it leads to the ruins of the participants. It is beyond us how those countries which regard themselves civilized allow financial gambling at such scales, which will not only ruin the participants in the market but also the working people and the taxpayers. If such free-for-all banking behaviour remains unchecked, then the whole economy would most certainly suffer from a severe cancer, eating it from within. This will lead the few to protect themselves in gated communities for fear of the rest of the community.'

I asked, 'How come the ordinary people who do not get involved in investment feel it is nothing to do with them? This only affects those who have money to invest.'

Newton being the mathematician could not keep quiet. He responded, 'The true wealth is what humans would like to consume and enjoy. The act of speculation does not produce such goods or services. So when the speculators make huge gains then it must be at the expense of others who are the true producers of the goods and services.' He smiled and continued, 'Simple maths my friend, simple maths. The ordinary people suffer the consequences through higher prices, unemployment and higher taxes without being able to work out the link with the true causes.'

Adam thanked Newton and continued, 'One can clearly see the damage done to business ethics and why it would be very painful to correct it if it is left unchecked for too long. Computers will start to replace shareholders as they trade at high speed, buying and selling shares of well-established companies for the sole purpose of making quick money. This short-term approach pushes the executives of most companies to go for short-term performance rather than long-term planning. This leads to squeezing salaries and ignoring customers' long-term interests for the benefit of the bottom line. Even the heads of monopoly companies, like utilities, start to demand higher pay, as greed becomes an accepted norm. Athletes and footballers follow the same pattern as they have rare abilities. Then the culture of overpaying all individual qualities in public demand is established irrespective of the principle of fairness. The end result is that those who do not make it to the ranks of the elite will live at mere subsistence levels while those who are well positioned will reap huge reward. A class system will develop between those who have some wealth and abilities, real or perceived, and those who have not.'

Adam continued, 'As technologies and export of jobs through globalization reduces the need for labour in the advanced economies, we find a higher portion of the nation's wealth is passed to the owners of capital and top executives at the expense of the rest of the population. This inevitably leads to greater income differential and ultimately to creating a class of privileged citizens, who have, and the rest, who have not.

History tells us that if those who make up the middle class in any society continue to fall below a critical mass, it will ultimately lead to the weakening of democracy, serious discontentment and probably uprising.'

I interrupted to get some clarification by saying, 'I understand that athletes may have special ability although excessive rewards are not justified. What does a banker have which is not common among the average intelligent people? What is this magic, which lets a hedge fund manager make billions of dollars in one year and everyone admire him for that?'

Adam, with some scepticism in his voice, responded, 'Mac, don't be fooled by what you are told. There is nothing magical in what bankers do. In fact, it is the simplest type of trading, yet they are rewarded obscenely. The terrible tragedy is that the financial gamblers have extended their hands into commodities including foods, energy, water and other basic necessities. You see Mac, something seriously immoral is going on. The majority seem to have no clue as to what to do about it. They are trusting democracy to produce a government to protect them.'

In disbelief I protested, 'Adam, you seem to be presenting only an anti-banking view point. Let me tell you what the counter arguments will be. 'Deregulations have led to: a) reduced red tape, b) freeing the movements of money to seek new opportunities at a truly global scale, c) to identify economic excesses and then force the hands of the politicians or business leaders to correct economic imbalances, d) to fund risky ventures that otherwise would not come off the ground, e) to identify inefficient or fragmented industries and push them into action to consolidate and so on.'

Plato laughed and said, 'Adam, you seem to have forgotten that Mac is involved in banking, although of the conventional type. If you cannot persuade Mac, you will have a problem persuading others with your argument. Please remember that there will be a huge attack by the guided media on those calling for regulating the banks in the name of avoiding bigger governments. A truly fair economic system should be based on rewarding true creativities in science, dealing with economic inefficiencies and rewarding fairly the toils of genuine hard work.'

Adam seemed very relaxed to deal with the counter arguments as he has heard them before.

He said, 'Let me deal with your points one by one:

'Deregulation has led to reducing red tape! There is no call for heavy regulations to deal with genuine banking transactions. The war on terror has created more regulations to stop funding the terrorists and rightly so. Why then, should one complain if a call is made to deal with financial terrorism, i.e. those who manipulate the economy for their selfish personal gain at the expense of others? It is not beyond the wisdom of man to simplify regulations and at the same time restrict or penalize only non-genuine or casino banking transactions.

'Free movement of money seeks new opportunities on a truly global scale! Yes, the big banks have made huge search to identify new opportunities in the developing markets and frontier markets. Usually, that money comes with many conditions to create huge, short-term profits for the bankers and the investors. We are calling for a much fairer system where money is passed to the poorer countries in the true spirit of partnership and not for speculative gains in properties, currencies or some other hot assets. This does not mean that all the investments by banks have been unhelpful. Any regulation should not hinder private banking or private equity funds where true investments are made in the right places. In fact Mac, you are making my point, if true bankers chase opportunities where capital could be put to create employment and improve efficiencies, then this will be a genuine part of fair and efficient use of banking services.

'To identify economic excesses and force politicians to correct the imbalances! This is an interesting argument. Let us look at some examples from recent history and see if this is what true, virtuous banking should be about. A well-known speculator attacked the value of the British pound sterling in nineteen eighty-two, through the hedge fund he ran and he made more than $1.2 billion dollars at the expense of the British taxpayers. He forced the UK to leave the European Exchange Mechanism during the time of the Conservative Chancellor Nigel Lawson. Should a speculator dictate to an elected government what they should decide as economically acceptable by the people? If sterling was overvalued and hurting UK businesses, then it is the role of other institutions to lobby the government. Is it good for democracy, when a foreign speculator forces the hands of the UK business community and the elected government to act? Let us take the example of bond vigilantes. These are speculators who are ready to attack any country or company that has issued bonds, if they feel that entity is not managing their budget or business correctly. With huge funds at their disposal, the vigilantes will create a distortion and usually administer the wrong medicine. One needs to remember that during 1998, excessive speculations in the bonds market almost brought down the world's financial system. The actions of the unregulated fund managers have led to great pain in the developing countries. Are these genuine benefits that cannot be replaced by other means?

'To fund risky ventures which otherwise would not come off the ground! It is the basic role of the banks to assist in raising capital, and not casino banking. Conventional banks have made huge progress in the past following this route. In

Germany and Japan, the banks, before deregulation, participated in funding long-term capital. The deregulations have made this unattractive, as short-term alternatives have become more attractive for quick bonuses.

'To identify inefficient or fragmented industries and push them into action! This is usually done by private equity funds and there is no reason that such activities should not continue. Some of the private equity houses specialize in asset stripping. They buy companies with the purpose of restructuring and returning excess cash to the investors. In the process, they increase the borrowing and improve the short-term return on equity. This is fine if it does not lead to bankruptcy at the first sign of a recession. By then, they would have sold out and made their regular fees and the 20% bonus on the excess profit.'

I looked at Adam and said, 'You seem to have come well prepared. I think this is one of the reasons why almost 50% of the people do not bother voting as there is a widespread belief that their votes do not lead to any change. It seems that the masses are doomed to serve the "masters of the universe" as the political system has been engineered to enrich them.'

Adam, with some emotion in his voice, said, 'This is not how the Scottish Adam Smith envisaged capitalism. This system works only if the people are virtuous and the controllers, the governments, are truly outside the powers of the few. This is why we are calling for human awakening. To galvanize support for decent politicians against those who rely on the evils of money. The decent politicians should include, in any bank regulations, strict disciplines to ensure true reforms to correct the damage done since the financial big bang. Without dealing with the spreading disease of naked greed, nothing can be done to save human salvation. People are living in a materialistic world, and the demand for excessive reward is at the centre of the current distorted capitalism.'

Adam continued, 'Bank regulations should include, among other things:

'1) Break-up of the banks which are "too big to fail" so that the state will not hesitate to let it go bust and the shareholders will fear the pain of total loss.

'2) Banks accepting deposits should not enter the financial casino business.

'3) Hedge funds, private equities and other currently non- or lightly regulated bodies should be subjected to supervision of the regulators accountable to the people.

'4) Worldwide financial transactions should be taxed, to generate income for the international bodies instead of relying on funding by the states. This will allow truly independent world organizations that will be trusted by all.

'5) Bonuses and high rewards should be linked to long-term performance and not pay packages only.

'6) Central banks must add to their armouries many tools to re-balance the economy and deal with potential bubbles.

'7) Smaller countries must be protected from the financial vultures, as many of the current hedge funds could attack any free-floating currency of a small country with impunity.

'8) Pure Speculation in commodities, currencies, agricultural lands and foods must be strictly regulated.

'9) All powers of the state, including the education system and civil institutions, should be employed to promote business ethics.

'10) Shorting of shares, bonds, currencies and commodities to be severely regulated, as no one should trade in any asset he doesn't own. Borrowing assets for the sake of short trading comes under this heading'

'Unfortunately, most politicians are unlikely to be interested in effective reforms as long as they are at the mercy of the donation of bankers. I can tell you now that when a serious financial crisis takes place, they will pretend to be regulating the banks to absorb public anger, while in reality they are only covering up, as the average voter will not have a clue of such complex matters. In a society where ethical behaviours are dominant, businesses must focus on providing services the people need at fair prices. Exploitation is seen as taboo. So successful executives, in the end are those who serve their customers and probably exceed their expectations.

'At present, shareholders have abandoned their supervisory responsibilities, as most of the shares are held by fund managers, who are usually day traders, and have no interest in what the company does in the long run.'

I couldn't help stopping Adam and said, 'You are drawing a gloomy picture. There are many regulations to protect the working of the system. Company laws are regularly revised to meet these challenges.'

'Yes that is true Mac,' Adam responded. 'The point I am making is to show that you cannot protect business ethics from going downhill if you have banking, or any other industry in the economy, out of control and massively enriching its participants legally at the expense of the other players in the society. This is a serious economic virus and it is infecting all the other players.'

I asked Adam, 'Are those who corrupt politics and work ethics immune from any human failings? After all, no one is perfect.'

Adam consulted with Plato trying to ensure that he would be as diplomatic as he could in responding to this question. In a very serious tone he replied, 'As they succeed beyond their wildest dreams in advancing their agendas, they get pushed by those who are less cultured among their lot for more extreme policies. This does not only involve distorting history but also committing greater acts of injustices. They allow their benefactors to break all sorts of international laws, they commit more cruelties and they bully countries and their politicians who manage to be elected outside their clutches.

'Then the time comes when the just elite start to speak out, as they no longer submit to their tactics. Ultimately, the ordinary people will see through the curtains of lies and deceits. They will make out that only the poor ordinary people and their taxes are being sacrificed for battles and wars of no interest to them. A strong reaction will follow which will lead to absolute rejection to being manipulated or blinded. Then a mass movement will ensure that this enormous distortion will be suppressed to near zero.'

Abraham smiled and said, 'God bless those who act to put an end to the trespasses of the arrogant and foolish among them. Damned are the countries where the powerful get away with his evil acts by the help of those in authority. Damned is the planet where the spoiled few get way with breaking God's Law of Natural Justice with the help of the most powerful countries.'

Adam then continued after this interruption, 'It is obvious that cultures play dominant role in economic prosperity. Cultures need to be understood in terms of those values that have direct influence on economic activities of the individuals, the organizations and the communities. It is not sufficient to know that hard work is important but it is also essential to know what guides and directs hard work. While education is important, the type and quality of education is even more so. Those who can afford to employ cultured nannies for their pampered children will escape the inertia of cultural ignorance. The world is full of youths who have the wrong attitudes and skills because the educational institutions and the business communities are not talking to one another. Unfortunately, in some countries they use education to indoctrinate the young in blind faith, leading to the creation of unemployable generations. Humans seldom realize that their thoughts and emotions are implanted in them as they pass through the journey of life. Only those who reflect relentlessly on the direction of where they are heading can change their destiny.'

Abraham, sensing that the Islamic countries need to work the hardest to catch up to the age of "knowledge economy" said, 'It is time for Muslims to wake up to the true teaching of their faith. The Quran says that God will not change the fortunes of any nation unless its citizens change from within. It is clear that God is not offering the Muslims or any other group a free ride. If the individuals don't work on changing their culture, then they should not expect that God will do it for them no matter how much they shout or pray.'

I looked at Adam and said, 'I am now confident that only if we can eradicate the evils of greed and craving for power, humanity would have a chance for a fairer world order. The way to do that is to identify those who use their talents to the detriment of the rest of the society. How could we identify the arrogant among us so that we can isolate them and avoid falling victim of their apparent charms and deceits.'

Plato took this challenge and said, 'You are right. These are usually people with above average intelligence and probably brought up to feel that what they are doing is acceptable and even commendable. Let me spell out their tactics so that one will not be fooled by them. They apply many positive characteristics that are not uncommon among virtuous business leaders. They are aware of the nature of envy and keep most important things away from people they are not sure of. They avoid fighting a losing battle or offending the wrong people as they are driven by realism. They prepare well thought out plans to avoid surprises. At the right place and time they act boldly, as they are aware that timidity kills the best laid plans. They understand what motivate others through deep psychological analysis and use it effectively.'

Plato continued, 'The key is to be aware of the negative characteristics they employ. They flatter and massage their bosses' egos. They tactfully manipulate and deceive others. They appear ruthless when they are in a position of strength and merciless in victory. They do not disclose their full intent and exploit others' weaknesses to throw them out of balance. They are often not frank or open and purposely appear ignorant. They are not predictable and frequently changing their positions. They apply the Machiavellian philosophy who once wrote, "Anyone who tries to be good all the times will bound to come to ruin among the great number who are not good".'

I looked at Plato and said, 'Isn't Machiavelli right? If the majority are bad then the goods people will be swallowed by the ocean of evils. Isn't this is what we are noticing in failing states?'

Plato responded, 'This is why the world should wake up to avoid the slippery slope of the weakening work ethics. This was not so common before the banking Big Bang. We are not dreamers. Virtuous people should not abandon their countries or bury their heads in the sand. They should have the talent and the courage to group themselves and speak out to make whatever little difference they can. Abandoning action, ethics and hope will lead to the worst outcome.'

After some lengthy discussion, we moved back to the cultural profiles based on differences in values that included ideas about what is good or bad and what is right or wrong and so on.

After a pause, Adam said, 'I can give you two examples on the impotence of culture in shaping economic realities. One involves the discovery of the New World in the last 500 years and the other is the economic progress of Germany and Japan after total destruction during the Second World War. I will be very brief in both cases and I will start with the first.

'Let us compare the economies of the English-speaking countries like USA, Canada, Australia and New Zealand with those of South America and Mexico. What is common between the two groups of countries? The first group of countries was tailored according to the prevailing cultures in northern Europe especially Britain and France. The then prevailing aristocratic values and legal systems where adopted as the foundation for those economies. The aristocracy or the enlightened elite were guiding the masses. They adopted the principles of free trade, rule of law and hard work. They engaged the people to continuously improve the government system, maintain family values, applied a liberal interpretation of Christianity, embraced education based on rational thinking and so on. Compare this with the second group of countries occupied mainly by Spain as in the case of Mexico and South America. Those countries adopted the culture of Southern Europe. They put more emphasis on the adherence to the rigid religious teachings of Catholicism and applied their own political inflexibility that did not evolve to meet the minimum aspiration of the people. While Northern European countries were embryonic democracies, Southern Europeans were lagging behind in this respect. Small variations in cultural and ethical values, including religious beliefs and quality of education, usually lead to major differentials in the political and economic performance over the years. This is an important message for establishing a Just World Order. If the developed countries truly want to see lasting economic progress in the less developed ones, they must focus on the contents of people's characters and not just on responding to the crisis resulting from starvation or natural disasters.

'Let me now move onto Germany and Japan. These two countries were almost completely devastated after the Second World War. Yet they have become super economic powers. The key to recovery lies again in the characters of their people. Over the years, with good work ethics their economies throve. They rebuilt their businesses on the principles of reliable qualities, respect to all stakeholders, detailed planning followed by quick execution, creating the correct processes to get the desired results, examining the true facts before decisions are made, evening out workloads to remove bottlenecks and so on. With such strong business ethics and attention to detail, people around the world will always prefer the "made in Germany" or Japan mark over the products of other exporting countries.'

I looked at Adam and said, 'Therefore every country, which aims to improve the living standards of its citizens, must start with addressing issues of work ethics and morality as top priority. I know of two examples of such successful transformation. Singapore and Dubai, where changes started by focusing on security of the state led by enlightened authoritarian leaders then followed with emphasis on reducing corruption. This was accompanied by building civil institutions, openness, education, gradual involvement of the population, equal opportunities and so on.'

Adam continued, 'Yes of course, no country can achieve sustainable economic progress in a globalised world if their work ethics are inferior to those of their competitors. Business

241

principles should be guided by Universal Virtues and instilled in the young through education, media, parenting, religions, etc. You cannot have a fair economic system, where a section of the society relies on handouts by the state while others work very hard to make ends meet. In areas where reliance on state handouts is widespread, special attention must be made to educate the young on the value of work. Parents are to guide their children about the need to excel with public services in mind. Everything depends on upbringing. Rewarding laziness should not be confused with compassion. Empowering the lazy who rely on lies and deceits is equal to condemning complete generations to a culture of criminality, poverty and reliance on aids. Through incentives and the tax system, a way should be found to shift the burden of the welfare state to the families, local communities and charities who should know the true needs of those individuals within their localities. Only in this way can they weed out those who are abusing the system.

'The state is usually to be blamed. If a welfare system hands out money without ensuring that those relying on the handout have the true passion to work, then more will follow this route to empower their wicked behaviours. It is evident that many refugees from various countries come to Europe and ask for support when they can adequately live within their own communities. Usually no questions are being asked and no penalties are imposed on those who are found to be lying. Many well-meaning people who defend the refugees' needs for financial support are actually condemning them to a culture of dishonesty and theft. They collect money from the state while they work in the black-market in addition to the wealth they have back home. This will undoubtedly lead to resentment from the indigenous hard-working people who have to foot the bills.'

Then Adam concluded this part of his teaching with a comment on the needs for establishing an appropriate legal system. He continued, 'No country can prosper unless it has a legal system which deals with commercial disputes fairly and speedily. This can only be achieved if the people who are in charge of this branch of government have the accumulated precedents and wisdom to deliver justice and fairness on completely impartial basis.'

We broke for lunch and realized that this subject could be very vast as human nature has broad applications to economic realities. As it was a question and answer session, Plato reminded me that I needed to be brief and focus only on the major world issues. He confirmed that Adam still needed to cover the subject of funding the international bodies for the Just World Order. He also needed to deal with external imbalances.

I tried to change the seriousness of the dialogue during the break. I said jokingly, 'If what Adam is preaching is truly workable, then why don't you show me a movie from another civilization where the economy is in such a Utopia?'

Newton, with his usual seriousness said, 'Do you doubt Adam?'

I was uncomfortable by his tone. I replied, 'No, it's just that his teaching is rather idealistic and requires reforming human nature first. We all know how hard that can be. Is modifying our genes a realistic alternative? If we are born with a selfish gene how could we use parenting to overcome those built-in handicaps?'

They realized that I was still harbouring some doubt about the difficulty of the task ahead.

Darwin walked next to me after lunch and said, 'You should know well, by now, that humans are still evolving with

243

the help of the monitoring gene. Humans need to mobilize as if they are being invaded by aggressive aliens. We need to start to instil the missing virtues. After two or three generations of good behaviours, the gene responsible for selfishness will be switched off, just like that responsible for the appendix in the human body. The genes driving kindness and care will become dominant. Economies based on fairness and equity will replace those based greed and craving for power. You see, it is not the time for humanity to doubt the importance of change. This will not happen in a year or two. Even a hundred year plan is a rather short time relative to human history. Those who will lead the movement will be immortal heroes for many generations to come. They would have achieved what humans have failed to do over thousands of years. The word "impossible" should be deleted from the vocabulary of the doers. Such a word is often used to maintain the status quo. It is used by the weak and lazy that fear challenges. The young should insist on creating a better world than their parents have managed to achieve.'

I realized that when I do get those moments of doubt, I should step back and ask if I want to live in an unfair world with the worst to come or in a world full of hope for future generations. I must train myself to remember that self-doubt is always the worst enemy within. Hesitation is to be controlled and not to let it control me.

I could see Adam was keen to return to his lecture. We all re-convened for the last formal session of the Encounter.

Without waiting for me to ask any questions Adam said, 'I will explain the economic gap between South Korea and Egypt and how to fund the new world order. Is that OK with you Mac?'

I smiled realizing that he has chosen two countries that have followed completely divergent economic paths in recent history.

Adam started, 'The reason I selected Egypt is to show how prevailing poor moral codes have led to the destruction of the fabric of the nation, while a similar country with similar economic development, some sixty years ago, has become an economic tiger. The removal of the monarchy in Egypt in 1952 destroyed in few years what was a growing elite with stable rules of law to replace it with an embryonic democracy but a destructive dictatorship. Under the grip of the army, and with very poor political philosophy on the part of those in charge, poverty and deteriorating work ethics led to a rapid break-up of the economic system. Business ethics were replaced by corruption. Acquisition of knowledge became superficial. Poverty and ignorance became widespread. The high birth rate meant the lower standard of living became even lower. The country was sucked into a cycle of continuous decline. Parents instilled fear of politics into the heart of their children due to the cruelty of the system in dealing with new ideas. This has led to a complete absence of political maturity. If the corrupt regime is to be replaced through a popular uprising then chaos will prevail due to the lack of decent civil institutions to debate and support such change. Religion is not the solution as some have advocated. Unfortunately, the religious institutions and most of the preachers themselves need to appreciate the process of rational thinking to comprehend the working of the modern state.

'In complete contrast, South Korea managed to create successfully the necessary escape velocity to break out of the cycle of poverty and joined the tiger economies. Maybe those preaching Islamic values in Egypt, who care about practical

Islam, should examine why Buddhism has led Korea out of its poverty while Islam, as it is practiced by the majority in Egyptians, have not. Those who care about Egypt's long-term prosperity must search for cultural differences with countries like Japan and South Korea and put forward a detailed plan of action to reform all aspects of building the character of the individuals in that country. The first act must be to reform the media and the film industry to deliver the correct moral message in an entertaining way, instead of peddling current failing moral codes. Films and TV shows can and do have great effect in moulding the characters of the young.'

Abraham was observing my discomfort with this approach, as I am very aware of the sensitivity of anything to do with faiths. He said, 'Do you remember the saying, "Only an inquisitive mind can challenge the status quo"? It is in this context Adam is making the call to awaken the true spirit of Islam. During the Islamic rule of Andalusia, the West was in deep darkness, while the enlightened scholars from the Islamic and Jewish faiths worked to maintain the human march for knowledge including philosophy.'

I looked at Adam and said, 'As a case study, how could we get Egypt out of the vicious circle of continuing economic decline?'

He replied, 'For sure, Egypt at present is economically a failed state. It needs a true Marshal Plan of a kind, to get it out of its current downward spiral. The plan must involve a revival of moral values through very strict actions on corruption and on raising work ethics. It must include reforming the media that peddles lies and half the truth according to the wishes of the paymasters. Religious clerics need to receive training on rational thinking. Attempts must be made by charities employing retired teachers, thinkers, executives to train Egyptians to improve the

246

delivery of modern and practical knowledge and know-how to the young. This can also be done through volunteers from many countries including the West and Japan. They can be planted in every nursery, school and major businesses to pass their knowledge and experiences which is badly needed to upgrade the work ethics of the country. This approach could be applied to many other countries in the third world.

'The second aspect of the plan is to invite major developed countries to invest in newly created free zones. Those leased areas must be managed for 100 to 150 years, where the laws of those countries will apply. Investors will be invited from major corporations. In other words, create a few mini Hong Kongs. The location of Egypt is ideal for this plan. As China gets relatively expensive then this country should be the engine for growth in the area. It will truly link the East and West. A flourishing Egyptian economy will be the greatest peace driver and will absorb many millions of workers from Egypt and other countries in the region according to the required skills. Israel will benefit from such growth and its people will no longer live in fear, as wealth created on a large scale in the region will address poverty, ignorance and injustices.'

I was really comfortable with this approach, as the war on terror is directly linked to the Middle East conflict and poverty. A true Marshal Plan with world technologies and Gulf money, plus international goodwill, will be the strongest wall to isolate terror and create bridges of trust. This approach will be much cheaper and practical than continuing with the current roadmaps for imposed solutions, based on demoralizing the opponents through continuous conflicts and civil wars.'

Adam continued, 'Let me move to the question of dealing with the big external imbalances and then the funding of the Just World Order. As a general rule, and other things being equal (as we economists love to say) countries where the individuals have lost their desire to save, will become net importing countries. The call to control overspending in all countries creates a dilemma for the world economic order. Excessive spenders must exist to counterbalance those with thrifty cultures. The desired current world economic equilibrium is based on the need to create full employment in the thrifty countries as well as the overspending ones. This can only be achieved by those who save to rely on export to those who love to indulgence in luxuries. This means that wasteful consumption is to be encouraged or at least tolerated. To solve this dilemma we need a world where the poorer countries get help from the rich ones through gifts and easy loan. In effect, the world needs to move away from excessive consumption to helping the poor. This will require a fundamental shift in the moral code of Mankind.'

I looked at Adam and knowing how difficult such a task would be, I asked, 'Could you comment on the economic tools in use to deal with imbalances?'

Adam replied, 'To have the correct economic tools we must understand the part of human nature which deals with the demand side of the economy, that is, investors and consumers. The key is to identify the economic symptoms very early and deal with them by applying a mild medicine instead of waiting until the patient gets too sick. If things were left for too long, then electric shock would be needed to revive the economy. This is what will happen if speculation is not brought under control; if China is not forced to float its currency; if consumers in America and Europe do not live within their means; if pension deficits are not addressed; if corruption in India is not tackled; if work ethics and education systems are not addressed in the Middle East, and so on. Many of these issues are staring humanity in the face and the politicians are refusing to lead, as most of the medicine to be applied is very bitter, and the politicians are finding it more convenient to kick the can down the road. In summary, economists must be become expert in psychology first. They must understand and develop tools to deal with excessive fears and greed to manage investment. They must also develop tools to deal with the irrational run for luxuries or extreme thriftiness to manage consumptions and saving. They must become Messiah-like and preach in support of charities.

'If, in the long run, economies are the reflection of the characters of its people, how can China and the West trade with each other under a free trade agreement without influencing each other to converge at the cultural level?' I asked.

'This is really a good example to make my point,' Adam replied. 'There couldn't be a bigger divergence between these two economic giants. Communists versus democracy, controlled exchange rate versus reserve currency, low wages versus high wages, low health, and safety net versus over-regulated H&S rules. This is an obvious case of a temporary marriage of convenience. In the long run, however, one of two things must happen.

'1) China is forced to play according to the rules of the game and remove all the barriers to free trade and at the same time, it must stop currency manipulation. This will then force prices of Chinese goods to go up and surpluses to shrink. The speculators would move in, and wide currency fluctuation would lead to a wider economic cycle and severe pain to the politicians to control the population under the one-party system. The call for liberalization of political decisions will then be louder and convergence with Western values will follow.

'2) China will resist the required economic changes and the West will call for protectionism. Hardship in China will rise and the political system will more likely move toward a greater rigidity. This will lead to divergence of cultures, greater suspicions and an inevitable Cold War or even worse.'

As the time was passing quickly, I urged Adam to address the question of funding World International Organizations.

'Yes', he replied. 'To avoid countries pushing for external payment surpluses and to create funds for the Just World Order, we are proposing a tax on all exports. This money could be collected through the banking system and then passed to the International Bank or other agencies. The fund is then used to assist poorest countries with deficits to industrialize, improve its export, and reduce its reliance on import. This assistance would be in the form of low interest loans, technical assistance, improving the education system, etc. This means that countries with surpluses should assist those with deficits or stop their over reliance on export. Only by improving the standard of living of the poor in Third World countries will migration and the clash of civilizations avoided. This will also allow international bodies with the financial power of large funds to improve work ethics, political systems and eradicate corruptions. This money will be truly international and administered by experts independent of the interest of any one state. We are also calling for taxing all financial transactions, as said before.'

I said, 'There seems to be a contradiction which I cannot find a way to resolve. Those countries with good work ethics and have not been corrupted to seek luxury goods, cannot sustain full employment unless they become net exporters. Therefore, they need the luxury seekers and over spenders. If you are preaching for moderation in consumption to prevail in all countries, then a nation like Japan will have to work less, consume more or give more to charities to sustain full employment.'

Adam apologized for not covering this inconsistency and said, 'Globalization and rapid balanced economic growth can only be maintained in the long run if human behaviour is guided to put moderation ahead of luxury, fairness ahead of selfishness and Earth's sustainability ahead of mindless destruction of the planet. You see Mac, humans have to find a way to speed up the evolution of their moral code at a speed compatible with scientific and economic changes. One should promote the culture of benefitting the society ahead of rewarding the individual. Business leaders need to be global in their thinking. They should stay ahead in embracing change and contributing generously to the community at large.'

Adam continued, 'Religions have dealt with the dilemma of excess wealth by asking the rich to give to the poor. This will give great pleasure to those who give and to those who receive. The individuals in the society will be closer to one another. Hate and envy will be replaced by love and gratitude. The same could be done at an international level where the emerging countries, for many years to come, will need the support of the rich ones. Regard these as gifts for peaceful co-existence rather than a tax on the rich. Those who are blessed with plenty should not hesitate to give to the less fortunate. You see Mac, I am sorry to say that you are thinking in the current human paradigm. Everyone thinks with their selfish interest in mind to accumulate wealth and differentiate their tribe or country at the expense of the overall well-being of Mankind as a whole. Would the world be a better place if there was high unemployment in a country and your neighbour is in need of you; or to have full employment and use the surpluses to help the needy to catch up?'

On the question of seeking moderation Adam expanded, 'I will never advocate spending on luxuries to achieve full employment as this will be the worst of all worlds. It will destroy the planet and corrupt moral values; create divergent cultures, lead to wars and cultural clashes. Truly, world-class leaders are required for such transformation in Mankind's thinking. Away from "what's in it for me?" to "what's in it for Mankind?" When those countries with surpluses are willing to serve humanity at large, Mankind will be ready for the big spiritual transformation. If assistance is not given to the poor, the fund will be lost via unemployment or the destructive force of the economic cycles, or worst, through spending on immigrants and wars.'

Adam continued, 'As the Earth has limited resources, an international tax should be imposed on the use of all natural resources to slow down human destructive force on the planet.' You see, Mac, humanity is heading toward a serious disaster. As technology improves, fewer people are needed to satisfy the basic needs of Mankind. In order to avoid unemployment countries try to encourage consumption to increase demand. This means that more of the Earth's natural resources must be extracted. Therefore, improvement in technology leads to a cycle of waste. Humanity will sleepwalk into accelerating the march to destroying their planet.'

I said, 'You are here not to raise doubts as to how man will survive on this planet, but to supply suggestions how to survive better. You are proposing that Man use his talents to advance knowledge. Now you are telling me improved technology will speed up the destruction of our planet. I am rather confused.'

They all looked at Adam to resolve this dilemma. He obliged, 'Mac, you are right to be concerned. This supports the basic message we are trying to tell you during this encounter. Virtues have to evolve continuously to deal with the changing world. As technology improves, as life expectancy increases and as world population increases at a fast pace, a new paradigm needs to be agreed to save the planet. We do recognise that the new paradigm must take into account the need to maintain full employment, continuous improvement of human health, fairer distribution of wealth, continuous improvement in technology and a sustainable planet. For all these objectives to be achieved, people should move away from excessive consumption to more cultural and spiritual endeavours. Working hours to be reduced, satisfaction based on enjoying nature to replace materialism. You see this shift is not a call for new religion but a call to survival on this planet.'

For the first time I felt overwhelmed with the changes required and how humans have ignored them seriously. I started to think seriously that wars and destruction are the result of these failures. Instead of dealing with these issues of upgrading human moral codes, we find it easier to assign blame and attack one another in continuous wars and conflicts. Now I can see why the world needs to fund the international organizations through means independent of any single state. In doing so, you are taxing the depletion of resources, speculation and currency manipulation. Only with availability of such fund, man can start to work on these fundamental issues.

I then asked, 'If it is doable why has Mankind not applied this medicine?'

Plato came with the answer, 'You must remember that in some countries the economy is run for the benefit of the politicians and their cronies. People need to deal with their distrust of other cultures. We know this is rather difficult. Calling for cultural proximity will have its own antagonists from all quarters. The Just World Order needs independent institutions with financial might to effect change. Many countries need to surrender some of their powers and influence. That would be a bitter pill to swallow. It would take a lot of courage, a lot of faith in the just order. Some would argue that humans should wait for the arrival of the Messiah. We think such thinking is defeatist thinking and as we said before, Earth will only be governed by humans.'

Adam thanked Plato and continued, 'I promised to touch on the doomed Euro. A single currency and a single economic policy works only if there is a unified culture in an economic block with effective mobility of labour. If this were not the case then the existence of a different currency and monetary policies would be unavoidable to rebalance different work ethics and cultural values. If workers in Greece, Spain and Portugal will not move in sufficient numbers to the countries with surpluses, then those with surpluses must move their industry to the poorer countries to even out the employment level. If neither of these is likely to happen within a reasonable time, then the break-up of the European Fiscal Union becomes inevitable, as the rich countries will not support the poorer ones indefinitely. You cannot have a boxing match between world heavyweight economic champions against a lightweight trainee and not expect the defeat of the latter.'

I noticed that Adam was about to conclude for the day. 'Please expand on the role of the business community in helping the needy,' I asked. 'It will be rather a tragedy if we get into the culture of relying on the state for every aspect of improving human life.'

'You are right,' said Adam. 'The sea is made of little drops. Therefore, we expect every decent-minded individual to assist as activists with ideas, campaigning, charitable contributions, and so on. Businessmen have greater responsibilities than the politicians do. They should all respect the communities where they operate and add value to the area. If all the employees, at each business unit are organized for one hour a week to come with practical ideas to assist the community where they work and raise money, then huge progress will be achieved. By the way, this is also good for business. If some do it, then many others will follow their example due to the competitive advantage they will get. What better public relation exercise than helping the community?'

Adam continued with some practical examples of how businessmen can help the poor and the communities where they operate:

'1) Micro Financing has helped millions of villagers in the poorest countries to cross the line of starvation and hardship into self-sufficiency. All that it took was for a caring individual to act as the banker for those who are not bankable. It has become a sustainable business for alleviating poverty. Over the past thirty years, the Micro Finance movement has built a global infrastructure that links millions of disadvantaged people to the global economy. There are more than 3,500 Micro Finance Institutions (MFI) worldwide offering financial services to more than 155 million impoverished households in remote places, isolated from proper infrastructure. Solutions to several issues need to be market-based at affordable prices.

'2) Voluntary training of the unemployed. Every company should allocate a small fund to train the youth in their areas. This task cannot be left to the state alone. Business people who are blessed with love and wisdom should truly care. Let me give you the example of a man in the car distribution business. He started by training a few jobless people as taxi drivers. Once they got their driving license, he guaranteed their car loans so that they could buy their own taxis. The scheme expanded to train people as technicians, sales people, etc. Then he asked his colleagues at the chamber of commerce to follow his example. In ten years, with the help of other companies, he lifted 500,000 people out of unemployment in several countries where his businesses were located. It was good for business, as he retained the good workers who wanted to stay with him. He was also very popular in those communities.'

Adam continued with the theme of Corporate Social Responsibility. He said, 'Business should give back to the community generously through volunteering and mentoring. The world would be a better place if more people join the army of contributors to a better tomorrow, and inspire others by sharing opinion and ideas.

Abraham smiled and said, 'Blessed are those who cannot sleep unless they have done something useful for the poor and the needy that day. Blessed are those who aim to be the first at being the best, in the act of helping others.'

I thanked Adam and Abraham and said, 'This is really refreshing and practical stuff. If we break the problem of transformation into small steps, engaging large numbers of people over a long period of time then everything becomes possible.'

I continued jokingly and said to Adam, 'Now I think you deserve to change your brand from the father of capitalism to the father of a 'Just Economy'. Business leaders can play a true role to tap the energy of youth for the Just World Order. Since you have placed so much emphasis on business leaders to galvanize the transformation, what is your advice for a good course on leadership?'

Adam looked at Abraham as if I had asked a question on theology. He said with a smile, 'I will let Abraham answer that.'

'Sorry I think you have misheard me,' I said. 'I asked about training businessmen.'

They all laughed and Plato said, 'We do understand your question Mac and Adam is right, the best one to answer is Abraham.'

I apologized to Abraham and said, 'I'm all ears!'

'Mac,' Abraham asked, 'who is the greatest man who has ever lived?'

Before I could answer he continued, 'For Muslims it is Mohammed, for Christians Jesus, for Buddhists Buddha and so on. Why are they still remembered and relevant?'

'Because they have received Divine messages' I answered.

'Well there are hundreds, if not thousands of people during the course of human history who have received Divine messages, yet they are hardly remembered,' Abraham replied. 'You see for a world class leader, he must think and act as his prophet, except instead of creating a religion he creates a world class business. Let me be brief and remind you of the fundamentals of forming a lasting religion. Let me also examine how these fundamentals could apply in creating world-class businesses.

'1) Just like a Prophet, a business leader must have great vision. For example Google's vision is, "to organize the world's information and make it universally accessible and useful".

'2) The vision must be supported by principles. All religions have their commandments to guide their followers. This is also the case in business. Every company must have its own guiding principles. For example, Toyota has its own fourteen principles. They call them the "Toyota Way". For example, the right process produces the correct result.

'3) No religion is established without disciples. This is the same in business. The business leaders must have great managers who understand and live the vision and principles.

Without well-trained managers who believe in the vision and principles, no leader will succeed in creating a world-class company.

'4) Many prophets had visions, principles and disciples but they were forgotten by history for the lack of continuous learning. Lasting religion created organizations and places of worship for weekly sermons and trainers to provide continuous learning. To last, businesses must also have evolving organizations and continuous learning. Those who do not train and upgrade the knowledge of their staff become second-class businesses and they are swept away by their competitors.

'5) Religion deals with problems of the day and it is supposed to adapt to last for eons. Those who fail this test bury their followers in darkness. Therefore, businesses must also have an R&D or a research and development department to stay ahead of the game.

'6) Religion builds cultures around all aspects of human life like marriage, death, christening etc. Therefore businesses must do the same to create a sense of pride and identity for the business.

'7) Religious leaders are approachable. Therefore, business leaders must have an open door policy where employees and other stakeholders can approach them and they can find the facts for themselves.

'8) Religion is full of symbolism and rituals. Business branding and handling of daily routines are the way to replicate that.'

Adam interrupted and said, 'So you see Mac, this is not an exercise in theology. However, it is a well tried and tested way for people to remember the path to lead their business to stardom. Let me also tell you that for a person to be a super boss, he must remember all the adjectives that have been given to God in the holy books. In Islam, for example, God has been given ninety-nine names, e.g. the Creator, the Just, the Compassionate, the Listener, the Strong, the Wise, etc. If everyone who hears these names tries to understand their true meaning and put them into practice by becoming just, compassionate, listener, etc, then he will truly become a super boss. This principle also applies to politicians. A good political leader is not how popular he is, but how he makes what matters most popular.'

Plato added, 'By the way, leadership quality starts at home. It is the role of parents and the education system to prepare the children. I believe that what children become, depends on their parents acting as role models and what they discuss at the dinner table.'

I asked if I could make a last question: 'How could we empower the ordinary consumer to penalize businesses who commit unethical conducts?

Adam obliged, 'You need to mobilize the masses into consumer activism. Boycott those who exploit child labour, those who do not provide decent wages and working conditions, those who commit corrupt practices, those who damage the environment, those who pay excessive bonuses to the few at the expense of fair pricing, and so on. This can be achieved by promoting investigative journalism and honouring whistle blowers. If a few businesses are shut down, the shareholders will wake up to the folly of getting business leaders who ignore their customers and the communities.'

As it was getting very late, Adam decided to conclude the formal teaching of this encounter, 'Let me leave you with a few economic guiding principles:

'• Respect individual ownership.

'•Reward long-term risk-taking and restrict short-term speculation

'• Reward individual creativity, work ethics, and genuine hard work.

'• Promote the creation of equal employment opportunities and the payment of fair wages.

'• Challenge and expose activities that create systematic risk to the economy.

'• Promote charitable activities and voluntary work.

'• Establish key indicators to identify human excesses and nip them in the bud.

I looked at Adam and said, 'This is an excellent conclusion to the day and to the formal teachings.'

They all laughed realizing that what I meant was, I couldn't wait for tomorrow's conference call. As Abraham had organized it for the next day, he stood up and recited:

O Man! Wake up, engage your talent, seek new heights
The peaks of wisdom are yours to conquer
Don't be fooled by the wicked picking a fight
Reject rigidities, all faiths can't be right
Don't judge, leave it to the Lord with all His might
Give the needy, help the weak, don't be tight
Start with the near and dear but don't forget those out of sight
Share what you have, be generous, be upright

The thought of being able to ask Moses, Jesus, and Mohammed any question I wanted to was overwhelming. Overflowing with emotion, I wished every one goodnight.

Chapter 8
The Conference Call

It was Friday, the last day of the Encounter. I woke up with strong pious emotions. Am I really going to see and speak to such great holy men? Can I include Jesus in the word men? How would I address them? Why are they here? Is it that serious? So far, my shadows seemed to give rational explanations of some religious texts. They seemed to reconcile differences of various faiths beautifully. Can they really help humanity in creating religious understanding and become a reliable driving force in achieving a Just World Order? Can they suggest ways for effective dialogue between the three monolithic faiths? After all, they have so much in common and they are all descendants of Abraham. Would they talk in one voice or would they show differences as theologians usually do? Would Mohammed recite the verse from Quran (Al Amran 64), "O people of the Book (Jews and Christian), let us come to an agreement on that which is common between us, that we worship no one but God, and make non His compeer, and that none of us take any others for lord apart from God."

As I was immersed in my thoughts and overwhelming emotions, I suddenly noticed that my teachers over the last six days were all staring at me with deep concern.

They walked to my breakfast table and Abraham said, 'Mac, I know this is not going to be easy for you. While we represented mere mortal Souls, you will be seeing the true spirits of the greatest and holiest men that have ever walked on this planet. What they will say and do will have a profound and lasting effect on your understanding of religions and your innermost value system.'

My hand shook like a leaf. As I was holding my cup of tea, I said, 'Thanks for that. You have really made me even more nervous now. Please tell me how this is going to be organized?'

As we were having a chat at the breakfast table, I heard unusual noises and saw flashes of very bright lights from the hall next door.

Plato held my hand and said, 'This is it, let's go.'

I could not stand on my feet as my legs were trembling so much. With the support of Plato on one side and Abraham on the other I was dragged to the hall where all the action was. I closed my eyes as I was assisted by them, thinking that I might wake up from a long and vivid dream. I don't recall how we entered the hall. I felt a gentle hand stroking my head. With some hesitation, I opened my eyes and there were three holy men with glowing white light surrounding their bodies. The one stroking me was Jesus. On his left was Mohammed and on his right was Moses.

As I established eye contact with Mohammed, he said, '*Al-Salam Alaykum.*' *Peace be upon you*, this being a formal greeting in Arabic.

The words to respond did not readily come out of my mouth as I was trembling and my throat felt dry. Finally I replied with, '*Alaykum Al Salam.*' *Peace be upon you, too*.

I was guided to a comfortable chair next to a big round table with the rest joining.

Abraham broke the silence and said, 'Let me explain why our guests are here. I will ask each of them to say a few words before we give you the chance to raise all the questions you may have. This is not a structured session and it has no formal setting. As you may recall Mac, we are here to strengthen the message of peace on Earth. At present, we are confident that Mankind will not endure the coming wars and destruction. Scientific progress is advancing at such a rate with the main aim of speeding up the power of destruction while human morality is moving completely in the opposite direction. The worship of Wealth and Power, combined with the dark forces of ignorance and religious bigotries, has created an explosive combination and it will only end up in bloodshed and tears. Our observations of human written and spoken words in recent times indicate a remarkable march to selfishness and greed compared to care and compassion.'

I could not help stopping him to try to find out how they identified these trends. I noticed that Abraham was pleased that my mind was still functioning.

He responded that it was by looking at the number of times the words: money, bonuses, power, influence, wars, scheming etc have been used as compared with the words: love, care, empathy, duty, responsibility and so on.

After this short digression, the three prophets of these great faiths were asked to make their contributions and give their moral support to the call for world peace and tranquillity. We all knew that without the support of all the open-minded spiritual leaders and just elites, very little can be done to stop and correct this dangerous plunge in individual immorality.

Moses, being the eldest of the three holy men, seemed to have a slight speech impediment. With a reassuring smile he said, 'Let me first apologize on behalf of our common father Abraham for not attending, as he was confident that all those present could adequately cover all the subjects being raised.'

Moses continued, 'By the way Abraham sent you his special regard as you are the direct descendant of Abraham and Jonah.'

I looked at him and said, 'How that can be, I am a Muslim?

Jesus smiled and said, 'Do you doubt our records? There are more Muslims and Christians who are descendants of Abraham than Jews. So don't be surprised if one day a genetic test is done to confirm that. For example, not all European Jews are the descendants of Abraham. One should not get mixed up between religion and ancestry.'

I said, 'God's covenant with Abraham regarding "the Promised Land" spoke of his ancestors inheriting the land.'

Moses smiled and said, 'I think this is an issue that will be clarified in some detail later on.'

I apologized for the interruption and Moses continued, 'I was the one who was chosen by God to lead the twelve tribes of Israel out of bondage in Egypt. I also do acknowledge that the Israelites did leave Palestine voluntarily to join Joseph who was the effective chancellor of the Pharaoh. At that time, Egypt was more than half the civilized world. We had several hundred years of very successful life there. We became very influential and wealthy. Due to the jealousy of some of the ruling elite, pressure was put on successive pharaohs to marginalize us and enslave our people. Finally those close to the pharaoh persuaded him that we were after his kingdom. He finally decreed to kill all newly born male Hebrew infants. I ended up in the pharaoh's palace and learnt all that needed to be learnt regarding the formation of a structured religion and leadership. I think the rest of my story is well known to you Mac, from your reading of the Quran and the Old Testament.'

Moses continued, 'I was ordered by Elohim (God) to lead my people out of Egypt. I refused to use force to enter Palestine, as it was not compatible with the Ten Commandments I had just received from my Lord. It would have been an act of utmost hypocrisy and great sin to breach Elohim's top commandment, "Thou Shall Not Kill" for the sake of a land that Jacob and his eleven children left to join Joseph. After all, only Isaac, Jacob and his twelve children were born in Palestine and they were all a distant history by the time we left Egypt. The rest of us were all born in Pharaoh's land over more than 600 years. The covenant with our father Abraham ceased to exist due to putting wealth in Egypt ahead of keeping the covenant. The only way to re-enter Palestine, as decreed by the Lord in Sinai, was through peaceful means and in agreement with its inhabitants. Let me repeat here and now, the Lord was angered when Jacob and his twelve children abandoned Palestine in pursuit of wealth and power in Pharaoh's Egypt. Elohim threatened to place a curse on the Hebrews who occupied the land, unless it was done peacefully and justly. This is why I elected to die in the wilderness. I refused to enter Palestine against the wishes of its people. I am telling you this in some detail Mac, because I know most of today's religious misunderstanding, including this war, has been manipulated to support a secular Jewish movement to reclaim Palestine under the pretext of the Promised Land. Therefore, you see, I am completely innocent of their deeds. There are also many Jews who are still bound by the teaching of the Torah and in complete opposition to this act.'

Jesus commented, 'According to my teaching, I fully agree with what Moses has just said as the Jews have already broken my Father's covenant with Abraham.' He then winked at me for using the words "My Father".

Moses continued, 'Let me also repeat what has already been said regarding the claim that the Jews are "God's Chosen People", and what this really means. Elohim blessed the descendants of Noah with a unique power to tune into the Divine Dimension through meditation. They are tasked to continuously update human morality by their ethical and moral conducts. After the establishment of a formal religion, instead of accepting and honouring this role, the rabbis in power refused to listen to subsequent messengers of the Lord. Elohim had no alternative but to send Jesus as the Saviour to warn the Israelites to stick to the covenant of serving God. To impress the descendents of Noah, Elohim empowered Jesus with many miracles so that they could not mistake or doubt His Divine mission.

'They chose to be blinded by the privileges they were enjoying rather than listen to the message of the Lord. They ultimately conspired with the Romans and had Jesus crucified. That was when Elohim finally declared that He no longer needed the Israelites to be his chosen people. Elohim then chose a Bedouin with no education to start a great religion without the help of the Israelites. Therefore, to say that Elohim favours the Hebrews in any way other than due to their good deeds upsets the Lord a good deal. The mere thought that Elohim is a discriminating Creator is obscene and a sin in the eyes of the Lord.'

Jesus quoted from the Bible regarding equality with slight modification in compliance with his explanation of his role in this universe. Galatians 3:28 ESV: "There is neither Jew nor Greek, there is neither slave nor free, there is no male and female, for you are all one in Jesus Christ (i.e. one in the eyes of the Lord)."

Colossians 3:9-11 ESV: "Do not lie to one another, seeing that you have put off the old self with its practices and have put on the new self, which is being renewed in knowledge after the image of its creator. Here there is not Greek and Jew, circumcised and uncircumcised, barbarian, Scythian, slave, free; but Christ is one, and in all."

Abraham smiled and looked at me to expand on the above biblical text. Then he said, 'You see Mac, "putting on the new self" means uplifting once moral code. "Being renewed in knowledge after the image of the creator" is to spell out that the purpose of the Lord creating man is for the latter to use his talents and ultimately to renew the seeds of life. Christ in one and in all, means that Christ with the help of the Holy Spirit is accessible by all who seeks his help.'

I thanked Abraham for this important clarification, looked at Moses and asked, 'How can one resolve this contradiction? You have been speaking about God's covenant with Abraham, yet during this encounter I have been told repeatedly that God does not get involved in the details.'

Plato could not stop himself from answering this question. He said, 'Like any human system of government, everyone issues orders in the name of the king. It is the same in the Divine Dimension or as Jesus calls it "The Kingdom of Heaven". Those Souls (Angels) trusted by the Creator to maintain the moral codes of all intelligent beings, are the ones who speak in the name of the Lord. To a human being what difference does it make if all the orders communicated by the Angels are released in the name of the Lord?'

They all looked at me for a comment. I replied, 'Nothing, nothing at all. I will then continue to use the word "God, the Lord, the Father" when I really mean Jesus and the Angles in the DD. Presumably the Angels address the one and only God as "My Father", being the ultimate Creator of the universe.'

They all looked at Jesus and smiled.

Moses continued and said, 'By the way, Elohim now regards all those who uphold the moral codes and conduct themselves virtuously as "God's Chosen People". Here in the DD we always talk about how all intelligent beings, on all planets, will be "God's Chosen People" if they keep cosmic virtues. Their souls will be chosen for activation to dwell in the Kingdom of Heaven.'

Mohammed thought it was appropriate to mention a verse from the Quran in this respect, "You were 'God's Chosen People' who command good deeds and prevent evil ones."

I was pleased to see how a better liberal and rational understanding of some themes in all holy books could stop so much misunderstanding and confusion. I was encouraged to ask another question.

I looked at Moses and said, 'If the Jews no longer hold to these two principles, namely the "Promised Land" and being "God's Chosen People", then what will be left to keep their tribal instinct together as they have done for more than 3000 years?'

Mosses felt very excited and actually came up to me and hugged me. 'You are absolutely right. There is no need to adhere to a tribal instinct in a global world. We are here to prepare Mankind for the giant leap to peace and tranquillity. There is no room for any group to bury themselves in the past.'

Mohammed said in a firm voice, 'This is also the case with some Muslims who insist on trying to physically imitate the way I dressed and looked more than 1400 years ago, while they ignore the fundamentals of my message. There are so many distortions to the true teachings of Islam.'

I asked Moses, 'What should the key message of Judaism be in today's world?'

Moses responded without hesitation, 'The true message is the continuous renewal of the moral code to free humanity from the bondage of money, hate and conflict. The Lord demands virtuous conduct and equal respect towards all human beings, which would lead to peaceful coexistence. Humanity at present is at the height of inequality, at the height of injustice and at the height of exploiting human weaknesses leading to widespread violence and destruction. It is vital for all men to walk, hand in hand, to the "Kingdom of Love and Justice". Tranquillity and justice are so precious and so eternally true. I tell you Mac, if one lives his life without finding an issue which deserves to be addressed, then he must be living on a different planet.'

I continued questioning Moses, as he seemed to recall his encounter at Mount Sinai and being uninhibited with his answers. 'What did you think of Jesus and Mohammed when they came after you and asked the Jews to believe in their messages?'

Moses responded after looking at Jesus and Mohammed. 'My answer is obvious regarding Jesus' and Mohammed's calls, although it may sound strange to you. In the Divine Dimension, there are no such labels as Jews, Christians, Muslims, Buddhists and Hindus and so on. What matters are the contents of peoples' characters and their belief in the one God. These labels apply to the rituals and the traditions of the religious institutions. The core of any religion is the moral codes as commanded by God. You see, Islam for example, regards everyone as Muslim if he submits to the teachings of the Lord. Unfortunately, rituals have become like women's make up. A human may be fooled by an attractive face but not Elohim. What matters is what is in the inside, no matter how beautiful that person is on the outside.'

'I see,' said I. 'So then you are supporting the teachings in this encounter and accept that the followers of all faiths should be true participants in leading the world to true peace based on quality and respect for all?'

The three holy guests strongly agreed. Moses's eyes were still locked onto mine, expecting me to continue.

As I kept silent, Moses continued to explain how all prophets receive holy messages. He continued, 'Messages or commandments are delivered as thoughts to be converted into spoken or written text by the messenger, or at a later date by his disciples. This is where weakness creeps into the wordings being used and leads to untold hardship when those words are treated as the absolute truth. In most cases, those ideas can only be understood by relating them to the specific reasons they were delivered to the named messenger at the relevant time. Often this conversion of thoughts to written text (in some cases after considerable time) and subsequent separation of the message from the causes of its uttering, leads to a completely different meaning from that originally intended. The background of the messenger has a great influence on converting thoughts and visions to spoken or written words.'

I looked at Moses and said, 'It is clear to me that at the heart of all religions are effective moral teachings, otherwise those religions would not have survived the test of time. Before you conclude, could you give us some quotes from the Torah relevant to this Encounter?'

He looked at me and said, 'I will be very brief, as I know we do not have much time.' He then started with his quotes by highlighting some principles of morality:

The Golden Rule Quotes: "Love your neighbour as yourself. I am God" (Leviticus 19:18). "Let the honour of your friend be as important to you as your own". "Do not rejoice when your enemies fall, or let your heart feel joy when they stumble, lest the Lord see and turn His displeasure to you".

A few quotes on Good Thoughts, Speech and Action: "Say little and do much, and receive all men with a cheerful face. Initiate a greeting to everyone, and it is better to be a tail to a lion than a head of a fox. Be careful of politicians, they are your friends when it is to their advantage, but they abandon you in your time of need."

Avoidance of Deadly Sins: "The more flesh you have, the more the worms will eat. Don't get angry easily, and repent one day before you die. Do not look at the flask but look at what is inside it. There is a fancy bottle with bad wine in it".

Avoidance of Greed and Speculation: "According to the effort is the reward". "I returned and saw under the sun that, the race is not to the swift, nor the battle to the strong, nor bread to the wise, yet they are all the same when a time of disaster falls upon them."

They all looked at me to see if I understood the profound implication of what is being said by Moses.

I said, 'It is obvious that if followers of the all faiths adhere to these principles, the world will be a different place today. I am sure that this will create a better interfaith dialogue to achieve world peace through core teachings of all religions?'

Moses looked at Jesus as if it was the time for him to commence.

Jesus looked somehow different from the other two venerable Holy men. I assumed that his virgin birth had something to do with that.

Jesus said, "My first task is to explain to Mac who am I. This is not going to be easy, as so much of humanity thinks I am literally the son of God. The decision in the Kingdom of Heaven was taken to lead from the front. The decision was made to send "Earth's Divine Governor" to dwell in a human body from birth.'

They all looked at Jesus. I got the hint. It was Jesus (Earth's Divine Governor) who was tasked to do the job himself. This would allow Him to live in accordance with the tradition of the Israelites in order to create a circle of trust and get them to adhere to their role in upgrading the human moral code.

Jesus continued, 'You see Mac, I am half human and half Divine Soul. I had full access to the powers of the Divine Dimension. This explains my abilities to perform all those miracles with the objective of creating the correct paradigm shift. I was hoping that those miracles would shake up the established Jewish religious institutions to recognise that God means business this time. I also hoped that they would return to the true virtues of the descendants of Noah.

'They did not take this last chance to repent. My original message was to the Jews only. I was fulfilling a Jewish prophesy of how the Messiah will enter Jerusalem on a donkey and be crucified on the cross and then this would be followed by a resurrection. It was only after my crucifixion that I instructed Paul, during my encounter with him "On the road to Damascus", to extend the message to the gentile. I think you have already been told that God is not of the physical form. He is neither similar to humans nor to any other intelligent being. No one can perceive his form or looks. I do confirm that we in the DD also do not know what God looks like. We know He is the ultimate Creator and he is in control of the Divine Dimension as was explained to you at length. How could one believe in the oneness of God and at the same time believe that he has children? There are thousands, if not millions of other intelligent beings that exist, or have existed during the continuous life of the universe. If God has one child per planet then he will have the biggest family one can imagine. The concept of oneness would then become really untenable.'

I looked at Jesus, 'You are adamant then, to explain away the concept of trinity in Christianity?'

He quickly responded, 'This should not be the case. God exists as one and this is not in doubt. The Holy Spirit exists as the Divine Dimension and gives powers to those who correctly tune into it. Moreover, there is me, Jesus, as Earth's Divine Governor being tasked to see human salvation until the End of Times. So in that sense, the trinity concept exists and there is no contradiction with the singularity of the Creator.'

Mohammed responded in support of Jesus by saying, 'According to Islamic teachings, the messiah will return at the End of Time and there will be no differences between Muslims, Jews or Christians as Moses said. After all, the oneness of God and adherence to the Universal Moral Code will determine the faith of the individual. The labels and rituals are completely of personal nature and relevant only to the structure of the religious institutions.'

Looking at Jesus I said, 'I think there will be many who will challenge this explanation, as your death on the Cross is at the core of Christian theology. You have been presented as the one who washes away all the sins of those who repent and believe in your resurrection.'

'Let me explain,' Jesus responded. 'The exact objective of this encounter is to get all men of faith and decency to become active missionaries for peace and justice. We are all confident that if one ignores religious institutional rigidities and focuses on core values, then universal virtues will be applied within a reasonable time. However, as human beings have a tendency to stray in search of wealth and power and these are deep-seated in their genes, the need for religious institutions with liberal leaderships becomes very helpful. The key is to get these institutions away from the domination by those who mix their personal interests with that of the fundamental teachings of their faith. This can only be done by the continuous vigilance of all decent people to challenge all men who preach hate and bury their heads in ignorance.

'The act of repentance applies to followers of all faiths. To repent is to rewire one's brain and free it from the inner evil. The act of repentance with great emotional feelings leads to the release of chemicals in the body which make the reprogramming of one's value system more permanent.'

I couldn't help laughing and said, 'Yes, Darwin explained how the chemical released when one is having one's first kiss makes that memory permanent. Let me ask you another question then. How do you explain the rigid teachings of Christianity when you said, "I am the truth and the light, and only through me can man pass to the kingdom of Heaven".'

He looked for an answer from Moses or Mohammed, as they knew what that meant.

Moses volunteered to answer. 'You see Mac, Elohim does not sit in judgment over every created intelligent being in the universe. I think you agree that that would be rather boring and a near impossibility. As you have been told, God creates processes. One of these processes is to judge if intelligent beings have passed the compliance test with the ethical and moral codes as explained before. Each planet has a Governor (or a Senior Divine Soul) to check observance of God's laws. To ensure fairness in the process, the one put in charge of judging all the people on Earth when they die, must be a Divine Spirit originated from another planet. This will ensure justice, transparency and independence.'

I turned to Jesus and said, 'I see, so you are then the one to judge, not in your capacity as a prophet of the Christian faith, but as the appointed "Divine Earth's Governor". Of course, this is why you have been mentioned in the Quran more than any other prophet including Mohammed. This is why you will return at the end of time. Therefore, you will judge the followers of all faiths as to the degree of their compliance with the evolving ethical values. You will not favour Christians over Jews, Muslims or followers of any other faith.'

'No,' he responded, 'and it will be an insult to think that I will be anything but just and impartial. I will treat all humans equally based on their deeds alone. You see, during my brief period of existence on Earth I did not ask for a new religion to be formed. It was Mankind who established a formal, unified Christian religion to preserve my calling for love and peace almost three hundred years after my birth.'

I thought the time had come to ask him about the crucifixion. 'Muslims believe that you were not crucified but it appeared that you were. This is one of the major points of contention between the two major faiths. How do you explain that?'

Jesus looked at Mohammed for the answer.

Mohammed obliged and said, 'Let me explain, although by now it must be obvious what the Quran meant. The essence of Jesus was not the physical son of Mary in flesh and blood, but Jesus the "Agent of the Lord" residing in that body. As you cannot crucify a Soul, the true Jesus was not crucified but returned to the Divine Dimension. The physical body was crucified and then stolen by the authorities to ensure that the prophecy of the resurrection within three days of the crucifixion would not come true. Remember, the Jews do not believe in the Divine Spirit of Jesus nor did they acknowledge his miracles. They called Jesus the son of Joseph, the carpenter from Ghalali. So, Jesus returned to his disciples in the same way we are appearing to you now and stayed with them for forty days travelling around without the impediment of the physical body.'

'Wow!' I exclaimed. 'This how he walked on water. You seem to have come well prepared to answer all the questions humans have been asking and sometimes fighting over. It really seems very silly now, how simple answers could strengthen the faith of the people and at the same time create religious harmony on Earth.'

I asked Jesus casually, 'Why then did you not make these revelations earlier to save all this confusion?'

Jesus answered with a rather serious tone, 'It is not Divine policy to regularly interfere with the debate of the people unless we see major disasters in the making.'

I was rather scared to hear that, and asked, 'What could occur worse than what is already happening? Invasion of Iraq by the mightiest power ever created on Earth is being waged under the pretext of "Weapons of Mass Destruction". Some are killing the innocent in the name of jihad and others are committing great injustices in the name of the Promised Land. What more should we expect?'

I continued, looking at my visitors, 'Before Jesus finishes his contribution for the day, I would like to hear from Him about His favourite quotes from the Bible to support your message for humanity.'

Jesus, with his usual long hair, flowing robes and gentle smile continued with his favourite quotes:

'God's original plan for all his creations: Jeremiah 29:11 "For I know the plans I have for you, declares the LORD, plans for welfare and not for evil, to give you a future and a hope."

'The Golden Rule: 1 John 4:7-8 "Beloved, let us love one another, for love is from God, and whoever loves has been born of God and knows God. Anyone who does not love does not know God, because God is love."

I interrupted and asked, 'I thought you said you do not know what God is made of? Now you are telling me that God is love.'

They all smiled, as they were happy to see me challenging everything that is not consistent with what I have been told.

Jesus looked at me and said, 'You seem to understand your fellow human beings very well. They will challenge every word you will convey from this encounter. I think you have been told in the holy books that the use of the word God is taken to mean the Almighty Allah, and the Holy Spirit. Therefore, when my disciples conveyed my message about the importance of Love, they wanted to equate all God's power to the power of love. With true love, humanity will see its salvation. It is time to give those morally defective biological units a "Love pill" to stop aggression and suicide."

Mohammed commented, 'In the Quran and in other holy books, the Lord has been given many names like, "The Just, the Tolerant, the Compassionate, the Merciful, the Patient, the Giver, the Wise, the Creative, the Listener, the Expert, the Knowing, and so on". These are adjectives or titles given to the Lord so that humans are reminded of what the Almighty God expects them to adopt in their daily activities if they are to be regarded as virtuous enough to dwell in Heaven.'

Jesus thanked Mohammed for the clarification and continued, 'The principle of evolving moral codes and seeking knowledge: Romans 12:2: "Do not conform any longer to the pattern of this world, but be transformed by the renewing of your mind. Then you will be able to test and approve what God's will is – His good, pleasing and perfect will."

'The Principle of Soul Activation: Romans 6:23: "For the wages of sin is death (non activation of the Soul after death), but the gift of God is eternal life (activation of the Soul as Abraham explained)"

'The Principle of humility: Micah 6:8: "He has showed you, O man, what is good and what does the LORD require of you? To act justly, to love with mercy and to walk humbly with your God."

'The Powers of the DD and definition of the Soul: Romans 15:13: "May the God of hope fill you with all joy and peace as you trust in him, so that you may overflow with hope by the power of the Holy Spirit".

'1 Corinthians 6:19: "Do you not know that your body is a temple of the Holy Spirit, who is in you, whom you have received from God? You are not on your own."

'New criteria have been declared to be regarded as God's New Chosen People: Colossians 3:12: "Therefore, as 'God's Chosen People', holy and dearly loved, clothe yourselves with compassion, kindness, humility, gentleness, and patience."

Abraham thanked Jesus, knowing that it takes months to summarize the good words of the Lord and winked at Mohammed to start his observations.

Mohammed thanked Abraham and all those present and said, 'It may be time for me to say something now. I am sure that Mac has heard the story of my background about being

278

from a prominent family in Mecca. I was not educated by a pharaoh nor was I half Divine. I was an orphan without any education. You could not have a bigger contrast in comparison with Moses and Jesus. At that time, there were Jews and Christians in Mecca and Medina but the majority where non-believers in the oneness of God. It was about the seventh century AD and the established religious institutions had already strayed from the core teachings. With much meditation and soul searching on "Mount Hara", I received the first revelation to call for seeking knowledge and confirm the powers of the Creator. My message was to supplement the moral messages in the previous holy books of Moses and Jesus. You see, I was the first prophet in the region outside the tribes of Israel.'

Mohammed continued, 'So my message was not to compel people to convert from one faith to another. This is not God's way of judging the actions of Mankind. I came to update the moral codes of those who have strayed from the true spiritual and moral teachings of their faiths. At that time, there was a lack of emphasis on spirituality. Too much importance was given to materialism. This is why a heavy emphasis was placed on praying and fasting in Islam compared to Christianity. Mercy and compassion was a key part of the new teaching. Muslims are reminded of that at the start of every Surah (chapter) in the Quran. Patience and tolerance were emphasized as people where easy to anger. My message was to urge people to be proactive in all aspects of their lives to lift the community from poverty and continuous conflict. The policy of live and let live with people of other faiths was encouraged.

'Islam flourished, and in the first 100 years or so it expanded at the fastest pace ever known to Mankind. Due to this rapid spread of Islam, many new converts to the faith did not have sufficient time to adapt to the true teaching of Islam.

Instead, they retained their tribal and other traditions. The deep-seated evils in every man resurfaced to replace the call for moderation, tolerance and compassion.'

Mohammed continued, 'Like in all other established religions, the search for worldly desires was the driving force among those in the religious hierarchy and very quickly Islam was used as a convenient way to control the population. Hereditary rules for Khilafa were introduced. Succession usually occurred through in-fighting or assassinations. With the absence of a formal education based on rationalism and with continuous division and conflict, the people reverted to their tribal cultures. Exceptional periods of Islamic revival appeared when the rulers were just and guided by its true ethical values. They allowed scholars to approach Greek and other literatures and encouraged education and science. Philosophy and Islamic theology were not seen to contradict each other. Islam, being the last major religion, had to embrace the principle of evolving ethical codes. The principle of *ijtihad*, or continuous improvement or deduction, was introduced to keep the faith relevant to the life of all Muslims.

'I tell you Mac, ignoring *ijtihad* is the same as ignoring the faith itself. When scholars were buried in ignorance, abandoned philosophy and sciences, a long period of darkness appeared, in all the areas governing Muslim life. While the rest of the world raced away in broad-mindedness and creativity, Muslims buried themselves in rigidity and irrational conformity to traditions incompatible with twenty-first century requirements. Over time, a huge gap developed between those who adhered to ancient tribal heritage and the West, who kept the scientific wheel of knowledge moving at an ever-faster pace. Today, some Muslims attach more importance on trying to imitate how I looked and dressed instead of adhering to the love and tolerance I was showing to those who disagreed with me. Such individuals find it easier to imitate than to be inquisitive and learned men.'

I looked at Mohammed and asked, 'What is the problem with people trying to imitate you in every little detail? You have been identified by some modern scholars as the greatest man who has ever lived on this planet. If individuals manage to look and perform their rituals like you did, then society will be wonderful.'

He looked at his colleagues and said, 'This is a good question. Let me see why it is not working, then. If I were to live on Earth today, should I dress up and look exactly the same as I did then? Is man to be judged by how he looks and the way he dresses? Would I use a car, a mobile phone, listen to music, be in an office with women working next to me, and travel on airplanes? Those who think that the essence of Islam is by dressing like me, growing their beards and shaving their moustaches like me and praying and fasting as I did, are missing the point.

'My essence is not how I looked, but how I handled issues that faced the community. My essence is how I applied ethics and compassion and how I met with love and tolerance those who abused me. I think all Muslims know that I adhered to top moral codes in all my business dealings. Most Muslims are taught how to pray and they are proud to say that they pray regularly. When you ask them about the essence of Islam, they stare you in the eyes as if you are speaking in a foreign language. Others are quick to say that the essence of Islam is to pray, fast and visit Mecca. I say to them: No, No, No, the essence of Islam is to commit to the moral code first and the rituals come second. You know Mac, corruption is more widespread in Muslim countries than in Europe? This does not mean that Islam condones corruption. Of course it doesn't. What it really means is that the millions, who call themselves Muslim, are in fact ignorant. The devil within each of them is highly in control, yet they claim to be Muslims. In doing so, they are distorting the message of Islam. As Adam explained to you, economic well-being is the reflection of the individuals' ethics and cultural heritage. Most failed states are in the Muslim world in recent times. Islamic teachers are graduating from schools that emphasize rituals rather than ethics, adherence to the past rather than preparing for the future, obedience rather than renewal, admiring perceived glorious past rather than working for a better future. There is an absence of emphasis on creativity, sciences and philosophy. Rational thinking is fundamental to the key Islamic principle of *ijtihad* (or continuous evolution of ethical values); yet it is almost completely absent in Muslims vocabularies.'

Mohammed continued, 'For countries inflicted with corruption, they should adopt zero tolerance to such practices. There is no room for the "Lion or the Insects" to be exempted". You see Mac, "Corruption should be seen as the worst type of economic terrorism whether it is committed by those in charge or those at the lowest levels of government.". It deprives the innocent from their equal opportunity in achieving success. It enriches the evil doers, it corrupts politics and creates a generation of sceptics. Corruption involves the wicked givers and the evil takers of bribes. No mercy should be given to all those who commit these obscene acts, no matter how global the organization is or how senior and powerful the individuals are. All countries need anti-corruption activists who are ready to risk all by blowing the whistle on this sinful practice. International foundations to fight corruption should be supported by all decent human beings. Whistle blowers and corruption

282

antagonists are to be nominated for Nobel Prize for Peace if they lead to removing the evil of corruption.'

Then Mohammed continued to explain how current teachers of faith, mostly unintentionally, are abusing religion. He said, 'The Quran and Hadeeths (my sayings and deeds) are misunderstood and frequently taken out of context. Those who are thoughtful and rational in their approach are drowned and intimidated by the few who are ready to use money and violence to shut them up. Let me give you a simple example of how virtues have been hijacked by ignorance and sold to people as the prophet's teaching. This is not supposed to be a joke but a real story. I am aware of a man who attended a lunch serving camel meat in Saudi Arabia in the last decade of twentieth century. This is a period of true rational thinking in human history. Before finishing the meal, the host said rather seriously, "He who has just eaten camel meat should do 'Ablution' before the next prayer". When he enquired about the logic behind this teaching, the reply came very quickly, "Because Prophet Mohammed Said So". That man had true faith in my ethical and rational thinking. He asked if someone could explain what exactly happened which made the prophet makes such pronouncement. The explanation went like this: At a similar luncheon invitation, in the presence of the Prophet, one of the invitees broke wind, and therefore he must re-do "Ablution" before next prayer according to the Islamic tradition. Therefore, the gentleman being educated and a rationalist screamed loudly, "Oh My God! What the Prophet did was to instruct all those who were present to do Ablution to avoid embarrassing the one who broke wind. This is nothing to do with eating camel meat. This is like ordering them to apply the Golden Rule, "Do unto others as you like others to do unto you".'

Mohammed continued, 'You see how sad I am? It is because of the many irrational things committed in my name and in the name of Islam. I tell you now Mac, any act of irrationalism or inflicting pain committed as part of Islam must be strongly challenged, reviewed and corrected. If they cannot find the correct interpretation in support of universal virtues, then I assure you that the Hadeeth is incorrect or that it is interpreted out of context as I have explained before. Any interpretation that advocates violence (not in self-defence) has nothing to do with Islam. I would like to see increased emphasis on rational thinking. I would like to see parents spending greater time and money on the education of their children and specially the girls who are the natural teachers at home. I would like to see Muslims learn philosophy and think independently. I would like to see them challenge all negative aspects of their traditions and build on the positive ones. They should learn foreign languages to fulfil Allah's command as stated in Quran, "I created you as male and female and made you nations and tribes to get to know one another. My blessings are to those who are virtuous." Look at the millions who are not Muslim. They are busy advancing knowledge and living mostly in harmony and peace. It is time for all Muslims to examine their ways. It is time to learn from other cultures, and it is time to act and build a better future for all. Those who call for reliving the past in the name of faith are committing their community to cultural poverty and perpetual stagnation.'

Darwin with some hesitation made the comment, 'The world around them will move on. They risk letting the unrelenting evolutionary process hard codes what they do into how their future offspring will be. This will be regrettable and cause irreversible damage which should be avoided at any cost.'

Mohammed looked at Darwin and recognized the stark consequences that could result from putting human talent in deep freeze in the name of adherence to religious teaching. He continued, 'How could so many Muslims have gone astray from seeking peace, wisdom and compassion? Islam's original message has called humanity away from the worship of the ego. Every individual bears the duties and responsibilities to serve others. True Muslims should be ambassadors to their faith. They should not shame it with labels of ignorance and violence. True Muslims should rise above their prejudices and selfishness. They should act for true peace on Earth, even if that takes centuries. Peaceful resistance and power of the argument is greater than the might of the fists and the sound of guns. History favours persistent rational thinkers who can touch the hearts of others in humility and the power of their argument. I am innocent of all the acts of terror committed in my name. All Muslims need a strong foundation based on love for genuine awakening.'

We all realized the strong passion Mohammed was expressing and continued, 'Muslims should master how to communicate with each other, no matter which sect they belong to. They should endorse fully interfaith dialogue at individual and group levels. For such dialogue to be effective, they need to:

'a) Reach beyond suspicion and fear of one another by sharing stories and experiences. Gain a true understanding of the core teachings of the various faiths and traditions. Understand how some of the verses and callings of one another's holy books are consistent with the core teachings and how some verses are not consistent and must not be allowed to hinder co existence.

'b) All parties must be willing to enter into a more difficult conversation like the injustices committed in the name of the "Promised Land".'

'c) Interfaith dialogue should address the issues of religious exclusivity and inequality between men and women. This need not be the case if we accept the principle of rational openness and apply the principle of "live and let live". It is written in the Quran, "you have your traditions, and I have mine". This means that all should deal with each other with civility and respect.

'd) One should keep in mind that relationships are healed by willingness to identify the differences and face them head on. Moses and Jesus have already dealt with some of what has been regarded as absolute truth within each religion.

I looked at Mohammed as he was reaching the end of his observations and asked him to mention a few quotes from the Quran and Hadeeths that will support what has been said during this encounter.

'Sure,' he quickly responded. Then he started with the quotes from the Quran:

'Principle of Moderation: "And let not your hand be tied (like a miser) to your neck, nor stretched forth to its utmost reach" (to be wasteful) [al-Isra' 17:29]

'Principle of Humility: And walk NOT on the Earth with conceit and arrogance" (al-Isra' 17:37)

'Al Fargan (83): "People of the Lord are those who walk with humility on the Earth and when they are addressed by the ignorant, they say: Peace."

'Principle of Sanctity of human life: "God does not forbid you to be kind and equitable to those who have neither fought against your faith nor driven you out of your homes. In fact God loves the equitable." Qur'an:60:8

'Principle for Religious Dialogue and unity of all faiths: "And in the footsteps of the earlier prophets we sent Jesus the son of Mary, confirming the law that had come before him. We sent him the Gospel, therein was guidance, light and confirmation of the law that had come before him, guidance and admonition to those who fear God." Qur'an:5:46

'Principle of holding the individual responsible for his words and actions: "Whoever recommends and helps a good cause becomes a partner therein, and whoever recommends and helps an evil cause shares in its burdens." Qur'an:4:85

'Principle that only the Soul of the righteous will be given eternal life: "Whoever works with righteousness, man, or woman, and has faith, verily, to them will we give a new Life, a life that is good and pure, and We will bestow on such their reward according to the best of their actions." Qur'an:16:97

Then Mohammed turned to quotes from Hadeeth.

'Principle of promoting family values: "The best charity is that given to a relative who does not like you." Fiqh-us-Sunnah: V3N100

'Principle of religious moderation: "Religion is very easy, and whoever overburdens himself in his religion will not be able to continue in that way. So you should not be extremists, but try to do things in moderation to receive reward." Bukhari: V1N38

'The Principle forbidding corruption and speculation: I was asked as to what constitutes honest earning: "From a man's decent work and every lawful business transaction". Al-Tirmidhi: 846

'The Principle that God favours creative people: "The learned are heirs of the prophets, and prophets do not leave any inheritance in the form of (monetary wealth), but they do leave knowledge as their legacy. A person, who acquires knowledge, acquires his full share (of this legacy)." Riyadh-us-Salaheen: 1388

'The Principle of activism for good causes: "The best *jihad* is to speak words of justice to an oppressive ruler." Sunan of Abu-Dawood: 2040

'The Principle of love thy neighbor: "A person will not enter Paradise if his neighbour is not secure from his wrongful conduct." Muslim: 15

'The Principle of having good thoughts, speech and action: "People who will receive God's reward are: a just ruler, a young man who passed his youth in humility and in the service of others, a person who was invited to sin but declined, saying 'I fear God' and the one who spends his charity in secret, without making a show." Riyadh-us-Salaheen: 376

'The Principle dealing with human rights: "*God* has revealed to me that you should adopt humility so that no one oppresses another." Riyadh-us-Salaheen: 1589

'The Principle of avoiding deadly sins: "Avoid jealousy, for it destroys good deeds as fire destroys wood." Riyadh-us-Salaheen: 1569

Mohammed looked at all those present and said, 'Islam is a religion of peace and moderation, of family values and virtues. I am deeply saddened by the few who are making the devil within them preach extremism. This is the ultimate *kiffer* (blasphemy). Unfortunately, due to their ignorance, they know not what they are doing. They should repent or they will be condemned to eternal rejection. Man's unforgivable sin is to believe blindly in all what he is being told without exercising his better judgment to do "Good Deeds and Reject Evil Ones" as God has commanded.'

During Lunch, I wanted to know what Mohammed thought of the use of talent, as it is the main reason God has created man.

Mohammed responded, 'First let me tell you what talent is not. It is not imitating what is most popular or profitable. It is not reciting verses from holy books without reflection and understanding. It is not accumulation of wealth or getting into privileged positions.

'Let me now give a hint as to what talent could look like. If you were hungry and lost in the desert, how would you survive? You will look for every unusual pattern in the surrounding sands and hope you will uncover some hidden food for you to pick up and eat. To search and to use one's energy productively is essential for survival. Talent is like that. It is to look in unfamiliar places for the unexpected and make sense out of it. It is to stay hungry for the unusual and to be recognized. If it were that obvious then it would not have been waiting for you to be found. Stay on the road of discovery, stay alert, and seek continuous improvement. Once you are satisfied with that you have achieved, you will experience the beginning of your decline.'

I looked at Mohammed and asked, 'Why is the same religion practiced differently according to this or that tradition of the people?'

Mohammed gave a brief response, 'Faith is a combination of tradition and moral codes. With time, they cannot differentiate between the two and the tradition becomes part of the religion. This in turn could subject society to backwardness, ignorance, and rigidities in the name of religion.'

Abraham asked if I had any more questions as we were to conclude the encounter. Uncontrollably, a lot of tears started to pour out of my eyes.

I said, 'Before I have a farewell message from each of their holinesses followed by some predictions, can I ask Abraham and Plato to tell me something about Buddhism and Hinduism. I am sure that all religions have something positive to offer.'

They looked at each other and Plato said, 'This is not going to be a quick farewell then. Let us sit down comfortably.'

Abraham started with a very brief summary on Hinduism and Plato chose Buddhism due the prevalence of rationalism in that teaching.

Abraham then commented on the basic teachings of the Hindu faith, 'Hindu ethics are related to reincarnation, which is a way of expressing the need for reciprocity, as one may end up in someone else's shoes in his next incarnation. Intention is seen as very important. Selfless actions for the benefit of others, without thought for oneself, is an important rule in Hinduism, known as the doctrine of karma yoga. Someone else's unfortunate situation, while of their own doing, is considered the observer's own situation since the Soul is shared by all. More emphasis is placed on empathy than in other traditions, and women are sometimes upheld, not only as great moral examples but also as great gurus.'

Then Abraham continued to explain how some of the elements mentioned during this encounter, like vibration, the Soul and the DD have already been incorporated into the Hindu religion. The quotes below are from Hindus teachings.

1. Recognition of the eternity of the universe:

Most humbly, we bow to You, O Supreme Lord. At Your command moves the mighty wheel of time (the photon). You are eternal, and beyond eternity.

The whole mantram AUM (the DD) is Indivisible, interdependent, goes on reverberating in the mind. Established in this cosmic vibration, the sage (the soul) goes beyond fear, decay, and death to enter into infinite peace (into eternal life). (*Prashna Upanishad*).

I looked at Abraham and said, 'This is very interesting. This is similar to Genesis revisited passed onto me during this encounter. God at his command created the photon and time resulted as the by-product. The DD is interdependent with the vibrating photon, with the atom creating gravity and with the living cell creating the Soul. I wonder why people of different faiths don't talk to each other more often and share experiences and find the truth.'

2. Minimize total conscious pain and sufferings of all living beings:

The one who loves all intensely begins perceiving in all living beings a part of oneself. He becomes a lover of all, a part and parcel of the Universal Joy. He flows with the stream of happiness, and is enriched by each Soul. (*Artharva Veda*)

Hinduism calls for vegetarianism and an ideology of reducing harm leading ultimately to nonviolence. It is about the active creation of truth through courage. It calls for rejection of cowardice and concern with pain or bodily harm.

After Gandhi's profound achievement of forcing out the British Raj from India, these views spread widely and influenced much modern thinking on ethics today, especially in the peace movement, ecology movement and those devoted to social activism.

I heard Mohammed whispering to Abraham, 'Muslims need to learn from the likes of Gandhi and Mandela and clothe themselves in tolerance and compassion?'

3. The human body interacts with the DD creating the Soul:

The human body is the temple of God (man is blessed with talent in the image of God). The one who kindles the light of awareness within (who complies the UMC), is the one who gets true light. The sacred flame of your inner shrine (Your Soul) is constantly bright. The experience of unity is the fulfilment of human endeavours (ultimate human objective is to dwell in the DD). (*Rig Veda*)

4. The existence of the eternal soul:

The all-knowing Self (The Soul) was never born, nor will it die. Beyond cause and effect, this Self is eternal and immutable. When the body dies, the Spirit (Soul) does not die. (*Katha Upanishad*)'

Bright but hidden, the Spirit dwells in the heart (the physical body). Everything that moves, breathes, opens, and closes lives in the Self (the interaction between the cells and the Soul). (*Mundaka Upanishad*)

5. All are in continuous evolution except the DD:

All is changing in the world of the senses (in the physical universe), but changeless is the supreme Lord of Love (The DD). Meditate on him, be absorbed by him, and wake up from this dream of separateness. (Current life is seen as a dream where the soul needs to be released from the body.). (*Shvetashvatara Upanishad*)

6. Mindfulness, enjoying the present:

Look to this day, for it is life, the very breath of life. In its brief course lie all the realities of your existence, the bliss of growth, the glory of action, the splendour of beauty. For yesterday is only a dream, and tomorrow is but a vision; but today, well lived, makes every yesterday a dream of happiness, and every tomorrow a vision of hope. Look well, therefore, to this day. (Ancient Sanskrit)

I was amazed to see how much has been said thousands of years ago to explain the existence of the DD and the interaction of the body to create the Soul. The spirituality within Hinduism far exceeds any I have seen in the monolithic faiths. 'Does that explain why materialism plays a smaller role within the Hindu society?' I asked.

Abraham responded, 'This confirms the teaching of Adam. Religion that focuses on spirituality leads to a culture of reliance on the spiritual rather than the material conducts. Living for tomorrow without ignoring the need of the present life will lead to a balanced economic growth. You don't really know a person unless you have deep understanding of his faith, his true compass.'

'This is really an eye opener for me,' I said. 'I strongly recommend that we get to know the teachings of all other faiths and learn from them. Those who have confidence in their faith can only enhance their understanding of the mystery of creation by learning from others. In fact, one can only arrive at the universal truth by combining the common rational thinking of all faiths and current scientific knowledge.'

Abraham was encouraged by my comments and continued, 'Let me spend a few minutes on some of the evils usually found in man according to another faith:

'1. Blind Conformity. It's too bad that blind conformity (stupidity) isn't painful. The failings of most political systems are due to the elite exploiting this human weakness as explained by Plato.

'2. Pretentiousness, empty posturing can be most irritating. Chasing luxuries and branded products does not make a man wiser or virtuous.

'3. Reciprocal Negative Action. Avoid the dictum of "Do unto others as they do unto you". It is practiced by most people, and it requires constant vigilance to avoid a spiral of violence.

'4. Counterproductive Pride. If pride works for a person, then great. When it stops working, when the person is cornered and the only way out is to say, "I'm sorry, I have made a mistake, I wish we could compromise somehow", then he must do it. If this principle is widely applied many civil wars and conflict could have been avoided.'

I thanked Abraham for his interesting comments and looked at Plato to move on to the next dominant faith.

Plato was rather excited to expand on the subject of Buddhism as this faith is based on rationalism. He went on to say that Buddha means "Awakened One", and sees things as they really are.

'A Buddha is a person who is completely free from all faults and mental obstructions. He is awakened from the sleep of ignorance and removed of all rigidities from his mind. Moreover, Buddha has great compassion. He is impartial and embraces all living beings without discrimination. The Noble Truths of Buddhism are timeless and reflect personal and spiritual developments which are incorporated in the UMC.'

Plato continued with passion and cited a few of Buddha's key principles as both inspirational and helpful, regardless of where one is in his personal development and irrespective to what faith he belongs to.

'Principle 1. A person is the result of his thoughts and reflections.

'What one thinks, one becomes. What one focuses on, grows in his life and what one ignores are diminished. Everything one gets is first created in the mind. A person becomes able if he thinks he is able. Supportive manners are avoiding negative thoughts and utilizing empowering thoughts.

'Principle 2. The formation of habits is the result of repetition and reflection that wires the brain.

'Train and develop the mind and free it from rigidity and negativity. Only you can become what you want to be if you have an open mind. The mind is the source of all the fortunes and misfortunes of the individual. The mind, if used correctly, constructively, with empowerment, in an action-oriented manner, positively, in a truth-seeking approach and on a regular basis will lead to a positive personality. However, if used poorly – i.e. in a blaming, egocentric and negative way, if it is blinded by envy, then it will create unhappiness.

'Principle 3. Courage and mental energy are the foundation for positive activism.

'The enemy of all virtues is indifference. Those who bury their heads in the sand are living in permanent darkness. Compare them with those who rekindle hope in the life of many. Always remember the saying, "Thousands of candles can be lit from a single candle, and the life of that candle will not be shortened". Beliefs with courage have the power to create and the power to destroy. Do the right thing and be on the right side of history. From difficult experiences and struggles, one can develop his strengths.

'Principle 4. Practice mindfulness:

'Do not dwell in the past; do not get absorbed in the future, concentrate the mind on the present moment. The essence of living is being in the present moment, the Now. The past and future are only concepts of our mind. Therefore, they are good for learning from the past or conceptual planning for the future. However, this is only when it is useful to do so. Beyond that, there is no need to relive the past or jump into the future. One mustn't dwell in them and get stuck there by constant thinking about them.

'Principle 5. Action is what counts.

'No matter how many holy words you read or speak, no matter how many prayers you recite a day, what good will they do you if you don't put the virtues you learn into practice? Only if one "walks the talk", one is authentic and truthful to oneself.

If there is no action and therefore no testing of reality, the prayers, the words or ideas themselves are of no real sustainable value. You judge people by their deeds and not by their words or appearances.

'Principle 6. Act wisely and ethically.

'It means to live to the highest truth one knows, and to rise to one's highest values and capabilities. Living wisely also means not to act on every thought that comes in the mind, but to live reflectively and then act.

'Principle 7 Peace and inspiration come from within.

'It means not to look to the outside world for liberation or happiness, but to take responsibility for oneself and become that what you are seeking.

'Principle 8. Blind faith creates distorted truth.

'In the sky, there is no distinction of East and West. People create distinctions in their own minds and then believe them to be true. Be open-minded to see other possible perspectives. To label an idea divine is to shut the door for dialogue.

'Principle 9. Appreciate the power of the Creator by observing his creation.

'If you could see the miracle of a single flower clearly, your whole life would change. The ultimate appreciation of the Creator's miracles is to understand the powers and designs behind converting the photons into a living flower.

'Principle 10. Dreams to be pursued with passion and knowledge.

'The only real failure in life is not to pursue one's dream the best way one can. Do not follow others blindly. Always ask: is this really in line with what I know and want?'

I thanked both Abraham and Plato for confirming that all faiths have in common the building blocks for shaping human character.

Then we all turned to the farewell ceremony for our holy visitors.

As usual, Moses being the senior took the lead and I could see he wanted to be brief.

He said, 'Based on my teaching and focusing on ethical values, the tribes of Israel have done well. However, they have experienced great suffering in the past and could experience some unpleasantness in the future unless they strongly comply with the natural law of justice and treat others as they like to be treated. They have achieved their new heights outside Palestine and they will continue to do so as leaders in all fields of knowledge including science and finance. I will end with a quote we regularly teach, "Wicked is the one who kills in My Name, I am the Giver of Life. Wicked is the one who commit injustice in my name, I am the Law, I am the Just. Wicked is the one who put himself above others, I am your Lord who created all equal."

After a long pause, I looked at Jesus for his farewell comment. He stood up and smiled like a true angel from the Divine Dimension.

He said, 'Love and tolerance have served Christians well. I am sure they will receive the message from this encounter with an open mind. This will then be followed by accepting the fact that this is the age of rational thinking. Incorporating the information exposed in this encounter will lead to the return of those who have strayed away from Christianity in the name of rationalism. I strongly call on all those with missionary zeal to focus on calling for peace and justice for all. I strongly call on all able men to embrace voluntary work. I call, especially, on all retirees to volunteer and venture into foreign lands to use their knowledge and experience to assist in nation building. I will be present at all times to bless their work. Talent is limitless. The Lord blesses those who give and those who teach. The more one gives the greater the reward. Those who bury their talent will be buried with it. Those who seek virtues will find, and when they find they test eternity.'

Jesus then paused for few minutes. We all thought that he had finished. Then suddenly and with deep passion, he stood up and said, 'Those who seek should not stop seeking until they find. When they find they will be disturbed. When they are disturbed they will marvel, and they will rule over all.'

I looked around to see if he was talking to the other guests, as I did not understand a word. Abraham, having been with me for almost a week, noticed that I was having some doubt about my sanity.

He came next to me and said, 'Don't worry; there is nothing wrong with your ears or your mind. You have heard correctly. This is the way Jesus spoke to some of his disciples. This is one of the secret sayings of Jesus that did not make it to the official Bible. You can find all of the 114 secret sayings of Jesus in the Gospel of Thomas.'

Only then, I relaxed and said, 'Yes, I have heard of that Gospel. I know many books have been written to try to understand these sayings with very little success. Now I see why they have been left out of the Bible and why they are difficult to understand.'

Abraham put his arms around my shoulder and said, 'This is your chance to ask him for explanations. Of course, we do not have the time to get through all of the sayings. By the way, not all those sayings as quoted in the English version are correct representation of Jesus' sayings. Some have been misquoted, changed, or wrongly translated.'

I looked at Jesus for an explanation.

Jesus obliged, 'I would like to remind you what Abraham said earlier during this encounter. To understand my secret sayings, Mankind needs to endorse the new explanation you have just been given during this encounter. Humanity needs to accept the existence and the roles of the Divine Dimension. They need to revise their understanding of Heaven and Hell and the role of the Souls. Once they incorporate these principles, then most of the secret sayings will become clear, provided that they rely on the original Aramaic text. Keep in mind that in some cases, even in Aramaic, I was misquoted as you appreciate the difficulty of memorizing sentences that do not make sense to the listener at the time.

'So, let me help you by explaining the first and the last three of my 114 sayings as a random sample. The first saying is: "Whoever discovers the interpretation of these sayings will not test death".'

I was rather excited, I shouted, 'Thanks Jesus, you are going to reveal to me the secret of eternal life. Are you really?'

They all were stunned and laughed very loudly.

Newton could not stop himself, stood up, and said, 'No one could have eternal life on Earth. All forms of life on Earth will cease once the Sun's energy is depleted unless man destroys the ecosystem much earlier.'

Jesus looked at me and continued, 'Let me explain. I am speaking of the human Soul. For those who adhere to my teaching and understand the meaning of my sayings, will pass the test and their Souls will be in the eternal service of the Lord. For those who fail the test will get their Souls ignored and will not get activated for eternal life as explained earlier.'

'Let's look at the second saying: "Those who seek should not stop seeking until they find, when they find they will be disturbed. When they are disturbed they will marvel, and they will rule over all". Those who seek the truth about the universe and the DD should continue with their search until they discover the truth. We have revealed to you the truth about the physical universe and the DD. All those who read what has been revealed in this encounter will be truly disturbed, as it will challenge some of their existing beliefs. When this new paradigm sinks in, great scientific discoveries will be made. With the application of the UMC and the scientific knowledge, great powers will be obtained to release man from Earth's gravity and Mankind will get the power of creation within the physical dimension.'

I was very pleased to see that the knowledge of this encounter has been supported by the mysterious sayings of Jesus almost 2000 years ago. Is there some Divine reason for making those sayings mysterious to the degree of rejecting their inclusion in the canonical Bible? Then an encounter in Nineveh in 2003 reveals all the knowledge to make such sayings intelligible, with Jesus himself confirming that!

I was anxiously waiting for the third saying.

Jesus continued, 'If your leaders say to you, "Look, the (Father's) imperial rule is in the sky", then the birds of the sky will precede you. If they say to you "It is in the sea", then the fish will precede you. Rather, the (Father's) imperial rule is inside you and outside you. When you know yourselves, then you will be known, and you will understand that you are the children of the Living Father. But if you do not know yourselves, then you live in poverty and you are the poverty.'

I waited for Jesus to explain but they all looked at me and Abraham said, 'You should try to explain this saying Mac, using our teaching.'

I felt I was truly being tested, however I agreed to try it.

I said with some hesitation, "The Father's Imperial Rule description confirms that God runs the universe as a huge Empire in the DD and not above us or below us. He appoints Angels who reside in the DD as governors and administrators. For those who use their talent to accept the existence of God and the DD will be known by God. Once we accept that God creates processes then we will know that we have been created in the image of the Lord from a seed created by Him. However, if we do not use our talent correctly and do not accept the existence of God and the DD then we are in poverty. The real wealth is that of eternal life when our Soul gets activated. We are the poverty means that we end up as inactivated Souls.'

They all clapped and Plato shouted, 'Not bad, not bad at all.'

They continued with the last three sayings in the Gospel of Thomas to help Jesus.

Abraham said, 'Jesus' saying 112: "Damn the flesh that depends on the Soul. Damn the Soul that depends on the flesh." This means that God will condemn the lazy person who waits for the DD to enrich him. One should toil with honest work to feed the flesh. God also condemns the Soul if one puts his worldly desires ahead of virtues.'

Plato was next to explain saying number 113. He said, 'His disciples said to him, "When will the (Father's) imperial rule come?" It will not come by watching for it. It will not be said "look, here" or "look there" rather, the Father's imperial rule is spread out upon the Earth, and the people don't see it.'

I felt this is rather an easy one to explain. The kingdom of the Lord is already in existence and we are floating in it, yet our physical senses cannot see it. When a person dies, his Soul will no longer be attached to the physical body. This is his day of judgment and not at some future date.

Plato continued with Jesus' saying 114 being the last in the Gospel of Thomas. 'Simon Peter said to them, "Make Mary leave us, for females don't deserve life". Jesus said, "Look, I will guide her to make her male, so that she too may become a living spirit resembling you males. For every female who makes herself male, will enter the domain of Heaven."'

They were all expecting me to explain this mysterious saying. Mohammed was smiling to see how I could explain this one as Islam has always been criticized in the West as being anti-females. I tried to recall all that I had learnt during this encounter; but I could not really justify such an outburst by Simon Peter except that he was jealous of Mary Magdalene. After all, human frailty does not go away just because we become pious. Could I explain it through the smile on Mohammed's face? Did it mean that religions are a mere reflection of the cultures at the time, with some new ethical codes to address the prevailing problems? Only by continuous liberal interpretations can a religion continue to be relevant. If Simon Peter had said that today, he would have been condemned for discrimination.

They all noticed my struggle to reconcile this dialogue between Jesus and his disciples.

Jesus came to the rescue and said, 'Let me help you Mac. God does not discriminate between men and women. After all, women are the ones who experience all the suffering of child bearing and birth. They are specially rewarded for that in the next life. If they pass the test of course. During the three years with my disciples, I went out of my way to raise the status of women within the Jewish culture. This was not easy. I thought of the risk of losing control over the acceptance of the message if I pushed too far in the direction of complete equality between the sexes. Therefore, like everything else in the universe, I adopted the gradual approach. I started to get women to be treated as equal to men wherever that seemed possible. Some of my disciples where bewildered by my attempt to raise women's status. Therefore, when I said to my disciples, "I will guide her to make her male" they all understood that what makes men deserve the afterlife are their deeds and I will guide Mary to the path of good deeds. In this way they understood that good deeds are not a monopoly to men.'

So, jokingly, Jesus continued with his explanation by saying, 'For all those who have eyes to see and ears to hear, women are not inferior to men in the eyes of the Lord and they should not be denied the right to lead any congregation of any religion.'

I realized that Jesus was aware of the current debate among some Church leaders regarding the role of women to lead congregations.

'Will the day come when a woman is a pope?' I asked innocently.

He laughed and said, 'Not in your lifetime Mac!'

I understood from his answer to mean *Yes*, but after human beings mature to the concept of complete equality between the sexes and they stop taking everything in scriptures literally.

Then he turned to Mohammed and looked at me and said, 'Don't be embarrassed to also ask your Prophet difficult questions. Mohammed is well prepared.'

Then he shouted, "Blessed are those who stand for Peace. Wars are too awful to bear. A world where more time is spent on how to hate than how to love is doomed until eternity. Those who pursue privileges and powers ruthlessly will reap wars and destruction.'

It was a very moving call for peace and at the same time, a reminder that I have been withholding some difficult questions.

Mohammed with his usual gentleness took note of Jesus' comment and said, 'Mac, please do not hold back any questions in your mind. I know that the Islamic Umma (nation) is in great pain at present. Only by calmly discussing what is wrong will it be possible to get things to improve.'

'How that could be?' I asked. 'There is so much ignorance and hatred even between the various sects of Islam. We need sufficient numbers of "Virtuous Elites" to guide the masses. This is unlikely to happen while the culture of fear is dominant among most Muslims. Most of those who are in charge are ruthless and they do not encourage gradual openness in the society.'

He replied, 'Only by patience and reforming the individuals in those communities. At present, there is a lack of enough rational thinking teachers who could create an escape velocity to reach twenty-first century thinking. Islam is not and it should not be made a rigid religion. It is, and must stay, a dynamic faith capable of dealing with all aspects of people's lives with full comfort. Unless Muslims change to become a part of the world here and now, then they will be buried in the past. Many Muslims confuse adherence to rituals and the true essence of the faith.

'For those who claim they love me and my teaching, and I know they are in the millions, I say to them: "If you do well in whatever job or task you do, if you adhere to my ethical teachings, if you fully respect human life and dignity, if you are patient and humble with others then your dedication to Islam will be accepted and you are welcome to join me. If on the other hand you are spending all your time praying, fasting, visiting Mecca, and dealt with one person unfairly, if you have received money through corruption or if you have ruled harshly, then you are not welcomed in the Kingdom of the Lord and you are not to be called a Muslim. God will not judge man by the time spent on rituals but by the qualities of his characters".'

After this lovely sermon, it was my chance to ask difficult questions. I started with, 'Islam is the only religion to ask its followers to fast from sunset to sunrise or even longer for a full lunar month. If this is taken literally, then how could one fast in summer in the North Pole as some today are living not far from there?'

Mohammed was very relaxed in answering this question. 'For Islam to be a religion for all time and for all places, it must be interpreted rationally to meet the requirements of the time and place and without fear from existing religious rigidities. There are many overriding statements in the Quran that are part of the UMC. For example, sanctity of life and its quality overrides any other text that breaks this rule. In the Quran, there is a verse that says, "Allah will not ask any person (Soul) to do anything beyond what that person can reasonably bear". Therefore, if one is in the North Pole or near the North Pole, then he must fast for the number of hours that the person is capable of doing comfortably but not less than their equivalent in Mecca. God does not get any benefit from man's hunger for one month. Fasting is for the individual to achieve self-discipline and humility. It is to appreciate what one has, and to share it with those who have not. Fasting is to discipline the self on moderation in every respect. If one can deprive the body from the most basic of life's necessities, i.e. food and water, then one should also be able to avoid excessive indulgence in life's luxuries. Currently the Muslims have turned Ramadan into a month of extravagance and entertainment instead of moderation. This is a complete reversal of the role of religion.'

With a very sad tone he continued, 'Most Muslims today are so by name only and they are shameful to their faith. To all those who say they love Islam and his Messenger, I say to them apply the golden rule, "Do unto others as you would like them to do unto you". No ifs, no buts, no "I will get my sins washed away in Mecca". All Muslims will be judged on their deeds, especially those who spend most of their time in rituals.'

I asked if he was aware of a person who expected to be in Heaven but ended up as a complete reject.

Without any hesitation he replied, 'There are more rejects among those who think that they are serving God and keeping his commandments than those who conform to the true ethical values without the rituals. A very pious person, praying and fasting, yet treating his wife harshly and stopping her from visiting her family is not a Muslim. The rituals did not add any credit to his score if when he died his wife harboured a bitter taste of the way she had been treated.'

'What is the point of all the rituals, if they do not add any credit to one's Divine score?' I asked.

Mohammed replied, 'How many times do we need to tell humans that rituals don't add to one's credit unless they make him more virtuous? Prayers by those unethical and corrupt people are seen by God as a way of trying to cheat Him and give a bad name to the faith. Prayers are to remind the faithful of their duties to adhere in all their deeds to the moral codes i.e. adhering to the straight and narrow path recited by Muslims every day hundreds of times. If the rituals do not achieve these objectives, why should it be rewarded then? If prayer is merely a physical exercise, then those who go to the gym will be more pious. If it is cleanliness, then those who shower regularly will receive a higher reward. If it is for the sake of meditation, then yoga is more effective. There are many who belong to what is called religious political parties, yet they commit the worst acts of robbery from the public's purse and justify atrocities. There are those who kidnap in the name of religion. The list is endless. The task ahead is difficult. The damage is great and the road to salvation is very long.'

Then Mohammed smiled at Jesus and said, 'God will not abandon his children. God will finally fulfil his promise to free the poor and the weak from the bondage of the "Selfish Elites". He will free the ruled from the wicked rulers. He will free the virtuous from the grips of the irrational teachers of the Faith. Every child's inalienable right to education, equal opportunity and true freedom will be achieved through continuous vigilance.'

Then he looked at me as if he was reminding me of what I need to do and said, 'I call on all decent top executives in major businesses to seek deeper sense of meaning of life. It's not just about the money. It's about doing the right thing, having a profound impact on the local community, and improving the lives of many others.

'It is about giving back and sharing. In their career as top executives or business owners, they accumulated valuable knowledge and experience. Now they have the opportunity to guide other business leaders who can learn from their life's successes and failures. The appreciation and satisfaction they will receive are real and deeply profound.'

To finally conclude Mohammed stood up and recited:

O Man wake up and see
A just World Order is awaiting thee

Don't be selfish, don't be greedy,
Think of the sick, help the needy
Your essence is not in luxury or in brand
Don't be fooled, it is all in the mind
Forget the sword, forget the bomb,
Don't be misguided, don't seek a fight
In tolerance and wisdom, go deep,
Through practice, reach your height
Use your talent, enjoy the sun
It is OK to play; it is OK to have fun

Throughout the whole encounter, I never saw anyone with such strong passion and seriousness as I saw in Mohammed, as he conveyed the depth of issues facing the Muslim world in the twenty-first century.

He then whispered in my ears, 'Revenge Cannot Contain the Wicked among men only Commitment to Love Can. Essence of Man is Not How Loud He Shouts But How He Gets His Message to Penetrate the Hearts of Man. Deliberate Ignorance and Conscious Stupidity are What Empowers the Enemies of Humanity.'

As everyone was ready for the final ceremony, I asked innocently, to test my understanding of politics after this encounter, 'Why do some opinion formers peddle the political theory that the West needs an external enemy to keep its cohesion? What is wrong with human morality and decency?'

The dialogue that followed was rather analytical and seriously scary. Plato, realising that this needed a brief response in these last few minutes of the encounter, stood up and said, 'Throughout Mankind's history great empires got destroyed from within when they did not find an external enemy to galvanise the population into submission to those who are holding the true levers of powers. The inability of man to maintain harmonious relationships with fellow human beings is present even at the family level. Almost in all cases, the trigger for enmity is the search for domination and recognition through accumulation of wealth and power. It is very common for wealthy families to disintegrate, on the death of the patriarch, who made the wealth, due to the feud between the children and the grandchildren, if no clear and legal succession plan has been spelled out in advance. The curse of money turns brotherly love to publicly expressed family in-fighting. The same drivers that destroy wealthy families are at work at national and international levels. Instead of taking the form of various individuals fighting for domination, it may take the form of tribal forces or pressure groups seeking domination. Once these groups get control they start to disintegrate from within for individual or smaller subgroups to dominate others. It is truly sad for human beings not to look inward and discover their own wrong doings. This exposes the great moral defect in man. If he has no external enemy then he brings his enmities to those around him.

'After the collapse of the USSR, very quickly some prominent politicians in the West did make it clear that the next enemy will be based on the cultural gap that already exists rather than on military oppositions. Would China come next then? Who will then follow China after that? It is sad that some politicians in the greatest nation on Earth need enemies and wars to put the "united" back into the United States. We repeat that human nature is still very flawed and imperfect. The American Constitution remains a big historical experiment. It has served the Americans well for over more than two centuries.

However, in modern times, due to the corruption of money and domination of politics by pressure groups, the ecosystems for the smooth working of the constitution are changing faster than any of the Founding Fathers could have dreamed off.

'Mankind should stop viewing peace as merely a matter of living safely within one's borders. Peace should be a universal requirement to include humanity as a whole. Otherwise, man will continue in the cycle of creating his own enemies and then congratulating himself on achieving a perceived temporary victory. Unfortunately, this cannot be done without a new moral code to kill the inner desire for selfish supremacy at the expense of others.'

I looked at my guests to absorb the impossible task ahead. 'You are telling me in no uncertain terms that in any small gathering of people there will be competition between individuals for domination. It is part of human nature to seek continuously a better tomorrow. The only dilemma is that most individuals cannot apply that in moderation. It seems that man cannot seek in moderation to enrich himself and his immediate associates over all others. To solve this problem, we need chosen people of high moral codes to dwell among all communities to act as role models and to guide them like a shepherd guiding sheep.' Then I stopped and shouted, 'O, My God! Is this why holy books speak of "God's Chosen People"? As long as human beings have not evolved to control the evil within, they need a shepherd within each community to inspire and guide others to pursue ethical conduct. This is why we should encourage religious and other institutions of morality, with the help of international bodies, to create philosophers of faith and wise men, instead of preachers of hate and domination. This message is of the utmost urgency to safe humanity from the definite self-destruction that lies ahead. Therefore, God's

Chosen People should spread out all over the planet to live with the people in need of mental inspiration and guidance, and not to live in isolated communities or in one location.'

Moses, taking great satisfaction to hear me reach this conclusion, said, "You see, to be one of God's Chosen People requires continuous vigilance and to ensure that he acts in moderation. He needs to reach a high level of learning and in compliance with the UMC in order to be in a position to provide guidance to others. Their greatest reward will not be in this life but in the next, when they will be selected as God's Agents for the continuous service of the Lord.'

I smiled and said, 'So if one wants to be an Agent of the Lord then he must be a shepherd on Earth first. So now I can call my teachers ex-shepherds.'

We all stopped for a break before everyone made his concluding prophecy. It was heartbreaking to see this journey into true illumination coming to its final stage.

I asked Plato, 'Who will start with his final remarks after the break?'

He replied, 'It will be in the same order as the lectures.'

As we were walking back to hear the prophecies, Mohammed came next to me and said, 'It is not all doom and gloom. Turkey, Malaysia and Indonesia will provide good Islamic examples for moderate Islam. Muslims in the West will enter into a meaningful dialogue with other faiths. They will embrace philosophy just as in the enlightened period in Andalusia.'

We re-seated around the big round table. I was full of excitement to hear the concluding prophecies.

1) Newton started with his prediction on science:

'a) Man will come to accept the fundamental explanation of the photon being the basis of everything in the universe.

'b) Man will accept the existence of the DD to support our General Theory of Physics and he will be able to explain all natural and supernatural observations.

'c) After many centuries, science will unlock the hidden knowledge of neutralizing gravity. Bending the photon will come much later and then will come the creation of energy from cold fusion. Of course, all this depends on Mankind succeeding in the next few generations in establishing peace and justice on Earth to allow him to strengthen the love and respect gene.'

2) Abraham also made three predictions:

'a) There will be destructive sectarian and religious wars in the troubled Middle East manipulated by the powerful few. This will be followed by a real awakening in the Muslim world through the adoption of rational thinking compatible with a new approach to their core faith.

'b) A strong world peace movement led by the youth and the liberal clergy will take hold and become an effective force for good within a few generations.

'c) The Universal Moral Codes will be discussed extensively, updated continuously, and used as the foundation for most laws and other human activities.

3) Darwin's three predictions were:

'a) Man will identify the monitoring gene and speed up the evolutionary process.

'b) Life expectancy will increase by several folds by genetically controlling and directing stem cells and enhancing the immune system to recognise rebel cells.

'c) Ultimately, man will succeed in creating the seeds of life and fulfil his role on Earth.'

4) Plato focused on politics and his three predictions were:

'a) Democracy will ultimately prevail by awakening the youth to be vigilant against those who corrupt politics with money and the controlled media.

'b) A Just World Order will have its own institutions by the end of this century.

'c) The Just Elites and liberal preachers from all faiths and in sufficient numbers will be the true guardians for lasting justice and peace.'

5) Adam's three predictions were:

'a) Great pains from the excesses of banks will lead to great misery and a worldwide uprising. This will be followed by stricter regulations.

'b) Voluntary work will be the key in closing the economic gap between the poor and the rich.

'c) World tax will be imposed to support a Just World Order.'

6) Moses and his three predictions were:

'a) There will be no state based on religion in the age of enlightenment. Talented people will follow where they will get greater rewards as in the time of Joseph 'b) By the end of this century, there will be no room for tribalism anywhere on this planet. Interfaith marriages will be very common as the brotherhood of man will replace all others.

'c) Jerusalem will be the capital for all Abrahamic faiths and the headquarters of the world for Spirituality and Learning

7) The three predictions of Jesus:

'a) Christianity will be stronger and more rational by accepting the fact that I am not the Son of God but I am the Divine Earth Governor.

'b) There will be a greater missionary zeal to strengthen family values and instil universal virtues.

'c) Christians will lead the movements for nation building and spreading knowledge and peace around the world. Only then will I return to bless this planet and its inhabitants.'

8) The three predictions of Mohammed were:

'a) Islamic teachers will adopt philosophy and rationalism to guide them to evolve their faith into moderation, silence the wicked among their lot, and actively endorse religious dialogue.

'b) After destructive wars, the two main branches of Islam will tolerate each other and will embrace each other's traditions.

'c) Muslims will participate effectively in the Just World Order and will embrace creativity.

I realized that the time had come for me to ask no more questions. I started to observe how this encounter would be concluded. The first part was for our three Holy Guests to depart. It was a very emotional goodbye. Moses was the first to hug me, followed by Jesus.

As Mohammed was embracing me, he whispered again in my ear, 'We need more Muslims like Gandhi and Martin Luther King Jr. The likes of them are regarded as top royalty in Heaven.'

Then all of us went out to watch the three holy men rise up and away into the infinite and invisible DD.

After they left, Plato continued with the farewell ceremony. He whispered in my ears, 'We trust that during this brief encounter, we have offered Mankind a beautiful and harmonious theory explaining all human observations, both natural and supernatural. We trust that people of different cultures will ponder upon and respectfully debate all that is revealed. We trust that they will commit themselves to the desired and necessary actions to improve their life. With peace and better understanding, humanity will receive the ultimate knowledge for their betterment.'

I asked him, 'What do you think I should do with all this knowledge?'

He looked at his colleagues and said, 'You remember when Jesus sat next to you and stroked your head?'

'I do not understand. What are you trying to say?' I asked.

Plato responded, "In the same way Jesus made his disciples speak several languages, he has given you the power to recall all the details of this encounter so that you can write them down for everyone to read. Go and walk tall among men, raise your head and shout "I have a vision for a Just World Order, I have a vision for a…"'

As I was hearing those words, I felt as if all the blood had drained out of my head and then I fell unconscious.

When I woke up, I found myself in an American army hospital in Mosul. I did not know for how long I had been there. As I had no pain or any sign of injury, I was not sure why I was there. I heard a nurse shouting, 'David, David, this Iraqi guy is regaining consciousness.'

I looked at her in disbelief and said, 'Who are you? Where are Plato and the team?'

David looked at me and said, 'Who? Who is Plato and what team are you talking about? Do you know where you are?'

'Yes I am in a cave in Nineveh.'

They all laughed and said, 'No, you are in a night club in Soho! Are you kidding me man? You are in an American army hospital. We found you unconscious in a cave. You had no apparent symptoms of injury and we couldn't find anything wrong with you.'

I asked, 'Then why are you keeping me here?

They looked at each other and David said, 'We don't really know. You were unconscious. We are just giving you drips to keep you alive. All our tests show that your body organs seem to be functioning OK. You are lucky we don't have any war casualties. You would have been regarded as a low priority to be kept here.'

'How long have I been here then?' I asked.

The doctor looked at his admission notes and confirmed, 'Seven days.'

'So why did you not wake me up earlier?'

'Because you were in a coma of some sort and we did not find anything on you to identify your relatives.'

I put my hand on my head in amazement. I was sad that my visiting shadows had left me. Then I said to the doctor, 'I want to see the nurse who was looking after me. Has she heard anything or seen anybody while I was here?'

'You can ask Linda,' David said as the nurse walked in.

She looked at me and said, 'By the way we don't even know your name.'

'Mac,' I replied. 'Did you hear me saying anything or speaking to anybody while I was in a coma?'

Linda laughed and said, 'You did not stop talking gibberish. We did not understand a word, although you repeated the names of very familiar people and many prophets. Are you a religious man, Mac?'

Linda continued, 'Mind you, although you were in a coma, you seemed to smile a lot and appeared comfortable with whatever you were experiencing.'

I asked if anyone had asked for me in the physical dimension.

Linda giggled again and said, 'The coma must have affected your brain, unless you have a funny sense of humour. In how many dimensions do you live, man?'

She looked at David and asked, 'Do you think Mac is stable mentally?'

David shrugged his shoulder.

Linda continued, 'Let me assure you that no one knows you are here or in whatever dimension you like. We didn't want you to be recorded as a war casualty and we don't know how and why you have lost consciousness. You have to stay with us until tomorrow then you can leave.'

'I am going to need help to get to my daughter and leave Iraq,' I said.

She replied, 'I don't know about that. It is not for me to decide I'm afraid.'

I could not sleep that night as my mind, after seven days of such an encounter, was not adjusting to reality. How could I

317

explain what happened? Am I really the same person who entered that cave while running from the American airplanes? If a man is what is stored in his brain, then certainly I am not the Mac I used to be. I started to think and talk differently. If all what I was experiencing was just a figment of my imagination, then does that mean all what I have been told is not real? If this is the case, then where did all this rationalism and ideas come from while I was unconscious? Who did plant all these concepts in my head? How come I have a vivid memory of every scene and every word said? Now, I know that there was no bending of the photons to feed me, and no hologram shadows creating those amazing experiences. Does that diminish my faith in what I have been told?

Then suddenly it hit me. Whenever I asked them about all the scenes and colours, they kept telling me that it is all in the mind. Is it possible that when I was in the cave in a state of fear and reverence, remembering Jonah and God, I started to communicate with my visitors in the DD? Therefore, in reality, they did not come to the physical dimension but my Soul that resides in the Holy Spirit was activated and was disconnected from my body. This is why I was unconscious. I was a body without a Soul. What and where were all those lights I had experienced at the very beginning of the Encounter? Was this what is usually described as a near death experience? Is this why they could not find anything wrong with me, except that I was unconscious?

As I was busy analyzing and trying to understand what really happened, I fell asleep. It was a deep sleep, as if I hadn't slept for many months.

The next day a military car was organized to take me to where my sister lived. I did not want them to enter the road leading to my sister's house, as I could be labelled as a corroborator. I sincerely thanked all those who saved my life and I was dropped off, as requested.

I knocked on the door and my eldest sister opened it. As soon as she saw me she shouted, 'It's Mahmoud, it's Mahmoud!' and then she fainted.

The entire family, including all the kids, soon assembled to greet me. I was lying with my head on Roxie's lap. She was worried to death about me. I spoke very little as I did not really know what to say. I was numbed by the experience of being in an encounter with shadows of all kinds and discussing centuries of total world knowledge with them to this general everyday chat.

I did not dare explain the encounter to anyone as they had already started to think that I must have suffered mentally during my ordeal and that I needed to see a doctor as soon as I got back to the UK.